Introducing statistics for socia   arch

Int.   *rch* describes when to apply, how to calculat   ad   comprehensive selection of statistical procedures comm   the social sciences. Ranging from chi-square and the *t* test to ana   of covariance and multiple regression, Duncan Cramer shows how to calculate these procedures by hand as well as with the computer program SPSS. He also covers a wide choice of statistics and includes tests not normally found in introductory texts, such as tests for determining whether correlations differ and the extent of agreement between observers.

Calculations are described with small sets of numbers and the minimum of statistical formulae. Where possible, important statistical points are illustrated with worked numerical examples. To test and to enhance the reader's understanding, exercises are provided at the end of chapters, with answers at the end of the book.

Introducing Statistics for Social Research also shows how these statistics can be more conveniently and efficiently calculated with one of the most widely used statistical programs, the Statistical Package for the Social Sciences (SPSS), available on both personal and mainframe computers. As such it provides a concise and handy introduction to this program. Minor differences between the various recent versions of SPSS are outlined.

This book assumes no previous knowledge of statistics or computing and will provide an invaluable introductory statistics text for first- and second-year social science students.

Duncan Cramer is Senior Lecturer in Social Psychology at Loughborough University. He is the author of *Personality and Psychotherapy* (1991) and co-author (with Alan Bryman) of *Quantitative Data Analysis for Social Scientists* (Routledge 1990).

D1434831

Introducing statistics for social research

Step-by-step calculations and computer techniques using SPSS

Duncan Cramer

London and New York

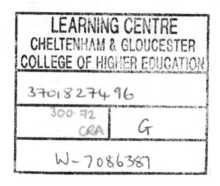
First published 1994
by Routledge
11 New Fetter Lane, London EC4P 4EE

Simultaneously published in the USA and Canada
by Routledge
29 West 35th Street, New York, NY 10001

© 1994 Duncan Cramer

Typeset in Times by Solidus (Bristol) Limited
Printed and bound in Great Britain by
Biddles Ltd, Guildford and King's Lynn

British Library Cataloguing in Publication Data
A catalogue record for this book is available from the British
Library.

Library of Congress Cataloging in Publication Data
Cramer, Duncan, 1948–
    Introducing statistics for social research: step-by-step
    calculations and computer techniques using SPSS/Duncan Cramer.
    p. cm.
    "Simultaneously published in the USA and Canada" – T.p. verso.
    Includes bibliographical references and index.
    1. Social sciences – Statistical methods.   2. Social sciences –
    Statistical methods – Computer programs.   3. SPSS (Computer file)
    I. Title.
    HA32.C7
    300'.72–dc20
                                                            93-4071
                                                                CIP

ISBN 0-415-07514-9 (hbk)
ISBN 0-415-07515-7 (pbk)

Contents

Tables

Figures

Preface

Statistics play a vital role in the description of the results of empirical research in the social sciences. Consequently, an understanding of the way in which such data have been analysed is essential to be able to evaluate those results fully and critically. This book describes when to apply and how to calculate, both by hand and with the aid of a computer program called SPSS, a comprehensive range of statistical tests used in the social sciences, ranging from chi-square and the t test to analysis of covariance and multiple regression. The widespread availability of computers and programs for carrying out statistics means that statistics can now be more efficiently and accurately computed with these means. SPSS (which is short for Statistical Package for the Social Sciences) was chosen because it was written specifically for the social sciences, has an extensive variety of statistical procedures and is well known, flexible, well documented and widely used.

However, in order to understand what these tests involve it is still necessary to work out the computations by hand. To make the calculations easier the examples employ small sets of data consisting of one-digit numbers. The same set of data is often used to illustrate more than one test so that the results of different tests can be compared and less time is spent on introducing new examples. Where possible important statistical points have been illustrated with worked numerical examples. Statistical symbols have been kept to a minimum so that there is less need to remember what these symbols represent. Exercises at the end of chapters (together with the answers at the back of the book) enable readers to test their understanding of the computational steps involved in the tests described, as well as providing additional examples of data and their statistical analysis. Once readers have learned how to operate SPSS, they can generate their own exercises and assess their knowledge by comparing their answers with those produced by SPSS.

The version of SPSS covered in the relevant chapters of the book is the fourth and, at the time of writing, the latest version written for personal computers. The differences between this version for personal and mainframe computers, as well as the differences between the third and fourth versions for both types of computer, are small and have been listed at the end of the book. To distinguish them, SPSS commands and output have been printed in bold.

I would like to thank Longman Group UK Ltd, on behalf of the Literary Executor of the late Sir Ronald A. Fisher, F.R.S., and Dr Frank Yates, F.R.S., for permission to reproduce Tables II, IV and VII from *Statistical Tables for Biological, Agricultural and Medical Research*, 6th ed. (1974).

Duncan Cramer
Loughborough University

Chapter 1

Role of statistics in social research

A major aim of the social and behavioural sciences is to develop principles which explain and provide new insights into human behaviour. One way of evaluating what appear to be sound and promising principles is to examine the extent to which they are found to be consistent with carefully controlled observations of human behaviour. In other words, the validity of principles needs to be tested by conducting empirical research wherever possible. If the data do not agree with the principle under scrutiny, then the principle may have to be modified and then re-examined. Alternatively, the way in which the controlled observations were made may have been mistaken and a new set of data may have to be collected. Suppose, for example, we tested the idea that dominant people are more likely to have submissive partners but found no evidence to support such a relationship. In this case, it might be necessary to make the principle more specific by proposing that individuals who like to *dominate their partners* are more likely to have a relationship with people who prefer to be submissive towards their dominant partners, and to test this revised proposition. On the other hand, the test of dominance–submissiveness we used may have been unsuitable for the purpose and may have to be replaced with a more appropriate test.

Statistics play a vital role in collecting, summarising and interpreting data designed to evaluate a principle empirically. Consequently, an under-standing of this important subject is necessary both to carry out research and to be able critically to evaluate research that has been, or is to be, conducted. The function that statistics serves in social research can best be briefly illustrated by looking at the ways in which it is involved in testing a principle. Take, for example, the simple idea that people tend to imitate what they have observed. If this is the case, then individuals who, say, have watched a violent incident shown on television should be more likely to behave in a similar way than those who have not seen this incident. One way of testing this idea would be to select two groups of people and to show one group (known as the *experimental* group, condition or treatment) a film or video with a violent incident while the other group (the *control* group) watched a similar film which did not contain the violent sequence.

After viewing the film, both groups of people would be observed in a comparable situation and the aggression they displayed would be recorded.

Suppose that the people who had watched the violent incident showed more aggression subsequently than those who had not been exposed to this violence. Before it could be concluded that these results confirm the principle that individuals tend to imitate what they have observed, at least two essential and related statistical considerations need to have been met. The first is that the participants should have been *randomly assigned* to the two groups. Random assignment means that individuals have an equal probability of being assigned to each group. The second is that the difference in observed aggression between the two groups is *statistically significant*, which means that it has less than a one in twenty probability of occurring simply by chance.

RANDOM ASSIGNMENT

One way of trying to achieve random assignment is to flip an unbiased coin. The two faces of the coin are used to represent the two groups. For example, it can be agreed beforehand that if the coin lands with the side containing the head showing ('heads up'), then the first of two people will be assigned to the group that will see the violent episode. The second person will be allocated to the group that will not be shown the violent incident. If, on the other hand, the coin lands with the side which does not contain the head showing ('tails up'), then the first person will be assigned to the group which will not see the violent sequence, while the second participant will be allocated to the group which will be shown the violent episode. This procedure of assigning two people at a time with one coin throw will ensure that the number of people in both groups will be similar, although a similar number of people in each group is not itself a statistical requirement.

The reason for random assignment of participants to conditions is to try and ensure that there is no bias in the way that people are assigned to the two groups and that every person has an equal chance of being in either group. If random assignment is not used, then there is the possibility that one group will contain individuals who may be more prone to show aggression. If this happened, then the results obtained could not be explained in terms of which films the participants had seen. Because this is a very important point to grasp, it will be further elaborated.

There are potentially a very large number of factors which may predispose individuals to be aggressive, some of which we may not readily recall or even be aware of. For example, participants who had had a poor night's sleep or had gone without breakfast that morning may be more irritable than those who had slept well or had had a hearty breakfast. Men may be more inclined to show their aggression than women, and so on.

Now, it is possible to control for some of these factors by holding them constant, such as restricting participation to men or to women. Alternatively, the role of these factors may themselves be investigated by including both women and men in the study. However, because we are not necessarily aware of all the factors that might influence aggressiveness and because it would be difficult to study or to hold constant all those variables that we were conscious of, it would be better to try to control for these extraneous factors through random assignment. By randomly assigning participants to treatments, it is more likely that the people in both groups will be similar in terms of a whole host of other characteristics. For example, random assignment will make it more probable that the two groups will contain the same number of people who had a disturbed night's sleep, who had missed breakfast or who were male.

However, when only a small number of participants are involved in a study and are randomly assigned to conditions, there is a greater probability that the number or proportion of people who have the same characteristic will differ in the two conditions. This point can be illustrated by looking at the possible results of tossing a coin a varying number of times. The two sides of the coin can be thought of as denoting any variable which can take on two equiprobable values such as being a woman or a man. If we tossed the coin once, then the probability of it turning up heads would be one of two possibilities (a head or a tail), which can be represented as 0.5 (i.e. $1/2 = 0.5$) or 50 per cent (i.e. $1/2 \times 100 = 50$).

If we tossed two coins once, there are four possible or theoretical outcomes as shown in Table 1.1: (1) a head on the first coin and a tail on the second; (2) a tail on the first coin and a head on the second; (3) two heads on both coins; and (4) two tails on both coins. The probability of obtaining both a head and a tail (regardless of the coin) would be two out of four possibilities or 0.5 ($2/4 = 0.5$). Since the probability of an outcome (or p value) is usually expressed as a proportion, we shall refer to it as a proportion although it may be easier to think of it as a percentage. The probability of obtaining two heads would be one out of four possibilities or 0.25 ($1/4 = 0.25$). Similarly, the probability of having two tails would also be one out of four possibilities or 0.25.

If we assume that we are randomly assigning only two participants to

Table 1.1 Four possible outcomes of tossing two coins once and their probability

	Coin 1	Coin 2	Probability (p)
1	Head	Tail	0.25 ⎫ =0.5
2	Tail	Head	0.25 ⎭
3	Head	Head	0.25
4	Tail	Tail	0.25

one of the two conditions, then we can see that the probability of having all women or men in this condition is 0.5. With three participants this probability decreases to 0.25, with four it decreases to 0.125, and so on. We can derive these probabilities in the following way. The number of possible outcomes that can be obtained from tossing any number of coins can be worked out by multiplying the number of possible outcomes for each coin by those of the other coins. So, as we have just seen, this number would be four for two coins ($2 \times 2 = 4$), eight for three coins ($2 \times 2 \times 2 = 8$) and sixteen for four coins ($2 \times 2 \times 2 \times 2 = 16$). The probability of obtaining any particular outcome from any number of coins can be calculated by multiplying the two outcomes of each of the coins being used. So, as we have already noted, this probability would be 0.25 for two coins ($0.5 \times 0.5 = 0.25$), 0.125 for three coins ($0.5 \times 0.5 \times 0.5 = 0.125$) and 0.0625 for four coins ($0.5 \times 0.5 \times 0.5 \times 0.5 = 0.0625$). For any number of coins there can only be one outcome which contains all heads and only one which consists of all tails. To work out the probability of obtaining both these outcomes we simply add up their separate probabilities, which is 0.5 for two coins ($0.25 + 0.25 = 0.5$), as we have already calculated, 0.25 for three coins ($0.125 + 0.125 = 0.25$) and 0.125 for four coins ($0.0625 + 0.0625 = 0.125$). It should be clear then that, as the number of participants increases, the probability that random assignment will lead to participants in any one group having all of one characteristic should decrease.

Of course, it is possible to check whether random assignment has resulted in the participants in the two conditions being similar in various ways before being shown the two films. However, in order not to overtax the participants' goodwill, it is preferable to limit this *pre-testing* to those variables of most direct interest, which in this case would be their aggressiveness before seeing the film. This pre-test information can be used in two ways. First, participants with similar pre-test aggressiveness can be *matched* or *paired* in terms of their scores and then randomly assigned to one of the two conditions. This matching procedure will ensure that the participants in the two conditions will be similar in terms of their initial aggressiveness.

Second, without resorting to matching, the pre-test aggressiveness scores of the participants in the two conditions can be compared after all the data have been collected. If the scores in the two conditions do not seem to differ, then it may be assumed that random assignment has been effective so far as the key variable of aggressiveness is concerned. The way of determining whether two groups of scores differ is itself a statistical issue which will be introduced below. If, on the other hand, the scores of the two conditions appear to differ, then there are statistical procedures which take these differences into consideration. These procedures will be discussed in later chapters.

STATISTICAL SIGNIFICANCE

The second statistical consideration that needs to be met before being able to interpret the findings of this study on violence (or indeed any empirical study) is to determine how likely it is that the results may be due simply to chance. Although there are various tests for assessing the statistical significance of a finding, which will be described in subsequent chapters, the general principle which underlies significance testing can be illustrated as follows.

There are three possible outcomes to the results of this study. First, the participants who saw the violent incident may behave more aggressively than those who did not see it. This result would be consistent with the principle that people imitate what they observe. Second, there may be no difference in aggressiveness between the participants in the two conditions. This finding might imply that watching violence does not affect how aggressively people behave. And third, the participants who saw the violent incident may behave less aggressively than those who did not see it. This outcome would be contrary to the imitation principle but could come about for various reasons. For example, people who viewed the violence may have been discouraged by what they saw as the potential harm that might result. Alternatively, seeing other people being violent may relieve some of their own aggressive feelings.

If these three outcomes are equiprobable, then the probability of any one of them occurring by chance would be one in three, or 0.33. Let us assume that there are four individuals in each of the two conditions and that all the four people who saw the violence were more aggressive subsequently than the four who did not. The probability of obtaining this outcome would be 0.012 when rounded up to three decimal places $(0.33 \times 0.33 \times 0.33 \times 0.33 = 0.0119)$. Since this probability of 0.012 is below the criterion value of 0.05 set for statistical significance, we could conclude that the participants who saw the violence were significantly more aggressive than those who did not. In other words, according to our criterion, this result is unlikely to be due to chance and we could infer that watching violence increases aggression.

We should note that if the number of people taking part in this study was increased and we found the same result, then the statistical significance of obtaining this finding would be higher still. Let us assume that five instead of four people participated in each condition and that all five who saw the violent film were more aggressive than the five who did not. The probability of finding this result by chance would be 0.004 when rounded up to three decimal places $(0.33 \times 0.33 \times 0.33 \times 0.33 \times 0.33 = 0.0039)$. In other words, there is a relationship between the level of statistical significance of a finding and the number of observations on which that result is based. The same finding is more likely to be statistically significant when the number of observations on which that finding is derived is increased, as we have seen. Consequently, it is important to note that the level of statistical significance is only concerned with the probability of obtaining a result and tells us nothing about the size of that result.

TRUE EXPERIMENTAL DESIGNS

The design of the study which has so far been used to illustrate the role of statistics in social research has been referred to as a *true experimental* design (Campbell and Stanley 1966). There are two essential features to such a design. First, only the presence of the factor (or factors) whose effects are of interest should be varied or manipulated. Everything else should be kept as similar and as constant as possible. Second, participants should be randomly assigned to the conditions which represent these variations, or to the order in which these conditions are run if participants take part in more than one condition. An example of the latter procedure would be where participants saw both the film with the violence and the one without it.

A design in which different participants (or *subjects* as they were traditionally called in psychology) are randomly assigned to different conditions has been referred to as a *between-subjects* design or one involving *independent, unrelated* or *uncorrelated* groups or samples, whereas a design in which the same participants are randomly allocated to more than one condition has been described as a *within-subjects* design or one involving *repeated measures* or *dependent, related* or *correlated* groups or samples.

The advantage of a within-subjects design, apart from requiring fewer participants, is that it holds constant all those factors which are unique to any one person (such as their genetic makeup and previous personal experiences) and which may affect the way they respond to the manipulation. However, since the order in which conditions are run may alter the responses to them, it is essential to control for any potential order effects by making sure that the different orders are conducted the same number of times. Suppose, for instance, that watching violent films does not increase aggression but that the more often people see a film (no matter what its content) the less aggressive they feel. If the violent film is shown first more often, then it will appear that seeing violence produces aggression. Random assignment of participants to different orders, on the other hand, is necessary to determine if the order of the conditions has an effect. With non-random assignment, it is more likely that people who are prone to aggression will be allocated to one or other of the two orders. If aggressive people are more frequently assigned to seeing the violent film first, then there may appear to be an order effect (such that seeing violence first makes people more aggressive) when there is none.

Within-subjects designs (where it is possible in principle to use them) have two potential drawbacks which may outweigh their advantages. The first disadvantage is that there may be a *carryover* or *asymmetrical transfer effect* where a change induced by the first condition will carry over to the second. For instance, watching the violent film first may increase a person's tendency to be aggressive so that they are more likely to act aggressively after seeing the non-violent film. If this happens, then the difference in aggressiveness between the two conditions will be less in a within- than a between-subjects design and consequently may not be statistically significant. The second potential disadvantage of the within-subjects design is that participants will have more information about the experiment as a result of being exposed to more than one condition. This knowledge may affect what they think the experiment is about which in turn may influence their subsequent behaviour.

The great strength of a true experimental design is that by virtue of trying to hold all other extraneous variables constant and to vary only those factors of interest, it enables us to determine with more certainty whether the effects we observe are due to the factors that have been manipulated. For example, suppose we find that, with everything else held constant, participants who watched the violent film behaved more aggressively than those who saw the non-violent film. Then, provided that this effect occurred more frequently than is likely to have happened just by chance, it seems reasonable to conclude that the greater aggression shown resulted from watching the violent film.

NON-EXPERIMENTAL DESIGNS

Experimental designs which do not entail the random assignment of participants to the systematic manipulation of one or more variables have been called *non-*, *pre-* or *quasi-experimental* designs (Campbell and Stanley 1966). Perhaps the most common of these designs is one in which two or more variables are measured at one moment in time. This kind of design is very similar to what Campbell and Stanley (1966) term the *static-group comparison*. Suppose, for example, we wanted to find out whether people who watched more violence on television also behaved more aggressively. In other words, we wished to determine if the amount of violence seen on television was related to the level of aggression displayed. The simplest way of examining whether there was such a relationship between these two characteristics would be to ask a number of individuals how much violence they watched on television and how aggressively they behaved and to work out what the association was between these two variables.

There are two main statistical approaches for determining whether there is a statistically significant association between these two factors. The first approach is essentially a test of difference. It examines whether there is a statistical difference in aggression between the two groups of people and it is the same as that previously used to find out in the true experiment described above if there was a significant difference between those participants who saw the violent film and those who did not. In the static-group comparison we could divide the participants into two groups according to how much violence they watched on television. Individuals in one group will have watched little or no violence on television, while those in the other group will have seen more violence on television. The exact criterion we use to form the two groups need not concern us here. We can then compare the amount of aggression reportedly shown by the people in the two groups.

As before, any difference we find between the two groups may be due to chance and so we would have to work out what the statistical probability was of coming up with any such difference by chance. Suppose we noted that those who watched more violence on television also reported being more aggressive than those who saw less violence. If the probability of finding this difference was calculated to be less than 0.05 (or one in twenty), then we could conclude that those who watched more violence on television behaved significantly more aggressively than those who saw less violence. If the probability of obtaining this difference was greater than 0.05, then we would have to conclude that there was no significant difference between these two groups of individuals.

The second statistical approach for calculating whether there is a significant association between two factors (such as watching violence on television and aggression) is essentially a test of the strength of that association. We are interested in estimating how strong the relationship is between two factors. To illustrate the principle behind this test, suppose we interviewed four people about their television viewing habits and aggressive behaviour and found that, of these four, two could be classified as watching little or no violence on television while the other two could be categorised as viewing violence on television. Furthermore, of the two who did not watch violence on television, neither of them behaved very aggressively, while of the two who viewed violence on television, both of them acted aggressively. We could summarise these results in the form of a simple table as shown in Table 1.2.

To work out the strength of the relationship between watching violence on television and being aggressive, we can count the number of people who watch violence and are aggressive (two) and the number of people who do not watch violence and are not aggressive (two). If we add these two figures together and calculate the percentage of the people in our study who fall into either of these two categories, then we can see that this comes to 100 per cent ($(2 + 2)/4 \times 100 = 100$). In other words, since both the persons who watch violence on televison are aggressive while both those

Table 1.2 Results showing a perfect relationship between watching violence on television and aggression

		Aggression	
		No	Yes
Violence watched	No	2	0
	Yes	0	2

who do not watch violence on television are not aggressive, we have a perfect relationship between watching violence on television and being aggressive. An index of association is usually expressed as a proportion which in this case would be 1.00 ($(2 + 2)/4 = 1.00$).

It should be noted that an index of association can also be worked out for the results of a true experiment between the manipulated variable (e.g. watching the violent or non-violent film) and the measured variable (e.g. aggression). However, this is done less often with data from true experimental designs. The important point to remember is that both statistical tests of difference and association can be used with either true or non-experimental designs and that the choice of which test to use depends primarily on the purpose of the analysis.

The static-group comparison design includes the following three advantages. First, it is relatively simple and inexpensive to carry out. Second, information on a large number of potentially relevant factors can be assessed which is useful in exploring which factors are likely to be the most influential. And third, these factors can be studied in the natural, everyday context in which they occur.

The main drawback of this design, however, is that it does not enable us to determine the causal nature of the relationship between any two variables. Suppose, for instance, we found that people who watched violence on television also behaved more aggressively in general. The causal connection between these two variables can be explained in four possible ways. First, as originally suggested, watching violence on television may produce aggression.

1 Watching violence ———————➤ Aggression

But this is by no means the only possible explanation. Indeed, the causal direction of this association may be reversed, with aggression resulting in watching violence on television. In other words, aggressive people may like to view violence on television.

2 Watching violence ◄——————— Aggression

In both these explanations, only one variable affects the other. Consequently, these causal directions are sometimes referred to as *one-way*, *unidirectional, unilateral, non-reciprocal* or *recursive.*

However, it is also possible that both variables affect each other. Watching violence on television may encourage aggression while aggression itself may lead to viewing violence on television.

3   Watching violence ◄————————► Aggression

Relationships in which both variables influence each other are sometimes described as *two-way, bidirectional, bilateral, reciprocal* or *non-recursive.*

Finally, two variables may appear to be related when in reality they are not because they are both associated with a third variable. For example, adolescents may both watch more violence on television and be more aggressive than adults. In other words, if age is strongly related to both these variables, then the two variables will themselves appear to be directly associated when they are not.

4   Watching violence ———————— Aggression

This kind of relationship is described as *spurious* because it is due to other factors.

It is important to realise that making claims about the causal relationship between two (or more) variables depends primarily on the experimental design used to examine the relationship and not on the statistical analysis of the results. True experimental designs enable causality to be ascertained with more confidence because an attempt is made to hold constant all other variables except the ones of interest which are systematically varied. Non-experimental designs, such as the static-group comparison, do not allow causality to be inferred because they do not systematically manipulate the variables of concern. The same statistical tests can be used to analyse the appropriate results of both non- and true experimental designs. What these tests do is to provide us with an estimate of the size of any relationship and the probability of finding that relationship by chance.

RANDOM SAMPLING

When testing a principle, we generally want to know how universally valid it is. Since it is not possible to involve everyone in testing a particular generalisation, we carry out our study on a *sample* or subset of people. The idea of a sample implies that there is a larger *population* from which it is drawn. This population is often not specified, perhaps partly because we assume the principles we are testing to be universal and because it is difficult to specify exactly what the population of interest is. Take, for example, the principle that we have been using as an illustration throughout this chapter. When we postulate that watching violence on television causes aggression, we presumably believe that this holds true for all people where watching television is part of their culture.

There are two main ways in which we can select a sample of objects or cases, which need not be people, of course. The first method is to draw a *simple random* sample where every object in a given population has an equal probability of being chosen. To do this, the population of objects needs to be specified and known and some random procedure employed for selecting objects. To give a simple example, suppose we wanted to draw a small sample of five people from a class of twenty which was the population of interest. We could assign a number from 1 to 20 to each of the individuals in the class. We could then go to a table of random numbers and select the first five numbers which fell between 01 and 20, which may be 13, 09, 17, 18 and 05. The five people who had those numbers would constitute our sample. In this method, everybody would have a one in five probability of being selected.

The second method of sampling is to generate a *non-random* sample where the probability of choosing an object from a specified population is not known. An example of this approach would be if we selected the first five people alphabetically using the first letter of their surname. This method would be non-random because people whose surname began with an A would have the highest probability of being chosen.

Simple random sampling is necessary when we want to know what the probability is of finding a particular result in a population. Suppose, for example, we wished to discover how many adults living in Britain viewed violent programmes on television. If we selected a non-random sample of adults, then we would not be able to estimate the extent to which watching violence on television was likely to occur among British adults because we would not know how representative that sample was of this population. If, on the other hand, we chose a simple random sample, then depending on the size of that sample we could work out how likely that result was for the population as a whole. Consequently, a knowledge of statistics is essential for being able to determine how probable any particular finding is provided that we can specify what the population is.

MEASURING CONCEPTS

Finally, an understanding of statistics is required for making decisions about how a concept or variable should be measured and for assessing how reliable and valid that measure is. For example, we have to decide how we should quantify or score how aggressive someone is. Do we simply categorise people as being aggressive or non-aggressive? Do we order them in terms of how aggressive they are from the most to the least aggressive? Or do we rate them in some way in terms of how aggressive they are? Furthermore, when comparing levels of aggressiveness in two or more groups, we have to summarise or aggregate the scores of the individuals in the groups being compared. How do we do this? Whatever method we use, we also need to know how reliable and valid our measures of aggressiveness are. By reliable we mean how similar the scores of aggressiveness are for a particular individual when measured on more than one occasion, or by more than one person or item. Whereas a valid measure of aggressiveness is one that behaves in a way which indicates that it seems to be assessing aggressiveness, the reliability and validity of a measure are usually assessed statistically. Because the use of these and other statistical tests depends on the manner in which a concept is assessed, the different ways of measuring concepts will be discussed in the next chapter.

SUMMARY

Statistics play a vital role in collecting, summarising and interpreting data in quantitative social science research. Random assignment of participants to experimental conditions is essential in increasing the likelihood that participants assigned to different treatments will be similar and that as a consequence any observed difference between conditions will be more likely due to the experimental manipulation. Random selection of participants from a population, on the other hand, is necessary when a sample is used to gather information about that population. The reliability and validity of the measures employed have to be ascertained. The data collected need to be summarised in order to determine the nature of the results. The size of the association between variables and of the difference between groups indicates how important a variable might be in relationship to one or more other variables. The statistical significance of a finding estimates the likelihood of that result occurring simply by chance.

Chapter 2

Measurement and univariate analysis

MEASUREMENT

Statistical analysis depends on being able to measure or to quantify those aspects of objects in which we are interested. Measurement involves the assignment of numbers to observations according to certain rules. Since the type of statistical procedure used to describe and to draw inferences from empirical observations partly rests on the way in which an attribute or variable is measured, it is important to be familiar with the kinds of measurement that have been distinguished. Stevens (1946) suggested four levels or scales of measurement which are frequently referred to in discussions on the types of statistical procedures to be followed with different kinds of measurement. Although each level has its own character-istics, the levels are hierarchical. The higher levels have more sophisticated properties than the lower levels but they also include the more basic features of the lower levels.

Nominal level

The nominal level is the lowest and crudest form of measurement. Numbers are simply used to identify or to 'name' the attribute or category being described – hence the term 'nominal'. The gender of participants may be coded as numbers, with 1 for females and 2 for males. Similarly, the treatments in a true experiment may be given a number. For example, participants who watched the violent film may be ascribed as 1 and those who saw the non-violent film as 2. The assignment of numbers is arbitrary. For example, males may be coded 5 and females 9. Since the numbers have no quantitative meaning, it makes no sense to carry out mathematical operations on them such as addition, subtraction, multiplication and division. The only mathematical operation that can be performed on them is to count the frequency of each number. For instance, there may be four 1s and six 2s, denoting four females and six males respectively. Data which correspond to this level of measurement are sometimes referred to as *categorical* or *frequency* data. Numbers are often used to label and identify people or objects, such as the participants in a study, consecutively. Some writers include this use of numbers as being nominal.

Ordinal level

The next higher level of measurement is the ordinal level in which the numbers indicate increasing amounts of a particular attribute. As the term 'ordinal' implies, individuals (objects or events) can be rank 'ordered' from the smallest to the largest in terms of the characteristic being evaluated. For example, ten participants can be rank ordered in terms of how aggressive they seem with 1 indicating the least aggressive person and 10 the most. The intervals between the numbers do not represent equal amounts of the quality being measured. For instance, the difference in aggressiveness between someone ranked 2 and someone ranked 4 need not be the same as the difference between someone ranked 6 and someone ranked 8. Further-more, the numbers do not indicate absolute quantities, so that someone ranked 8 is not necessarily twice as aggressive as someone ranked 4. In some instances, it is not possible to distinguish between cases and no attempt is made to order the cases. In this situation a *tie* is said to exist and the tied cases receive the same number.

Interval level

With interval level measurement, the intervals between numbers denote equal amounts of the attribute being assessed – hence the term 'interval'. A clear example of a measure having an interval scale is a Celsius ther-mometer. The difference in temperature between the two readings of 5°C and 10°C is said to be the same as that between the two readings of 15°C and 20°C. However, because interval scales have no absolute zero point, we cannot say that a value which is twice as big as another value denotes twice the amount of the quality being assessed. Although a Celsius thermometer has a zero point, this point does not represent absolute zero since the scale registers temperatures below zero. Consequently, while we can say that 20°C is hotter than 10°C, we cannot claim that it is twice as hot as 10°C. This point will be easier to demonstrate when we consider the highest level of measurement.

Ratio level

The ratio scale represents the highest level of measurement and so has all the properties of the lower measurement levels in that it has equal intervals and it also categorises and rank orders scores. Unlike the other levels, however, it also includes an absolute zero point which means that a value which is twice as large as another reflects twice the amount of the attribute being measured. Age is an example of a ratio measure. Someone who is 20 is twice as old as someone of 10. If age was made to be an interval scale in which zero was arbitrarily set at 5 years, 10 would become 15 and 20 would become 25, in which case the interval scale value of 25 is not twice that of 15.

As we shall see, many social scientists treat what appear to be ordinal scales as if they were interval or ratio ones. Suppose we developed a simple rating scale for participants to report how aggressive they generally saw themselves as being. The rating scale has four points which represent the following degrees of aggression: 0, not aggressive; 1, slightly aggressive; 2, moderately aggressive; and 3, very aggressive. Participants have to select the number which best describes them. Although this scale has a zero point, it is neither an interval nor a ratio scale since it cannot be argued that the interval or difference in aggression between, say, points of 0 and 1 is the same as that between 2 and 3. In effect, this scale is a simple ordinal one in which the numbers indicate increasing degrees of aggression and nothing more.

None the less, many social scientists will interpret ordinal scales as interval or ratio ones. Perhaps the main reason for this is that in many cases the main interest is not with the level of measurement as such but with whether two (or more) conditions differ or whether two (or more) variables are related. Since the statistical tests themselves only apply to numbers and not to what they mean (Lord 1953), no attention has to be paid to the measurement scales when undertaking the statistical analysis. Furthermore, there is no need to be primarily concerned with measurement levels should we, for example, find that those who watch more violence on television also rate themselves as being more aggressive. However, the failure to find a difference between the two conditions may result from using a relatively crude (i.e. ordinal level) measure of aggression. Consequently, the absence of a difference or association may be due to the low level of the measure employed. Because ordinal scales are often treated as if they were interval or ratio scales, we shall primarily make a distinction between nominal and non-nominal measurement, unless otherwise necessary.

UNIVARIATE ANALYSIS

Once we have collected the data of our study, we usually need to carry out one or more *univariate* analyses in which the data for a single variable are looked at on their own. For example, we may begin by wanting to know how many participants are married or what the average number of hours of television watched per week by each participant is. Marital status is a nominal variable while hours of television is a non-nominal variable.

Proportions and percentages

With nominal variables, all that we can do is to count the number or frequency of participants within each category and to report the total number for each category or as a proportion of the total sample. Suppose, for example, we had three categories of marital status (married, divorced and single) and that 40 people were married, 20 divorced and 10 single.

Rather than simply presenting the total numbers in each group, the numbers in any one category can be expressed as a *proportion* or *percentage* of the whole sample. A proportion is the frequency of cases within a category divided by the total number of cases. So, the proportion of single people is 0.14, rounded to two decimal places ($10/70 = 0.143$). The sum of proportions always equals one ($10/70 + 20/70 + 40/70 = 70/70 = 1$), so that the largest proportion can never be bigger than one. A percentage is simply a proportion multiplied by 100. Thus the percentage of singles in the sample is 14 ($0.14 \times 100 = 14$).

Describing frequencies in proportions or percentages is particularly helpful when comparing some variable across samples of different sizes. For example, suppose we want to compare the number of married and non-married people in two samples. The number of married people is 40 in one sample of 70 and 30 in another sample of 50. It is easier to grasp and to compare these figures when they are converted into a percentage for each sample, namely 57 ($40/70 \times 100 = 57.14$) and 60 ($30/50 \times 100 = 60.0$) per cent.

Note that percentages can be misleading when the total number of cases is small. For example, if we had a sample of only seven people, 14 per cent of them only represents one person. Similarly, if we expanded the size of our sample by one person from seven to eight people, then this is an increase of 14 per cent which seems large although it is only an increase of one person. Consequently, what the numbers represent is more important than their absolute size.

Rounding numbers and number of digits

When dividing one number by another we frequently obtain more digits than in the original number. To take an extreme example, if we divide 1 by 3, the resulting number is 0.3333 recurring. When this happens two questions arise. The first is how many digits in the number should we present and the second is how we go about reducing or rounding the numbers. Some writers have suggested that generally we should have only one or two digits more than the original number. If we restricted ourselves to having two more digits than the original number, then dividing 1 by 3 would become 0.33. We would now have three digits instead of the original one.

The general rule for rounding numbers to the nearest whole number or to the nearest decimal place is that if the digit (reading from left to right) following the one to be rounded is less than 5, it is dropped. So, in our example, the 3 (0.33*3*) following the 3 to be rounded (0.3*3*) is dropped since it is less than 5. If the following digit is more than 5 (say, 0.33*6*), then the digit to be rounded (0.3*3*) is rounded up or increased by 1 (to 0.3*4*).

The only complication arises when the following digit is 5 (0.33*5*). One rule for handling this situation is that when the digit preceding the 5 is an odd number (e.g. 0.3*3*5), it is rounded up by 1 (to 0.34). On the other hand, when the digit preceding the 5 is an even number (e.g. 0.3*2*5), the 5 is dropped (so the rounded number becomes 0.32). The reason that some numbers ending in 5 are rounded up and some down is that, over many instances of such rounding, about half the numbers will have been rounded up and about half rounded down. If numbers ending in 5 were always rounded down, there would be a bias towards lower numbers.

An alternative and more simple rule is to round up numbers that are equal to or greater than 5 and to drop numbers that are less than 5. So, rounding to two decimal places, 0.3*35* becomes 0.34 while 0.3*34* becomes 0.33. Because of its simplicity and because this rule is employed by the statistical program we will be using, we shall adopt this method.

Different procedures of rounding numbers will lead to different results. One way of avoiding these differences (which may be large) is to follow the further rule that each number in a series of computations is rounded to one more decimal place than the number of places used in the final answer. The rules described in this section will generally be applied to the examples worked out by hand throughout this book to ensure that a consistent practice is adopted.

Measures of central tendency

When dealing with non-nominal variables which can have a large number of different values, it is useful to be able to summarise these scores in some way. One way of doing this is to describe the scores in terms of their typical or central value. These indices are known as *measures of central tendency*, of which the three most commonly discussed are the *mode*, the *median* and the *mean* or *arithmetic mean* (to distinguish it from other means such as the geometric and harmonic mean).

Mode

The least used and simplest of these three measures is the mode, which is the score that occurs most frequently. Suppose we have the following set of seven scores which may be number of hours of television watched by seven people:

6 3 5 7 1 3 4

The most common score is 3, of which there are only two. Consequently, the mode is 3. Note that the mode is the most commonly occurring value (3) and not the frequency (2) of that value. If a number of the scores had the same frequency, then there would be more than one mode. For example, if there was another score of 5, then this set of scores would have two modes (3 and 5).

Median

The median is that score in a set of scores which divides the scores into two equal parts in such a way that all the scores above the median are higher than those below it. To obtain the median the scores should be placed in ascending order of size from the smallest to the largest score. For the seven scores used previously, this order becomes

1 3 3 4 5 6 7
       ↑

The median is 4 since the number of scores above the median are equal to the number below it and all the scores above the median are higher than those below it.

When the total number of scores is even, then the median is the average of the middle two scores of the ordered set of scores. So, in the following set of eight scores

1 3 3 4 5 6 7 7
       ↑

the median is 4.5 ((4+5)/2 = 4.5).

Calculating the median becomes more complicated when the frequency of the middle score is greater than one. Take the following set of eight numbers:

1 3 3 4 4 4 6 7
       ↑

The median lies between the first and second 4 but there is also a third 4 to take into account.

The median in this case is worked out as follows. First, however, we have to realise that although all these scores are whole numbers or integers, they can vary anywhere between these numbers. In other words, they can take on fractional or non-integer values such as 1.7 or 8.53. Thus, an integer has *exact* or *real limits* which determine what fractional values it can have and these are set as 0.50 units below and above that number. The exact limits define the *interval* of any score which for 4, for example, ranges from 3.50 to 4.50 with the exact midpoint being 4 itself.

Since there are three 4s in this instance, we assume that the three values are equally spread between 3.50 and 4.50. This means that each value occupies a third (0.33) of this interval. The limits of these three values, therefore, are 3.50, 3.83, 4.16 and 4.50. Consequently, the median is midway between 3.50 and 4.16, which is 3.83.

```
  4    4    4
3.50 3.83 4.16 4.50
       ↑
```

To give another example, take the following set of seven values:

```
1 3 3 4 4 4 6
      ↑
```

The median of these scores will lie midway in the interval of the first 4, which is the middle score. Since the interval of this 4, as we have seen, ranges from 3.50 to 3.83, its midpoint is 3.67 $((3.50 + 0.33)/2 = 3.67)$ which is therefore the median of this set.

Mean

The mean is the most commonly used measure of central tendency. To obtain it all the scores in a series are added together and this total score is divided by the number of scores. Take the following set of seven scores which we have already used initially to illustrate the calculation of the mode and the median:

```
1 3 3 4 5 6 7
```

These scores are first added together $(1 + 3 + 3 + 4 + 5 + 6 + 7)$ to give the sum or total score of 29, which divided by the number of scores (7) gives a mean of 4.14 $(29/7 = 4.14)$.

Comparison of mode, median and mean

Which of these three measures of central tendency should be used to describe the typical value of a set of scores depends partly on the distribution of those scores when ordered according to size. When the distribution is unimodal (i.e. has one mode) and symmetrical, then the mode, median and mean will have very similar values. Take the following set of seven scores, whose distribution is unimodal and symmetrical:

```
1 2 3 3 3 4 5
```

The mode or most frequent score is 3, of which there are three. The median or middle score is also 3 with two scores lower and two scores higher than it. The mean is 3 which is the sum of the seven scores $(1 + 2 + 3 + 3 + 3 + 4$

+ 5 = 21) divided by the number of scores (7). What this means in practice is that when the distribution of scores has one mode and is approximately symmetrical, then the mode, median and mean will have roughly the same value so that it matters less which measure we use to describe the central tendency of the array of scores.

When the distribution of scores is symmetrical but bimodal (i.e. has two modes), then the median and the mean will have very similar values which will obviously differ from the modes since there are two of them. For example, in the following symmetrical and bimodal distribution of seven scores

1 2 2 4 5 5 6

the two modes are 2 and 5 while the median is 4 and the mean 3.57 (25/7 = 3.57).

When the distribution of scores is asymmetrical, then all three measures of central tendency will differ. Examine the following asymmetrical distribution of seven scores:

1 2 2 3 7 8 9

The mode is 2, the median is 3 and the mean is 4.57 (32/7 = 4.57). When most of the scores in a set are relatively low, the mode will generally have the lowest value, the median the next lowest and the mean the highest.

Conversely, when most scores are relatively high, the mode will have the highest value, the median the next highest and the mean the lowest, as in the following example:

1 2 3 7 8 8 9

Here the mode is 8, the median is 7 and the mean is 5.43 (38/7 = 5.43).

Further complications arise when the data contain a few extreme scores (sometimes called *outliers*) since the mean is more strongly affected by such scores than either the mode or the median. We can see this if we substitute 90 for 9 in the preceding set of numbers. The mode and the median will remain the same (at 8 and 7 respectively) while the mean will be increased from 5.43 to 17 (119/7 = 17). In such situations, it may be more appropriate to use the median than the mean. Alternatively, the mean can be employed but calculated by either omitting the extreme values or making them less extreme. In this example, the mean would be 4.83 (29/6 = 4.83) if 90 was excluded or 5.43 if it was reduced to, say, the next highest score after 8 (i.e. 9).

Another possibility is to transform all the scores so that the differences between the extreme values and the other values are less. The two most common methods of doing this are to take either the square root or the (base 10) logarithm of the scores. These transformations are given below (to one decimal place) for the following set of scores which was previously used to illustrate the influence of an extreme value.

	1	2	3	7	8	8	90
Square root	1.0	1.4	1.7	2.6	2.8	2.8	9.5
Logarithm	0.0	0.3	0.5	0.8	0.9	0.9	2.0

For the untransformed scores, the difference between 8 and 90 (i.e. 81) is at least eleven times ($81/7 = 11.6$) as great as that between 1 and 8 (i.e. 7). For the square root transformations of the same scores, however, the difference between 2.8 and 9.5 (i.e. 6.7) is less than four times ($6.7/1.8 = 3.7$) as big as that between 1 and 2.8 (i.e. 1.8). While for the logarithm transformations, the difference between 0.9 and 2.0 (i.e. 1.1) is about the same size ($1.1/0.9 = 1.2$) as that between 0.0 and 0.9 (i.e. 0.9).

Measures of dispersion

Measures of central tendency only describe the typical value of a distribution of scores and do not indicate the spread or variation in those scores. Two distributions may have exactly the same mean but very different spreads of scores as the following two sets of scores illustrate.

3 3 4 4 4 5 5
1 2 3 4 5 6 7

The mean of both sets of scores is 4 but the spread of the first set is more restricted than that of the second. Indices of spread are called *measures of dispersion*, of which the three most often described are the *range*, the *interquartile range* and the *standard deviation*.

Range

The range is the simplest measure of dispersion and is just the difference between the highest and the lowest values in a set of scores. So, the range for the first set of scores above is 2 ($5 - 3 = 2$) while for the second set it is 6 ($7 - 1 = 6$). One disadvantage of the range is that, since it is only based on the two extreme scores, it gives little indication of what the distribution of other scores is like. If either or both of these extreme scores differs greatly from the other scores, then the range will solely reflect the difference between the extreme scores. So, if the 7 in the following set of scores is replaced with 17, then the range is 16 ($17 - 1 = 16$) rather than 6 ($7 - 1 = 6$).

1 2 3 4 5 6 7

Interquartile range

A measure of dispersion which is less dependent than the range on the two extreme scores is the interquartile range. To calculate it, the scores have to be arranged in ascending order and divided into four quarters containing equal numbers of scores. The *first quartile* is the value below which the lowest quarter of scores fall. The *second quartile* is the value below which half (or two quarters) of the lowest scores lie and corresponds to the median, while the *third quartile* is the value below which three quarters of the lowest values congregate. The interquartile range is the difference between the third and first quartiles.

To work out the number of scores which fall within the first quartile of a set of scores, we add 1 to the total number of scores and divide by 4. Similarly, to calculate the number of scores which lie within the third quartile, we add 1 to the total number of scores and multiply by 3/4. So, for the following set of seven scores

1 2 3 4 5 6 7
↑   ↑

the first quartile lies at the second score ($(7 + 1)/4 = 2$) which is 2. The third quartile falls on the sixth score ($(7 + 1) \times 3/4 = 6$) which is 6. Consequently, the interquartile range of this set of scores is 4 ($6 - 2 = 4$).

Note that the interquartile range of the following set of scores

1 2 3 4 5 6 17
↑   ↑

is also 4 since the third quartile is still 6 ($(7 + 1) \times 3/4 = 6$). Sometimes the *semi-interquartile range* or *quartile deviation* is used instead of the interquartile range. This measure is simply the interquartile range divided by 2, which in this example is 2 ($4/2 = 2$).

Calculating the first and third quartile is slightly more complicated where the number of scores is not equally divisible by 4. Take the following sequence of nine numbers:

1 1 5 6 6 6 6 9 9

The first quartile falls at the 2.5th score ($(9 + 1)/4 = 2.5$) while the third quartile lies at the 7.5th score ($(9 + 1) \times 3/4 = 7.5$). In other words, the first quartile lies halfway between the second score (i.e. 1) and the third score (i.e. 5). The difference between these two scores is 4 ($5 - 1 = 4$) which halved is 2 ($4/2 = 2$). Therefore, the first quartile is the second score (1) plus half the distance between the second and third scores (2) which comes to 3 altogether ($1 + 2 = 3$). Similarly, the third quartile is the seventh score (i.e. 6) plus half the difference between the seventh and eighth scores ($(9 - 6)/2 = 1.5$) which makes 7.5 in total ($6 + 1.5 = 7.5$).

Standard deviation

The most frequently used measure of dispersion is the standard deviation which is based on all the scores in a set. The standard deviation of a sample is the square root of its *variance* (strictly speaking, the *estimated* variance) which is each score subtracted from the mean, squared, added together and divided by the total number of scores minus 1:

$$\text{variance} = \frac{\text{sum of (mean} - \text{each score)}^2}{\text{number of scores} - 1}$$

As we shall see the notion of variance is an important one since it forms the basis of the parametric tests described in this book.

If the difference or deviation between the mean and each score in a set were simply added together, they would sum to zero and so give no indication of the distribution of scores. The reason for this is that the mean lies at the centre of a distribution where the sum of scores above it (i.e. positive) is equal to the sum of scores below it (i.e. negative). This fact can be illustrated with the following set of eight scores:

4 4 5 5 6 7 8 9

The mean of these scores is 6 (48/8 = 6). If 6 is subtracted from each score, then the differences between the mean and each score are

−2 −2 −1 −1 0 +1 +2 +3

The sum of the negative differences (−6) is equal to the sum of the positive differences (+6) which added together would equal zero. However, if the differences are squared before being added together,

4 4 1 1 0 1 4 9

then the *sum of squares* is 24 and the variance or *mean square* is 3.4 (24/7 = 3.4).

The variance is expressed in squared units, which are not directly comparable to the original values. For example, if the eight scores represented the number of hours of television watched, then the variance would refer to 'squared hours'. The square root of the variance is used to convert the squared units into the original ones. As can be seen, the square root of the variance (3.4) of the eight scores above is 1.8, which describes more closely than the variance the average deviation of the positive scores (6/3 = 2) and the negative scores when the negative sign is disregarded (6/4 = 1.5).

Because the standard deviation, like the mean, is based on all the scores in a sample, it is strongly affected by extreme scores. This point can be demonstrated with the following set of eight scores where 89 replaces the value of 9 in the previous example.

4 4 5 5 6 7 8 89

The mean of this set of scores is now 16 (128/8 = 16) instead of 6. The differences between the mean and these scores are

−12 −12 −11 −11 −10 −9 −8 +73

which when squared become

144 144 121 121 100 81 64 5329

The sum of these squares is 6104, the variance is 872 (6104/7 = 872) and the standard deviation 29.53 ($\sqrt{}$(872) = 29.53). Once again, we can see that the standard deviation is closer than the variance to the mean *absolute* (i.e. ignoring the signs of the deviations from the mean) deviation, which is 18.25 ((12 + 12 + 11 + 11 + 10 + 9 + 8 + 73)/8 = 18.25).

Because the above procedure for calculating the variance initially involves the arithmetic operation of division in arriving at the mean, it can result in greater rounding error than a process in which adding, subtracting and multiplying is done before dividing and taking the square root. There is an alternative computational procedure which is generally used in deriving the variance since the division occurs at a later stage. This procedure consists of (1) squaring each score; (2) adding them together; (3) subtracting from this number the sum of scores squared and then divided by the number of scores; and (4) dividing this figure by the number of scores minus 1:

$$\text{variance} = \frac{\text{sum of squared scores} - (\text{squared sum of scores}/\text{number of scores})}{\text{number of scores} - 1}$$

We can show that this procedure produces the same figure for variance as that previously calculated from the following set of numbers:

4 4 5 5 6 7 8 9

The sum of these numbers is 48 which squared is 2304. When these numbers are squared they become

16 16 25 25 36 49 64 81

The sum of these squared numbers is 312. Dividing the squared sum of scores (2304) by the number of scores (8) and subtracting this figure (2304/8 = 288) from the sum of squared scores (312) gives a sum of squares of 24 (312 − 288 = 24). Dividing the sum of squares (24) by the number of cases minus 1 (8 − 1) produces a variance of 3.4 (24/7 = 3.4).

$$\frac{312 - (48^2/8)}{8 - 1} = \frac{312 - (2304/8)}{7} = \frac{312 - 288}{7} = \frac{24}{7} = 3.4$$

As can be seen from this example the numbers involved in the inter-mediate stages of this procedure become large. Furthermore, the way in which the procedure is related to the idea of variance is less obvious. Consequently, this more accurate computational procedure for calculating variance will not generally be used in the book. However, if greater accuracy is required, then its use is recommended.

SUMMARY

Four levels or scales of measurement have been distinguished, called nominal (or categorical), ordinal, interval and ratio. Ordinal scales are often treated as interval or ratio scales in the social sciences. The distri-bution of nominal or categorical data can only be quantified in terms of the frequency of each category, which can be further summarised as a proportion or percentage. The distribution of non-nominal or non-categorical data, on the other hand, can be described in terms of measures of central tendency (such as the mode, median and arithmetic mean) and dispersion (such as the range, interquartile range and standard deviation). The sum of squared deviations from the mean (i.e. the sum of squares) and the mean of that sum of squares (i.e. the mean square or variance) provides the basis of parametric tests of association and difference. Extreme scores can disproportionately affect the mean and standard deviation of a sample.

EXERCISES

1 Which is the highest level of measurement that socio-economic status represents?
2 Which is the highest level of measurement that number of persons in a household represents?
3 For this set of scores

  7 2 5 3 8 6 1 4 3 4

provide the following statistics: (a) mode; (b) range; (c) median; (d) interquartile range; (e) mean; (f) sum of squares; (g) variance; and (h) standard deviation (to two decimal places).

Chapter 3

Introducing the Statistical Package for the Social Sciences

To understand the way in which statistical values are arrived at, it is necessary to work through the calculations ourselves since this practice will check our grasp of the steps involved. These calculations are relatively easily and quickly carried out by hand when the data consist of a small set of low whole numbers and when the statistics are comparatively straightforward like those presented in the previous chapter. However, with larger sets of bigger numbers, the manual calculation of even these simple statistics can be time-consuming and may result in elementary mistakes being made. The inconvenience of these two drawbacks becomes more serious when we need to employ more complicated statistics and/or when we want to examine the data in different ways, as is often the case. The advent of computers has led to the development of various computer programs for calculating statistics. These programs are not difficult to operate and carry out the required computations very quickly. With the ready accessibility of these packages, calculating statistics by computer is generally more efficient than doing so by hand, once the principles underlying the statistical tests have been grasped.

Knowing how to work one of these programs has three further advantages. First, our understanding and ability to carry out these tests by hand on new sets of numerical data can be simply checked against the results given by the program. If our calculations are different from those of the program, then the reason for this discrepancy needs to be determined. Since the error may lie in either our calculations or the way in which we ran the program, this procedure will test our comprehension of both these processes. In other words, these programs can be used to assess the accuracy of our own efforts in conducting the tests by hand as well as by computer. Moreover, we can explore our knowledge of various statistical principles by generating and running examples of data which either confirm or disconfirm our expectations about what should happen. In this way we can try out our understanding of statistics on as many problems as we like, knowing that we can easily verify whether our work is correct.

Second, these programs can be employed for other aspects of data analysis such as selecting subsets of individuals for further investigation or creating new variables. For example, we may wish to examine the scores for females and males separately as well as together. Or, we may want to create a new variable which can be routinely worked out from information we possess. For example, we may wish to calculate for each person in a sample the total number of hours of television watched per week from the number of hours watched per day.

And third, we can write our own programs to perform tests we need to use repeatedly but which are not part of the package. In addition, provided that the necessary information is reported, we can construct programs which enable us to conduct tests on other people's data which have not been carried out or we can check the accuracy of what has been done by repeating them. For example, if we know the mean and standard deviation of two groups of participants, we can work out whether these measures differ significantly between the two groups. Needless to say, in order to do this we have to know how to run the test as well as the program.

Consequently, there are considerable advantages in learning how to use a computer program for performing statistical tests. The aim of this chapter is to introduce you to one of the most widely used, comprehensive and flexible statistical programs in the social sciences, which is aptly called the Statistical Package for the Social Sciences and which is usually referred to as SPSS for short. It has also been readily available on both mainframe and personal computers for a number of years. For these reasons, SPSS has been chosen to illustrate the benefits of using computer programs. It is hoped that sufficient information has been presented in this book for you to operate this package without having to refer to the large manuals which SPSS has produced to instruct users. However, if you run into any problems, then it may be necessary for you to turn to the appropriate volume for further help. Once you have learned the material presented in this book, you may wish to find out about the other statistical techniques included in SPSS.

As SPSS is continually being revised and the revisions take time to be implemented in different institutions, various versions of it may be accessible at any one time and these versions may be periodically replaced with new ones when these become available. At present, the latest revision for the personal computer (PC) is called SPSS/PC+ 4.0 (Norušis/SPSS 1990a, b) while that for the mainframe computer is known as SPSS Release 4.0 (Norušis/SPSS 1990c, d; SPSS 1990). The immediately preceding versions for the personal and mainframe computer were respectively referred to as SPSS/PC+ Version 3 (Norušis/SPSS 1988a, b, c) and SPSS-X Release 3.0 (SPSS 1988). The differences between SPSS/PC+ 4.0 and SPSS 4.0 are few in number and relatively minor. However, to make the presentation easier to follow and to use, one version has been generally described in this and subsequent chapters which is SPSS/PC+ 4.0. A

summary of these commands is provided in Appendix 1 for quick reference. The small differences between the fourth version for the personal and
mainframe computer and the third and the fourth versions for both types of
computers are listed in Appendices 2, 3 and 4. Unless there is a need to be
more specific, the general statistical package will be referred to as SPSS.

GAINING ACCESS TO THE STATISTICAL PACKAGE FOR THE SOCIAL SCIENCES

As already implied, to use SPSS it is necessary to have access to it via a
personal computer, or a *terminal* connected to a mainframe computer.
Both a computer terminal and a personal computer consist of a *keyboard*
on which we type in or put in (hence the term *input*) the instructions. They
also usually have a video display unit (VDU) or television-like *screen*
which shows what we have typed. Since the screen only displays a limited
number of lines at any one time, information will disappear from the top
once the screen becomes full. This should not cause any concern as there
are keys (on the keyboard) for moving into view what we have typed or
entered. Furthermore, a *printer* is normally attached to the computer which
allows us to print out a *hard copy* of what we have typed.

Because the exact procedure for using SPSS will vary according to the
operating system of the computer, these details will have to be obtained
from the appropriate sources open to you. To simplify the presentation
further, only the *batch* method of running SPSS commands will be
described in which a group of instructions are first put together before
being run. Such a batch of information is often referred to as a *file*.
Information is put into a file by means of an *editor* or editing system, which
can, of course, also be used to change, delete or add further information.
Since the procedure for editing and running SPSS files is standard for
SPSS/PC+ (and is now also available as SPSS Manager on SPSS 4.0), this
system is described at the end of this chapter to show you how it operates.
In addition, some brief comments about using personal computers are
included.

Instructions or *commands* that SPSS employs will be printed in bold in
the body of the text to make clear the sense in which these terms are being
used. Similarly, the names given to identify SPSS information such as files
and variables will also be presented in bold as will any SPSS output which
is displayed in the text. These commands can be typed in either capital or
small letters (or a combination of them). SPSS commands are printed in
small letters throughout this book since these are easier for the inexperi-
enced typist to use. SPSS is a very versatile program and there are often
many different ways of carrying out the same procedure. To help you get
started using SPSS as quickly as possible, preference has been restricted to
what are considered to be the most generally useful methods of working.

TABULATING DATA

A collection of quantitative data is easier to read if it is presented in a table in which the values for each variable are placed in the same column(s) and the value for each *case* is placed in a separate row. Cases are often people but can be any unit of interest such as years, shops or newspapers. Suppose we were gathering information on the age, gender and the number of paid hours worked in the last week for a sample of not more than a hundred individuals whom we wanted to remain anonymous. We could arrange this information in table form as shown in Table 3.1.

In many situations, the way in which the cases are ordered does not matter and they can be entered as the information becomes available. Although the cases do not have to be numbered, enumerating them is an advantage when we want to refer to any of them. Since numbers are read from left to right, single digits of a two or more digit number (such as the number of hours worked) should always be placed in the right-hand column for that variable. If this is not done, then it is possible when, say, adding 7 to 42 to add the 7 to the 4 rather than the 2 making 112 instead of 49.

Incorrect	7	Correct	7
	42		42
	112		49

Gender in this example was recorded as F for females and M for men. However, any code could be used such as 1 for females and 2 for men, or vice versa. Sometimes data for a particular variable will be missing. Someone may not have given their age or it may not have been reported on the form. In such circumstances, the fact that this information is missing needs to be indicated in some way. In this example, the relevant column has simply been left empty or blank.

Table 3.1 Tabulating data

Case no.	Age	Gender	Hours
1	33	F	42
2	51	M	7
3	33	M	42
4	27	M	0
⋮	⋮	⋮	⋮
100	67	F	0

FILING DATA IN THE STATISTICAL PACKAGE FOR THE SOCIAL SCIENCES

When using SPSS, however, it may not be necessary to tabulate our data first since this will have to be done when the data are entered into a file. When we have a large amount of data, the task can be very time-consuming. If your institution employs people for this purpose, then this job is best left to them since they will do it more efficiently and accurately than you can. The examples of data in this book have been kept deliberately small so that you should be able to type them in quickly for yourself. Although these are not physically displayed on the screen, the file space into which the data are put consists of a potentially very large number of rows. Each row, however, is made up of a limited number of columns which is restricted to eighty in many computers and in SPSS/ PC+. Each column in a row can only hold one character such as a single letter or digit.

To illustrate the way in which a small set of data is arranged in an SPSS file, we can use the simple example above. Although SPSS does not require data to be tabulated in a *fixed-field* format where the values of a variable are always placed in the same column(s), this procedure is recommended since it is easier to read and to locate values, particularly where there are large numbers of variables. Consequently, the data for the five individuals can be entered into a file in the same form as above. Since it is generally more convenient to process data expressed as numbers, females will be coded as 1 and males as 2.

Furthermore, to make the data more realistic, the age of case 100 will be missing. SPSS will automatically assign as missing spaces which are blank but where it expects to find a number. However, it is more convenient to choose our own numerical code for identifying missing values. This number should not be easily confused with potential values that a variable could have. For example, it may be ambiguous to designate a missing age as zero since it is possible (although unlikely) that the age of the person was less than 1 year old. It is better to ascribe this missing value as -1 since there is no such age. We will also assume that the number of paid hours which case 4 worked is missing as well and that the missing value for this variable is also coded as -1.

If we make these minor changes, then the data for the five individuals can be arranged in the SPSS file as follows.

```
   1  33  1  42
   2  51  2   7
   3  33  2  42
   4  27  2  -1
 100  -1  1   0
```

Two blank spaces have been left between the four columns of figures to make them easier to read, although this need not be done. In this table, the case number has been placed in columns 1 to 3, age occupies columns 6 and 7, gender is in column 10 and number of hours worked lies in columns 13 and 14.

Although we know what these numbers represent, SPSS at this stage has no idea. Consequently, we have to tell SPSS how to read these data. This information is contained in the **data list** command, which states where the data set is to be found, what the variables are called and where they are in the set itself. This instruction will also remind us of this information. Data can be kept in a separate file on their own or they can be included in the file which contains the commands for defining what they are and what is to be done with them. Where the amount of data is large, storing them separately from the command file may be more convenient. Where the set is small, as in the examples generally used in this book, holding them in the same file as the SPSS commands may be more appropriate, which is the procedure illustrated here.

Unless otherwise specified, the **data list** command assumes that the data are included in the *command file* and the format is fixed. Thus, the only other information that has to be given is the number of rows of data per case (which in this example is one), the SPSS names for the variables and their column numbers. SPSS names must meet certain criteria to qualify as such. They must be no longer than eight characters and must begin with an alphabetic letter (a–z) or an @ (at) sign. The remaining characters can be any letter, any number (1–9), a period (.) and certain symbols (_, $, £, @). Blanks are not allowed within the name and each name in a file must be unique. In addition, certain words called *keywords* cannot be used because they are interpreted as part of commands by SPSS. They include **all**, **and**, **by**, **eq**, **ge**, **gt**, **le**, **lt**, **ne**, **not**, **or**, **to** and **with** in SPSS/PC+. If we inadvertently use one of these words as a name, we will receive an *error message* telling us of our mistake when we run the command file.

The name we choose should help remind us of what the variable is and should be as short as possible to save typing. So, the SPSS name for case number can be **cno**, age can remain as **age**, gender can be shortened to **gen** and number of paid hours worked can be abbreviated as **phw**. The column location of the variable should follow the variable name if the number of columns per variable differ as they do in this instance. If a variable only occupies one column as does **gen**, then only the number of this column is listed which is **10**. If, however, a variable is located in two or more columns (e.g. **age**), then the number of the first and last column for this variable is given separated by a hyphen (e.g. **6-7**). So, the **data list** command for this data set reads

data list/cno 1-3 age 6-7 gen 10 phw 13-14.

The forward slash (/) after **data list** indicates that what follows lies in the first row of the data set. If there was a second row of data for each case, then the variable names and column locations in that row would come after a second slash. The end of all SPSS/PC+ commands is indicated with a full stop. The blank spaces shown in the command need to be inserted in order to identify the terms in it. For example, if there was no empty space between **phw** and **13-14**, then SPSS tries to interpret the term **phw13-14** as a variable name.

If we do not wish to indicate in which columns the variables are we could use the following **data list** command where the keyword **free** is inserted before the forward slash and the column numbers are omitted:

data list free/cno age gen phw.

Since we have missing values, we also need to tell SPSS what these are, which we do with a **missing values** command. The names of variables having the same missing values are listed together, followed by the number(s) placed in parentheses which signify these missing data. Thus, the **missing values** command for this data set is

missing values age phw (-1).

SPSS commands can be abbreviated to the first three letters of each keyword so that this command can be

mis val age phw (-1).

SPSS only uses the first three letters of the keyword to recognise it and ignores the subsequent letters. So, for example, if we mistype **missing values** as **misng valeus**, this command will still be correctly identified because the first three letters of each word are right.

The rows of data come next but these must begin with a **begin data** command and finish with an **end data** one. So, the file containing the data and the *data definition* commands is

data list/cno 1-3 age 6-7 gen 10 phw 13-14.
missing values age phw (-1).
begin data.
```
    1 33 1 42
    2 51 2  7
    3 33 2 42
    4 27 2 -1
100 -1 1  0
```
end data.

The keywords in this file could be shortened as follows:

dat lis/cno 1-3 age 6-7 gen 10 phw 13-14.

mis val age phw (-1).
beg dat.
   1 33 1 42
   2 51 2   7
   3 33 2 42
   4 27 2 -1
100 -1 1   0
end dat.

STATISTICAL ANALYSIS WITH THE STATISTICAL PACKAGE FOR THE SOCIAL SCIENCES

To carry out a statistical analysis of these data we need to use the appropriate SPSS statistical *procedure* command. So far, we have only described the relatively simple descriptive statistical measures of central tendency and dispersion. One SPSS command which calculates the mode, median, mean, range, quartile, variance and standard deviation among some other statistics is the **frequencies** procedure command which takes the following general form:

frequencies variable names
 /ntiles 4
 /statistics mode median mean range variance stddev.

The command for computing these statistics for both **age** and **phw** at the same time is

frequencies age phw
 /ntiles 4
 /statistics mode median mean range variance stddev.

which can be shortened to

fre age phw
 /nti 4
 /sta mod med mea ran var std.

So, the complete SPSS command file now reads

dat lis/cno 1-3 age 6-7 gen 10 phw 13-14.
mis val age phw (-1).
beg dat.
   1 33 1 42
   2 51 2   7
   3 33 2 42
   4 27 2 -1
100 -1 1   0
end dat.

fre age phw
 /nti 4
 /sta mod med mea ran var std.

All that has to be done next is to run this file.

STATISTICAL PACKAGE FOR THE SOCIAL SCIENCES OUTPUT

The output from this command file is displayed on the screen when the file is run. Among other information, the output includes the original SPSS command file (excluding the data) as well as the statistics requested for both **age** and **phw**. The section containing the statistics for **age** is presented in Table 3.2. This command automatically lists the frequency of each value, the percentage of each value in the whole sample (including missing values), the percentage of each valid value (i.e. excluding missing values) and the cumulative percentage of valid values. From this list, we can see that the most frequent value or mode is 33 which is given below the frequency table with the other statistics. We can check the accuracy of these descriptive statistics by calculating these values by hand. If only the mean of **age** is required, then the **frequencies** command can be shortened to

fre age
 /sta mean.

In other words, we need only request what we want.

The mean, variance, standard deviation and range (as well as a few other descriptive statistics) are also produced with the **descriptives** procedure command which takes the following general form:

Table 3.2 **Frequency** output

Value Label		Value	Frequency	Percent	Valid Percent	Cum Percent
		27	1	20.0	25.0	25.0
		33	2	40.0	50.0	75.0
		51	1	20.0	25.0	100.0
		−1	1	20.0	MISSING	
		TOTAL	5	100.0	100.0	
Mean	36.000	Median	33.000	Mode		33.000
Std Dev	10.392	Variance	108.000	Range		24.000

Percentile	Value	Percentile	Value	Percentile	Value
25.00	28.500	50.00	33.000	75.00	46.500
Valid Cases	4	Missing Cases		1	

descriptives variable names
/**statistics 1 5 6 9.**

The numbers in the **statistics** subcommand refer to the following particular statistics

1   Mean
5   Standard deviation
6   Variance
9   Range

The short form of this command for producing these statistics for the two variables of age and paid hours worked is

des age phw
/**sta 1 5 6 9.**

The statistics output for this command is shown in Table 3.3. As can be seen, the values of these statistics for **age** are the same as those given by the **frequencies** command. There are no entries under **Label** because a **variable labels** command has not been included in the command file. This command, which is not essential, provides names for variables that can be longer than eight characters. The number of *listwise* valid observations is also displayed, which in this example is three. Listwise refers to the number of cases which have no missing values on any variable listed in the **descriptives** command. In these data, three cases (i.e. cases 1, 2 and 3) have valid observations for both **age** and **phw**. Excluded are case 4 (where **phw** is missing) and case 100 (where **age** is missing).

Unless specified, the **descriptives** command will automatically (i.e. by *default*) exclude cases on a variable-by-variable basis, in which the statistics are based on the number of cases with valid observations for that variable. Consequently, the number of cases on which these statistics are based is given for each variable in the column labelled **N** since this number may vary for different variables. Although this number is identical for these two variables in our example, the exact same cases are not involved in calculating these statistics. The statistics for **age** are based on cases 1, 2, 3 and 4 and those for **phw** on cases 1, 2, 3 and 100.

If we want the listwise option of selecting cases, then we have to ask for

Table 3.3 **Descriptives** output

Number of Valid Observations (Listwise) = 3.00

Variable	Mean	Std Dev	Variance	Range	N	Label
AGE	36.00	10.39	108.00	24.00	4	
PHW	22.75	22.41	502.25	42.00	4	

this by incorporating an **options** subcommand. The appropriate sub-command is inserted in the following **descriptives** command where the **5** requests SPSS to exclude cases with any values missing on these two variables.

des age phw
 /opt 5
 /sta 1 5 6 9.

The statistics output for this command is displayed in Table 3.4. These statistics are based on the same three cases. Consequently, the number of cases is not presented separately for each variable. Once again, the accuracy of these values can be easily verified by calculating them manually.

Table 3.4 **Descriptives** output with listwise exclusion of missing values

Number of Valid Observations (Listwise) = 3.00

Variable	Mean	Std Dev	Variance	Range	Label
AGE	39.00	10.39	108.00	18.00	
PHW	30.33	20.21	408.33	35.00	

Conversely, SPSS procedures can be used to check the manual calcu-lations in the previous and subsequent chapters. For example, in Chapter 2 the mean was worked out by hand to be 17 for the following set of numbers:

 1 2 3 7 8 8 90

This value can be checked with the following SPSS command file where **no** is the SPSS name for the set of numbers.

dat list/no 1-2.
beg dat.
 1
 2
 3
 7
 8
 8
90
end dat.
des no/sta 1.

A **missing values** command is not needed since there are no missing values. The relevant output of this file when run is presented below:

Number of Valid Observations (Listwise) = 7.00
Variable   Mean N   Label
NO   17.00   7

which shows that the mean is 17.

ERROR MESSAGES

It is easy to make mistakes when typing commands. There is no need to
worry about these mistakes, since SPSS will recognise them, display the
likely reasons for them and will not run the command file until they have
been corrected. Although mistakes are readily made, their causes are not
always immediately obvious. Consequently, examples of some common
mistakes will be presented together with the error messages which SPSS
gives in response to them.

No blank space between variable name and column number on **data list**
command

With no space, for example, between **phw** and **13-14** as in

dat lis/cno 1-3 age 6-7 gen 10 phw13-14.

SPSS displays the following error message:

ERROR   73,   Text: -14
INVALID START COLUMN FOR A VARIABLE ON DATA LIST
COMMAND—Check for a missing or negative start column.
This command not executed.

SPSS tries to read **phw13-14** as a variable name and expects to be told in
which column(s) this variable is to be found. Since a hyphen cannot be
used as part of a variable name, SPSS interprets **phw13** as the variable
name and then points out that either the start column in which this variable
is to be located is missing or that it is negative which is not possible. In this
instance, the start column (**13**) is missing since it is now seen as being part
of the variable name (**phw13**).

No forward slash on **data list** command

If the forward slash is inadvertently omitted from the **data list** command

dat lis cno 1-3 age 6-7 gen 10 phw 13-14.

SPSS produces the following error message:

ERROR   51,   Text: CNO
INVALID KEYWORD ON DATA LIST COMMAND—Keywords

FILE, FIXED, FREE, TABLE, and MATRIX are valid.
This command not executed.

The only valid keywords that can come after **dat lis** are those mentioned in the error message. Note that SPSS does not alert you to the possibility that the forward slash may be missing. In other words, the actual mistake in the command is not always identified in the error message but may have to be deduced as in this example.

No full stop at end of **data list** command

Another example of an error which would have to be worked out is when the full stop is accidentally left out at the end of the **data list** command:

dat lis/cno 1-3 age 6-7 gen 10 phw 13-14

This mistake gives the following error message:

ERROR   57,   Text: AGE
DUPLICATE VARIABLE NAME ON DATA LIST COMMAND.
This command not executed.

Because the full stop (which signifies the end of a command) is missing from the **data list** command, the next line

mis val age phw (-1).

is read as a continuation of the first line. SPSS indicates that **age** occurs twice on what it interprets as being the **data list** command. Notice that SPSS stops after picking up the first error. Other errors resulting from reading the **missing values** command as part of the **data list** command are not given.

Misspelt variable name

If the name of a variable such as **age** is subsequently misspelt, say as **ag**,

dat lis/cno 1-3 age 6-7 gen 10 phw 13-14.
mis val ag phw (-1).

SPSS displays the following message:

WARNING   420,   Text: AG
UNDEFINED VARIABLE NAME—Check for a misspelled
variable name.

In this example, the message is self-explanatory. **Ag** is undefined since it was not listed as such in the **data list** command. SPSS asks you to check the spelling of this variable as it does not recognise its name. Note, however, that the same error message appears if you inadvertently forget to include

age (and its location) on the **data list** command. In this case, **ag** obviously has not been defined rather than simply misspelt.

No **begin data** command

If the **begin data** command does not precede the data, then the following error message results:

ERROR   1,   Text: 1 33
INVALID COMMAND—Check spelling. If it is intended as a
continuation of a previous line, the terminator must not be specified on
the previous line.
If a DATA LIST is in error, in-line data can also cause this error.
This command not executed.

SPSS expects a new command to start with letters. When it comes across numbers, it suggests that these numbers may be part of a previous command which has been prematurely ended (with a full stop in SPSS/PC+) or that they may represent data which is what they do here.

As we have seen, although SPSS cannot necessarily identify the exact error you have made, it does notify you of the subsequent errors caused by that initial mistake. This information should help you work out what that initial mistake is. SPSS also displays the line in the file which contains the error. So, if you have difficulty in seeing what your mistake is, compare the line causing the problem with similar commands illustrated in this book. Any discrepancies in the general form of the two lines should indicate where the mistake may lie.

DATA TRANSFORMATIONS

In addition to carrying out statistical tests, SPSS has commands which can transform variables by changing their value (e.g. by multiplying them by 10) or by combining two or more variables (e.g. by adding the value of one variable to that of another). These data transformation commands will be used to show and to carry out some of the computations needed to calculate a particular statistic.

For example, to add up the following set of numbers,

1 2 3 7 8 8 90

we first have to define them as a case with the **data list** command and include them in the command file as follows:

dat lis/n1 to n7 1-21.
beg dat.
  1 2 3 7 8 8 90
end dat.

Note that where the variables are similar in nature and are consecutively ordered and each occupies the same number of columns (three in this instance), it is convenient to include as the last part of the name (i.e. the suffix) a number that corresponds to the position of the variable. Where this is done, the **data list** command need only contain the first variable name in this series (**n1**) and the last one (**n7**), separated by the keyword **to**. This keyword indicates that there are five other names not mentioned (i.e. **n2, n3, n4, n5** and **n6**) which begin with the same name (the prefix **n**) but end with consecutive numbers. These seven variables each occupy three columns (the first of which is the blank space making the seven numbers easier to read). Consequently, only the first column (**1**) of the first variable and the last column (**21**) of the last of these seven variables need to be specified, together with a hyphen (**-**) between the two numbers.

To add together the seven variables, the **compute** command is used to create a new variable (called **sum** in this example) which is placed after the keyword **compute**. The variables to be added together are listed after an equals sign (**=**) and are connected by the plus sign (**+**). So, the complete command reads

compute sum=n1+n2+n3+n4+n5+n6+n7.

The **list** command is needed to display the results of this arithmetic operation. It follows the **compute** command.

The complete command file for this computation is

dat lis/n1 to n7 1-21.
beg dat.
  1 2 3 7 8 8 90
end dat.
compute sum=n1+n2+n3+n4+n5+n6+n7.
list.

The relevant output for this command file is

N1 N2 N3 N4 N5 N6 N7   SUM
 1   2   3   7   8   8 90 119.00
Number of cases read = 1 Number of cases listed = 1

The values of the seven variables are listed together with the sum of their values.

To calculate the mean, another **compute** command can be employed to form a new variable called **mean** which is (**=**) the previous variable (**sum**) divided (**/**) by seven (**7**).

compute mean=sum/7.

If this new command is added after the first **compute** command

dat lis/n1 to n7 1-21.
beg dat.
  1 2 3 7 8 8 90
end dat.
compute sum=n1+n2+n3+n4+n5+n6+n7.
compute mean=sum/7.
list.

then the following output is presented:

N1 N2 N3 N4 N5 N6 N7   SUM   MEAN
  1   2   3   7   8   8 90 119.00   17.00
Number of cases read = 1   Number of cases listed = 1

Alternatively, a single **compute** command can be used to produce the **mean** in which the seven variables are first added together and then divided by seven:

compute mean=(n1+n2+n3+n4+n5+n6+n7)/7.

Since arithmetic operations on a **compute** command take place in a particular sequence, this order of priority needs to be known. Operations enclosed in parentheses are carried out first while multiplication (*) and division (/) are performed before addition (+) and subtraction (−). Consequently, the seven variables are placed in parentheses to ensure that they are added together before being divided by **7**. Without the parentheses, **n7** would have been divided by **7** first and then added to the other six variables, resulting in a value of 41.86 rather than 17.

If this single **compute** command replaced the previous two used, the following output results:

N1 N2 N3 N4 N5 N6 N7   MEAN
  1   2   3   7   8   8 90   17.00
Number of cases read = 1   Number of cases listed = 1

Other **compute** functions will be introduced as the need for them arises.

OPERATING SPSS/PC+

To operate SPSS/PC+, it has to be already installed on the personal computer we want to use, which we will assume is the case. After switching on the machine, we need to access SPSS/PC+. This procedure will vary somewhat depending on how the program has been set up. To ensure that we have a copy of any work we want to keep, we should store this information on a separate *floppy disk* which we can take away with us once the session has ended. Otherwise, the copy which can be held on the computer may be wiped out by a subsequent user. The floppy disk is inserted into a slot called a *drive*. The disk may first have to be *formatted* if it is new or if its present format is not compatible with the machine.

To call SPSS onto the screen, type **spsspc** after the *prompt* sign and press the (carriage) *Return* or *Enter* key to indicate that that is the end of the command, which will then be carried out. On many keyboards, the Return key is identified by having a ⮐ sign on it. After we have called SPSS/PC+, the SPSS/PC+ logo will briefly appear followed by a horizontally split screen (with two windows). At this stage, we need only be concerned with the lower window which we shall use to type in and edit information and which is called the *scratch pad.* The scratch pad will be initially blank apart from a small flashing light called a screen *cursor* in the top left-hand corner of the lower window.

The cursor indicates the point on the screen where the next item you enter will be placed. You should also note that in the bottom right-hand corner of the lower window is a number (**01**) which states the column where the cursor is. This information is particularly helpful when typing data into specific columns. The cursor can also be used to remind us which columns the data are in by moving it to the data we are interested in locating and reading off the column number at the bottom right-hand corner of the lower window.

The cursor can be repositioned within a file by the cursor keys. These keys have an arrow on them pointing either leftward, rightward, upward or downward which are the directions in which the cursor can be moved. To move the cursor more quickly, the following keys can be used. To shift the cursor to the end of the line it is on, hold down the key with Ctrl (for Control) on it and then press the key with the rightward pointing arrow on it. To move the cursor to the beginning of the line it is on, hold down Control and press the key with the leftward pointing arrow on it. To move the cursor up one screen, press the key with Pg Up (for Page Up) on it, while to move it down one screen, press the Pg Dn (for Page Down) key. To shift the cursor to the very top of the file, hold down Control and press the key with Home on it, while to move it to the very bottom of the file, hold down Control and press the End key.

SPSS/PC+ automatically takes us into the *Menu and Help* mode unless this default setting has been altered. To change into *Edit* or *Review* mode, we have to hold down the key with Alt (short for Alternative) on it and press the E (for Edit) key. You will notice that the cursor changes from a flashing block to an underscore (_). In addition, the border on the top left portion of the screen (the *Main Menu*) changes from lines to dots. These two changes should help to remind us that we are now in edit mode. However, since it is inconvenient to have to change from Menu to Review mode every time an SPSS/PC+ command is run, it is recommended that the default setting be altered so that we automatically stay in Review.

To change the default setting, we have to create a file called **spssprof.ini**. In edit mode, type the following command:

set automenu=off.

Press the F9 key (F for *Function*). The function keys are usually either at the top of the keyboard or on the left-hand side. The functions that these keys perform in SPSS/PC+ are displayed at the very bottom of the screen when the keys are pressed and the first option is always highlighted. If we press the wrong function key, we can always cancel this action by pressing the key with Esc (for Escape) on it. Pressing the Return key will carry out the highlighted option while the cursor keys will move the highlight. Alternatively, instead of highlighting the appropriate option and pressing Return, the function key can be pressed followed by the key with the letter which is capitalised in the relevant option. For example, the F9 key (which we have to use) has the two options of writing (i.e. saving) and deleting files. Since the write option is already highlighted, the Return key can be pressed. Alternatively, since the W in the write option is capitalised, we can simply press the key with W on it.

We now have to label the file (containing the **set** command) **spssprof.ini**. At the bottom of the screen, we will see **Name of file** displayed with **scratch.pad** highlighted. Type in the name **spssprof.ini** (which will over-write **scratch.pad**) and press the Return key. We have just created and saved our first file using SPSS/PC+. This file will only operate the next time we enter SPSS/PC+. So, let us finish our present session in SPSS/PC+ by moving the cursor one column to the right in the row it is in (i.e. past the full stop of the **set** command) and by pressing the Return key to move the cursor to the next line.

To end a session, we simply type **finish** (or **fin** for short) and press F10. The option we want (**run from Cursor**) is already highlighted and is the one we will always use for running any SPSS/PC+ command files. So, press the Return key and we will leave SPSS/PC+. To go back to SPSS/PC+, type **spsspc** and press the Return key.

We will see that SPSS/PC+ is now in edit mode and that the upper window is blank apart from an SPSS/PC+ heading, the date and the **set** command. This upper window contains a *listing* of all the output we produce in a session which is held in a file called **spss.lis**. At present, the only output is the **set** command which briefly appeared on the screen after the SPSS/PC+ logo. If we want to go over what we have done, we look at the information in this window. How to do this will be described a little later.

Next, type in the following SPSS/PC+ command file (which was described earlier), pressing Return at the end of each line to start the next one.

dat lis/cno 1-3 age 6-7 gen 10 phw 13-14.
mis val age phw (-1).
beg dat.

```
   1  33  1  42
   2  51  2   7
   3  33  2  42
   4  27  2 −1
 100 −1  1   0
end dat.
fre age phw
 /nti 4
 /sta mod med mea ran var std.
```

Information in a file can be deleted with the following keys. To delete one or more previous characters, press the Backspace key, which may have a leftward pointing arrow and Del (for Delete) on it. The key with Del on it (and no arrow) removes the character which the cursor is currently on. If we do this when the cursor is in the space at the end of a line, the next line will appear where the cursor is. We may need to use this key when we wish to join two adjacent lines. To erase the whole line the cursor is on, hold down either Alt or F4 and press the D (for Delete) key.

To remove a number of lines at the same time, we move the cursor to the first line we want deleted, press F7 and Return. The text on this line will now flash slowly to make it stand out. Then move the cursor to the last line we wish to delete, pressing F7 again. We have now defined the lines we want to remove, the text of which will flash slowly. To cancel what we have done, simply press F7 again. Otherwise, to delete this marked area, press F8 and the D key. Alternatively, we can press F8, highlight the **Delete** option and press Return. Using F7 and F8 to remove lines is particularly convenient when editing the SPSS listing file which may have large areas we want removed.

To run this command file, move the cursor to anywhere on the top line (i.e. the **data list** command) and then press F10 followed by the Return key. The F10 key will run the file from the line the cursor is on. So, for example, if we initially return F10 when the cursor is on the bottom line of this command file (i.e. the **frequencies** command), the data and the data defining command will not have been read with the consequence that no statistics can be computed.

The output produced by this command file will be displayed on the full screen. If the message **MORE** appears on the top right-hand corner of the screen, press any key to display more output. When all the output has been presented, we will be returned to the original command file. We can now change or add any information and run the file from where the changes have been made. If there is an error in our command file, an error message will be displayed, and when we are returned to the command file the cursor will be on the line in which the mistake was made. Correct what you think is the mistake and run the file again. If we have inadvertently activated the

SPSS/PC: prompt, type **review**. and press Return which will bring us back to the editor.

To save this command file on a floppy disk, press F9 and type in the letter of the disk drive that the floppy disk is in (say, drive A), followed by a colon and the name we want to give the file. The file name can consist of a prefix or stem of up to eight characters and a suffix or extension of up to three characters. So, for example, we could call this command file **phw.sps** where the prefix (**phw**) may remind us that the file contains information about the number of paid hours worked while the suffix (**sps**) informs us that it is an SPSS command file. In this case, we would type **a:phw.sps** to save the file called **phw.sps** on the floppy disk in drive A. To display this file in the scratch pad on a future occasion, press F3, Return and type in **a:phw.sps**. To save any subsequent changes made to this file, press F9, Return and type in the name of the drive and the file as before if they are not already displayed.

To read the output we have produced in the session, press F2 when **Switch** will be highlighted. Press the Return key and the cursor will now be in the upper window. Note that the size of the window that the cursor is in can be increased with either the **Change size** or **Zoom** option of F2. We can read the output in the list file by appropriately moving the cursor. A hard copy of the whole file can be printed after the session is over. Alternatively, we may delete those parts of it we do not want to keep. However, this edited file needs to be given a new name (such as **phw.lis**) using the F9 key. If we do not save the edited file with a new name, it will be lost. Note that both the **scratch.pad** and the **spss.lis** file will be wiped clean the next time we enter SPSS/PC+, so do save any information you want to keep in files which have names other than these two.

A system which is similar to that used by SPSS/PC+ is available on SPSS 4.0 and is known as SPSS Manager. However, since some of the keys for operating this system may be different from SPSS/PC+, you may need to check what the appropriate keys are. For example, the operation of function keys in SPSS/PC+ may be invoked by pressing the Escape key together with the appropriate number (with 1 for F1 to 0 for F10).

SUMMARY

Statistical programs allow statistics to be calculated quickly and accurately. One of the most widely used and comprehensive statistical programs in the social sciences is the Statistical Package for the Social Sciences or SPSS for short, available on both mainframe and personal computers. Commands are also available for selecting particular subsets of data and for creating new variables. The basic information needed to carry out a statistical analysis is a computer file containing the data, a command describing the names and the location of the variables in that file and a command which requests the particular statistics required. A computer file consists of a potentially large number of rows made up of a fixed number of columns which is restricted to 80 in most machines. The values of variables are listed in columns and data for each case or unit begin on a new row. Spaces which are empty and where SPSS expects a number are treated as missing. If missing values are coded numerically a command specifying these values is required. The statistical results are usually displayed visually on a screen and can also be printed.

EXERCISES

1   How would you numerically code the variable of marital status which has the following five categories: single and never married; married; separated; divorced; and widowed?
2   How would you code someone who had said they were both single and widowed?
3   In your data file you have information on the year of birth of your respondents. What command would you use to calculate their age in the year 2000?
4   For 10 respondents you have collected information on their age, gender and their responses to 10 dichotomous questions measuring self-esteem.
    (a) How would you input this information in your SPSS command file?
    (b) What command would you use to add up the scores of the 10 questions to give a total score for each person?
    (c) What command would you use to find the mean score for each person?
    (d) If some of the responses were missing what effect would this have on the total score?
    (e) What command would you use to find the mean of the total score for the whole sample of 10 individuals?

Chapter 4

Statistical significance and choice of test

As outlined in the first chapter, one of the main uses of statistics in the social sciences is to determine the probability of three different kinds of events or outcomes happening. The first kind is estimating whether a sample drawn from a population is representative of that population. Suppose, for example, we know that the population of interest consists of an equal number of women and men and we draw a sample of five women and seven men. How likely are we to obtain this particular number of women and men by chance? The second kind is deciding whether one sample differs from another. Assume, for instance, that ten people are randomly assigned to watching the same episode on television either with or without violence. Three of the five viewing the violent episode behave more aggressively than three of the five seeing the non-violent sequence, while there is no difference between the other two. What is the likelihood of finding this difference by chance? The third kind is estimating the probability of two events being associated by chance. Imagine, for example, that three out of four people who watch violence on television behave aggressively whereas three out of six people who do not view violence on television act aggressively. How likely are we to come across such a relationship by chance?

The probability of obtaining any particular event by chance on any occasion is one divided by the total number of possible events. So, the probability of randomly selecting a woman or man from a population containing an equal number of women and men is 0.5 ($1/2 = 0.5$). The probability of finding a person randomly assigned to watching a violent episode on television behaving more aggressively than another randomly assigned to viewing a non-violent episode is 0.33 ($1/3 = 0.33$), since that individual can be either more, less or as equally aggressive as the other. While the probability of someone being by chance both aggressive and having watched violence on television is 0.25 ($1/4 = 0.25$). If the probability of being aggressive is independent of watching violence on television, then the probability of both events occurring is the product of their separate probabilities ($0.5 \times 0.5 = 0.25$).

The probability of obtaining a particular sequence of independent events is the product of their separate probabilities. So, the probability of randomly choosing two women from a population consisting of the same number of women and men is 0.25 ($0.5 \times 0.5 = 0.25$). The probability of finding two people randomly allocated to watching a violent sequence on television acting more aggressively than two individuals randomly assigned to seeing a similar non-violent episode is 0.11 ($0.33 \times 0.33 = 0.11$). Whereas the probability of two people being by chance both aggressive and having watched violence on television is 0.06 ($0.25 \times 0.25 = 0.06$).

Since the procedure for determining the probability of independent events is similar for the three kinds of situations described above, we shall use the simplest case of randomly selecting women and men from a population containing an equal proportion of women and men. This situation is the same as tossing a number of unbiased coins once. If we select one person at random, then there are only two possible outcomes since that person can only be a woman or a man. Consequently, the probability of selecting either a woman or a man is 0.5 ($1/2 = 0.5$). If we pick two people, there are four possible outcomes: (1) two women; (2) two men; (3) a woman followed by a man; and (4) a man followed by a woman. If these four outcomes are equiprobable, then the probability of any one of them occurring is 0.25 ($1/4 = 0.25$). Since there are two different orders in which a woman and a man can be selected, the probability of obtaining a woman and a man is the sum of the probability of these two orders, which is 0.5 ($0.25 + 0.25 = 0.5$). If we plot the distribution of the probability of choosing these three different numbers of women and men, then this distribution will take the form of an upturned 'V', as shown in Figure 4.1.

If we select four people, there are sixteen possible outcomes, as presented in Table 4.1. If these sixteen outcomes are equiprobable, then the probability of any one of them happening by chance is 0.0625 ($1/2 \times 1/2 \times 1/2 \times 1/2 = 0.0625$). As there are four different ways in which either three women and one man or one woman and three men can be selected, the probability of obtaining either of these two outcomes is 0.25 ($0.0625 + 0.0625 + 0.0625 + 0.0625 = 0.25$). Similarly, as there are six different orders containing two women and two men, the probability of finding this outcome is 0.375 ($0.0625 + 0.0625 + 0.0625 + 0.0625 + 0.0625 + 0.0625 = 0.375$). If we plot the distribution of the probability of selecting these five different numbers of women and men, then this distribution takes the shape of an inverted 'V' once more, as drawn in Figure 4.2.

As can be worked out, the larger the number of people selected from a population, the less likely it is that the sample will consist of all women or men. For example, the probability of obtaining five women and no men from a population consisting of equal numbers of women and men is 0.031

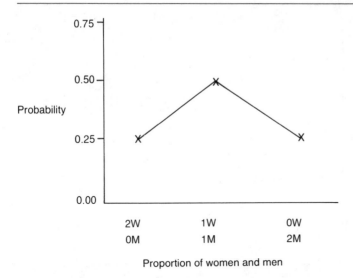

Figure 4.1 Two-case example of a probability distribution

Table 4.1 Four-case example of equiprobable gender outcomes

Possible outcomes	Probability
1 WWWW	0.0625
2 WWWM 3 WWMW 4 WMWW 5 MWWW	0.2500
6 WWMM 7 WMWM 8 WMMW 9 MWWM 10 MWMW 11 MMWW	0.3750
12 MMMW 13 MMWM 14 MWMM 15 WMMM	0.2500
16 MMMM	0.0625

$(0.5 \times 0.5 \times 0.5 \times 0.5 \times 0.5$ or $0.5^5 = 0.031$ rounded to three decimal places), while the probability of obtaining six women and no men is 0.016 ($0.5^6 = 0.016$ rounded to three decimal places). However, even with very large samples of people, there is always a very small probability that the sample will contain all women or all men. Consequently, the question

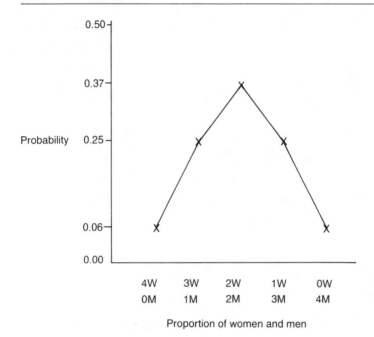

Figure 4.2 Four-case example of a probability distribution

arises as to when do we decide that a sample is or is not representative of the population from which it is drawn. The same issue, of course, is also raised when determining whether there is or is not a difference in the scores (e.g. aggression) between two groups (e.g. those watching the violent or non-violent episode on television) or whether there is or is not a relationship between two variables (e.g. being aggressive and having watched violence on television).

The conventional probability or *p* value for deciding that a result is not due to chance is less than 0.05, or five times out of a hundred. If the probability level of an outcome is below 0.05, then the result is *statistically significant* in that it is thought unlikely to have been due to chance. If, on the other hand, the probability level of an outcome is 0.05 or above, then that result is *statistically non-significant* in the sense that it is considered likely that it could have been due to chance. Note that this result is *non*-significant and not *in*significant.

When analysing the probability of an outcome, we can either specify the direction of the results we expect to obtain or we can leave the direction unstated. In terms of the three kinds of situation outlined at the beginning of this chapter, we could predict that the sample will contain a greater proportion of women than the population, that the people watching the violent episode on television will show more aggression than those viewing the non-violent episode, and that aggressive people will have watched more violence on television. Take the case of expecting that the sample will consist of a greater proportion of women than the population. Suppose we obtain a sample of only four women. Since the probability of selecting such a sample is 0.0625 which is greater than 0.05, we would conclude that the sample does not differ significantly from the population. If, on the other hand, we had a sample of five women only, we would assume that the sample varied significantly from the population since the probability of finding such a sample is 0.031, which is below the 0.05 level. When the hypothesis is *directional*, we adopt the *one-tailed* probability level since only one end or tail of the probability distribution is used.

When, however, the hypothesis is *non-directional* in the sense that we do not predict what the results will be, we employ the *two-tailed* probability level which takes account of both ends or tails of the probability distribution. Suppose, for instance, we wanted to know whether the proportion of women in the sample differed from that in the population but did not have any expectations about the way in which it differed. Since the sample may contain either proportionately more or proportionately less women than the population, both these probabilities have to be included. Consequently, the criterion of 0.05 for deciding whether the sample differs significantly from the population is made up of the 0.025 probability that the sample will contain proportionately more women than the population and the 0.025 probability that the sample will comprise proportionately less women than the population.

For example, if a sample of five women was obtained from a population containing equal numbers of women and men, then this sample could be interpreted as not differing from the population since the probability of obtaining five women (0.031) combined with the probability of obtaining five men (0.031) is 0.062 (0.031 + 0.031 = 0.062), which is greater than 0.05. If, on the other hand, a sample of six women was selected from the same population, then this sample could be said to differ from the population since the probability of selecting six women (0.016) added to the probability of selecting six men (0.016) is 0.032 (0.016 + 0.016 = 0.032), which is less than 0.05. Since the one-tailed probability level is half that of the two-tailed probability level, statistical significance is more likely to be obtained when the direction of the hypothesis is stated. However, the one-tailed probability level can only be used when the direction the results will take has been specified before the data are analysed. If the direction of the results are not predicted before the data are examined, then the two-tailed probability level has to be employed.

The convention of adopting the 0.05 probability level as the cut-off point for determining the statistical significance of a finding is arbitrary, since there is always the probability that any result is due to chance. For example, although we assume that a sample containing only six women differs significantly from a population known to consist of an equal number of women and men, there is a two-tailed probability of 0.032 that this result could have occurred by chance.

Because we can never be certain about whether a sample differs from its population, whether two groups differ from each other or whether a relationship exists between two variables, we can make one of two types of error. The first type of error, known as *type I error* or *alpha error,* is when we accept that there is a difference or relationship when in reality there is none, as shown in Table 4.2. For example, we may assume that the sample differs from its population when it does not. *Type II* or *beta error* is when we accept that there is no difference or relationship when in actuality there is one.

We may reduce the possibility of making a type I error by lowering the significance level from 0.05 to, say, 0.01 (one in a hundred) or less. If, for example, we adopt the 0.01 probability level, then a sample of only six women would not differ significantly from a population containing equal numbers of women and men, since the two-tailed probability of obtaining this result (0.032) is greater than 0.01. However, employing a more conservative probability level has the effect of increasing a type II error. One way of decreasing the probability of making this kind of error is to increase the size of the sample. For instance, the two-tailed probability of finding that a sample contains all women is 0.062 for a sample of five but 0.032 for a sample of six.

DIFFERENT KINDS OF STATISTICAL TESTS

What particular statistical test we use for deciding whether a result is statistically significant depends on five main considerations. First, are we interested in determining whether two variables are related or whether two or more groups differ on some variable? Tests of association assess the size and often the direction of a relationship between two variables, whereas tests of difference ascertain whether two or more groups differ on some

Table 4.2 Type I and type II errors

		Real difference or relationship	
		Yes	No
Difference or relationship accepted	Yes	Correct decision	Type I error α
	No	Type II error β	Correct decision

variable. Second, are the data categorical or non-categorical? With categorical data, the number or frequency of cases in each category is simply counted, whereas with non-categorical data the data can be described in terms of measures of central tendency and dispersion. Third, do we need to make assumptions about the way the values of the variables are distributed? *Non-parametric* tests do not depend on the distribution of variables whereas *parametric* tests do under certain circumstances. Fourth, do the two or more groups being compared consist of different (*unrelated*) individuals or ones which are the same or have been matched (*related*)? And fifth, are there only two groups to compare or more than two?

The major tests of difference and association covered in this book are displayed in Tables 4.3 and 4.4 respectively, together with the considerations for their application.

PARAMETRIC AND NON-PARAMETRIC TESTS

One of the unresolved issues in statistics is the question of when parametric rather than non-parametric tests should be used. Some writers have argued that parametric tests should only be applied when the data fulfil the following three conditions: (1) the variables are measured with an equal interval or ratio scale; and the samples are drawn from populations (2) whose variances are equal or *homogeneous* and (3) whose distributions are *normal*. A normal distribution is a theoretical or idealised one which is based on a population of an infinite number of cases and which takes the form of a bell or an inverted-U as shown in Figure 4.3. The extent to which a normal distribution looks like a bell depends upon the values of its parameters. Greater variances will create flatter distributions. The term *parameter* refers to a measure which describes the distribution of the population such as its mean or variance. Parametric tests are so called because they are based on assumptions about the parameters of the population from which the sample has been drawn.

Whether these three conditions have to be satisfied before parametric tests can be employed has been seriously questioned. Concerning the first condition, it has been suggested that parametric tests can also be used with ordinal variables since tests apply to numbers and not to what those numbers refer (Lord 1953). Suppose, for example, we compare the number of violent films watched during the last year by three individuals judged to be aggressive and three people thought to be non-aggressive. The number of violent films seen by the three aggressive individuals is five, seven and eight respectively, and is one, three and six for the three non-aggressive ones, as shown in Table 4.5. Consequently, the aggressive group has viewed twenty violent films in all while the non-aggressive group has seen ten. The variable of the number of violent films watched is a ratio scale since it has a zero point and the numbers indicate equal intervals.

Table 4.3 Tests of difference

Nature of variable	Type of test	Type of data	Number of groups	Name of test	Page numbers
Categorical (nominal or frequency)	Non-parametric	Unrelated	2	Binomial	75–9
			2+	Chi-square	79–92
		Related	2	McNemar	93–5
			3+	Cochran Q	131–2, 135
Non-categorical	Non-parametric	Unrelated	2	Kolmogorov–Smirnov	101–4
			2	Mann–Whitney U	104–9
			3+	Kruskal–Wallis H	109–12
		Related	2	Sign	111–14
			2	Wilcoxon	114–16
			3+	Friedman	116–19
	Parametric	Unrelated	2	t	121–8
			2+	One-way and two-way analysis of variance	129–35, 140–53
		Related	2	t	156–9
			3+	Single factor repeated measures	161–4
		Related and unrelated	2+	Two-way analysis of variance with repeated measures on one factor. One-way analysis of covariance	163–70, 171–84

Table 4.4 Tests of association

Nature of variable	Type of test	Name of test	Page numbers
Categorical (nominal or frequency)	Non-parametric	Phi coefficient	187–9
		Contingency coefficient	188–91
		Cramer's *V*	190–2
		Goodman and Kruskal's lambda	192–4
		Goodman and Kruskal's tau	194–5
Non-categorical	Non-parametric	Kendall's tau *a*	196–7
		Kendall's tau *b*	197–200
		Kendall's tau *c*	200–2
		Goodman and Kruskal's gamma	201–3
		Somer's *d*	202–5
		Spearman's rank order correlation	204–7
		Mantel–Haenszel's chi-square	207–8
		Kendall's partial rank order correlation	211
		Partial gamma	212–13
	Parametric	Pearson's product-moment correlation	216–20
		Pearson's partial correlation	231–8
		eta	238–9
		Unstandardised regression coefficient	243–9, 252–3
		Standardised regression coefficient	249, 253
		Part correlation	260–4

Indeed, the aggressive group has seen twice as many violent films as the non-aggressive group.

Now, assume that instead of asking people how many violent films they had seen, we had them rate how often they watched violent films on a four-point scale where 1 signifies 'not at all', 2 'rarely', 3 'occasionally' and 4 'often'. This measure would be an ordinal scale since someone scoring 4 would not necessarily have seen twice as many violent films as someone

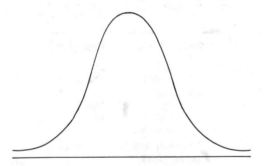

Figure 4.3 A normal distribution

Table 4.5 Ratio and ordinal measures of frequency of violent films watched by three aggressive and three non-aggressive individuals

	Aggressive		Non-aggressive	
	Ratio	Ordinal	Ratio	Ordinal
	5	3	1	1
	7	3	3	2
	8	4	6	2
Total	20	10	10	5

scoring 2. As indicated in Table 4.5, the three aggressive individuals rated themselves as 4, 3 and 3 and the three non-aggressive ones as 2, 2 and 1. Therefore, the total score is 10 for the aggressive group and 5 for the non-aggressive one. Since the measure is an ordinal one, we cannot say that the aggressive group saw twice as many violent films as the non-aggressive one. However, we can state that the aggressive group viewed more films with violence than the non-aggressive group. Since a parametric test applied to these two measures simply determines whether the mean scores of the two groups differ, the measure can be ordinal, equal interval or ratio.

With respect to the second and third conditions, a number of studies have been conducted to see what effect samples drawn from populations with non-normal distributions and unequal variances have on the values of parametric tests (e.g. Boneau 1960). Violation of these two assumptions generally had little effect on the values of these tests. One exception to this general finding was where both the size of the samples and the variances were unequal. Another exception was where both distributions of scores were non-normal. In such circumstances, it is necessary to either transform the scores to normality (Tabachnick and Fidell 1989) or use a non-parametric test.

F TEST FOR EQUAL VARIANCES

The *F* test or ratio is used to determine if the variances of two groups of scores differ. As described in Chapter 2, the variance of a sample is calculated by subtracting each score from the mean score for the group, squaring these differences, adding the squared differences together and dividing this total by the number of scores minus 1. The *F* test is simply the greater variance of one group divided by the smaller variance of the other:

$$F = \frac{\text{greater variance}}{\text{smaller variance}}$$

To find out if the two variances differ significantly, we look up the statistical significance of the *F* value in a table like that in Appendix 5.

Suppose we have the two sets of scores shown in Table 4.6 which, for example, reflect the number of violent films watched by seven aggressive and eight non-aggressive individuals during the past year. The mean of the aggressive group is 5 $((5 + 6 + 8 + 5 + 2 + 4 + 5)/7 = 5)$ and of the non-aggressive group is 2 $((1 + 2 + 2 + 2 + 3 + 1 + 2 + 3)/8 = 2)$. The variance of the aggressive group is 3.333 $((0 + 1^2 + 3^2 + 0 + 3^2 + 1^2 + 0)/(7 - 1) = 3.333)$ and of the non-aggressive group is 0.571 $((1^2 + 0 + 0 + 0 + 1^2 + 1^2 + 0 + 1^2)/(8 - 1) = 0.571)$. The *F* value or ratio is 5.83 $(3.333/0.571 = 5.833)$.

We look up the statistical significance of this ratio in the table of *F* values in Appendix 5, the relevant proportion of which has been reproduced in Table 4.7. In this example, the number of people in the group with the larger variance (the numerator) is seven while the number in the group with the smaller variance (the denominator) is eight. The *degrees of freedom* (*df*) for each group are the number of people in that group minus 1, which is 6 for the aggressive group and 7 for the non-aggressive one. The

Table 4.6 Number of violent films seen by an aggressive and non-aggressive group

Group 1 (aggressive)	Group 2 (non-aggressive)
5	1
6	2
8	2
5	2
2	3
4	1
5	2
	3

Table 4.7 Part of the table of two-tailed 0.05 values of *F*

df_2	...	5	6	7	...
6		4.3874	4.2839	4.2067	
7		3.9715	*3.8660*	3.7870	
8		3.6875	3.5806	3.5005	

concept of degrees of freedom is a difficult one to understand and it is explained more fully elsewhere (Walker 1940). Basically it means that the value of one of a set of scores is determined if we know the sum of that set of scores and the values of the remaining scores. For instance, if we know that the sum of seven scores in the aggressive group is 35 and that six of the scores are 5, 6, 8, 5, 2 and 4, then we can work out that the remaining score must be 5. If, on the other hand, we know the sum of the seven scores and the value of one of them, then the remaining six are free to vary.

According to this table, for an *F* ratio to be significant at the 0.05 per cent two-tailed probability level with 6 degrees of freedom for the numerator and 7 degrees of freedom for the denominator, the *F* ratio must be larger than 3.8660. Since an *F* ratio of 5.83 is larger than the critical value of 3.8660, we can assume that the variances of the two groups are not equal. If the *F* ratio had been less than the critical value of 3.87, then we would have inferred that the variances of the two groups were equal.

An *F* test comparing the variances of two independent samples is carried out as part of the SPSS procedure for calculating an unrelated *t* test which is used to determine whether the means of two independent or unrelated samples differ. To compute an *F* test for comparing the variances of the seven aggressive and eight non-aggressive individuals, set up the following SPSS command file.

data list/grp 1 nvf 3.
end data.
1 5
1 6
1 8
1 5
1 2
1 4
1 5
2 1

```
2 2
2 2
2 2
2 3
2 1
2 2
2 3
end data.
t-test groups=grp(1,2)/variables=nvf.
```

A variable called **grp** has been created to indicate whether people belong to the aggressive or the non-aggressive group. Individuals assigned to the aggressive group are coded as **1** and those allocated to the non-aggressive group are coded as **2**. The label **nvf** refers to the *n*umber of *v*iolent *f*ilms watched by the people in both groups. The unrelated *t* test command specifies the two groups being compared (**groups=grp(1,2)**) and the variables on which they are being compared (**variables=nvf**).

The relevant output for this command file is displayed in Table 4.8. As can be seen from this output, the *F* value is 5.83 which represents the 0.035 two-tailed probability level.

SKEWNESS

The extent to which a set of scores deviates from a normal or bell-shaped distribution is estimated by two statistics called *skewness* and *kurtosis*. Skewness is a measure of the extent to which the distribution is not symmetrical while kurtosis is an index of the degree to which there are either too many or too few cases in the middle of the distribution.

The formula for skewness is:

$$\text{Skewness} = \frac{[\text{sum of (each score} - \text{mean)cubed}] \times N}{\text{std dev cubed} \times (N-1) \times (N-2)}$$

where N is the total number of cases.

Table 4.8 *F* test as part of **t-test** output

	Number of Cases	Mean	Standard Deviation	Standard Error
Group 1	7	5.0000	1.826	.690
Group 2	8	2.0000	.756	.267

		Pooled Variance Estimate			Separate Variance Estimate		
F value	**2-Tail**	**t**	**Degrees of**	**2-Tail**	**t**	**Degrees of**	**2-Tail**
5.83	**Prob.**	**Value**	**Freedom**	**Prob.**	**Value**	**Freedom**	**Prob.**
	.035	4.27	13	.001	4.05	7.78	.004

Skewness is calculated by carrying out the following steps (Bliss 1967).

Step 1   Compute the mean.

Step 2   Subtract the mean from each score.

Step 3   Cube this difference.

Step 4   Sum the cubed differences for each of the scores.

Step 5   Multiply this sum by the number of cases.

Step 6   Compute the standard deviation, cube it and multiply the cubed standard deviation by the number of cases less 1 and the number of cases less 2.

Step 7   Divide the result of Step 5 by that of Step 6 to give the value for skewness.

When the distribution of scores is symmetrical, this statistic will have a value of 0. Take, for example, the following set of four scores which are symmetrically distributed.

1 3 3 5

Step 1   The mean of the four scores is 3 $((1 + 3 + 3 + 5)/4 = 3)$.

Step 2   Subtracting the mean from each score gives the following differences

−2 0 0 2

Step 3   These differences when cubed become

−8 0 0 8

Step 4   The sum of these cubed differences is 0 $(-8 + 0 + 0 + 8 = 0)$.

Step 5   This sum multiplied by the number of cases remains 0 $(0 \times 4 = 0)$.

Step 6   To compute the standard deviation of the four scores, the mean is first subtracted from each score and squared to give

4 0 0 4

These squared differences are then summed and divided by one less than the number of cases to give a variance of 2.66 $((4 + 0 + 0 + 4)/(4 - 1) =$

2.66). The square root of the variance is the standard deviation which is 1.63. The standard deviation cubed and multiplied by the number of cases less 1 (4 − 1 = 3) and the number of cases less 2 (4 − 2 = 2) is 25.98 ($4.33^3 \times 3 \times 2 = 25.98$).

Step 7   Dividing the result of Step 5 by that of Step 6 gives 0 (0/ 25.98 = 0).

The value of skewness is zero when a set of scores is symmetrically distributed because the sum of the cubed differences below the mean is equal to the sum of the cubed differences above the mean. The need to cube the differences will become apparent when the two examples of asymmetrical distributions are presented. When most of the scores are to the left of the mean, the distribution is said to be *positively skewed* as the value of skewness is positive. This point can be illustrated with the following set of four scores which is positively skewed:

2 2 2 6

To show the steps involved in the calculation of skewness for this set of scores, the scores will be arranged in a column as displayed in Table 4.9. The sum of these scores is given at the bottom of this column followed by the mean. The difference (d) between these scores and their mean is presented in a second column while the differences squared (d^2) and cubed (d^3) are displayed in a third and fourth column. The result for Step 5 of the calculation, which involves multiplying the sum of the cubed differences by the number of cases, gives 96 (24 × 4 = 96). The variance is 4 (12/(4 − 1) = 4) which yields a standard deviation of 2 ($\sqrt{4} = 2$). Consequently, the value for Step 6 is 48 ($2^3 \times 3 \times 2 = 48$). Dividing the result for Step 5 by that for Step 6 gives a skewness value of 2 (96/48 = 2).

The reasons for cubing the difference between each score and the mean should be clearer from this example. First, since the mean is the central point in any distribution, the sum of differences below the mean is equal to the sum of differences above the mean regardless of the shape of the distribution. Second, as negative signs become positive when squared but

Table 4.9 Positively skewed scores: initial computations

	Scores	d	d^2	d^3
	2	−1	1	−1
	2	−1	1	−1
	2	−1	1	−1
	6	3	9	27
Sum	12	0	12	24
Mean	3			

remain negative when cubed, cubing the difference indicates the direction of any asymmetry in the distribution.

When most of the scores are clustered to the right of the mean, the distribution is *negatively skewed* and takes on a negative value as shown by the following set of negatively skewed scores:

   1 3 4 4

Once again, to make it easier to follow the steps in calculating skewness, the scores and the three indices of their difference from the mean will be displayed in columns as shown in Table 4.10. Multiplying the sum of the cubed differences by the number of cases gives -24 ($-6 \times 4 = -24$) for Step 5. The square root of the variance is 1.414 ($\sqrt{(6/3)} = 1.4142$) which in Step 6 becomes 16.97 when cubed and multiplied by the number of cases less 1 and the number of cases less 2 ($1.4142^3 \times 3 \times 2 = 16.97$). Consequently, skewness equals -1.414 ($-24/16.97 = -1.414$).

To determine whether the distribution is significantly asymmetrical, the value of skewness is divided by the *standard error of skewness* and the resulting value is looked up in the table of the *standard normal distribution* in Appendix 6 (Bliss 1967). The standard error of skewness is a measure of the extent to which skewness may vary as a function of the size of the sample. It is most conveniently described in terms of the following formula where N is the total number of cases:

$$\text{standard error of skewness} = \sqrt{\frac{6 \times N \times (N-1)}{(N-2) \times (N+1) \times (N+3)}}$$

To calculate the standard error of skewness for a sample containing four cases, we substitute 4 for N in the formula:

$$\sqrt{\frac{6 \times 4 \times (4-1)}{(4-1) \times (4+1) \times (4+3)}} = \sqrt{\frac{6 \times 4 \times 3}{3 \times 5 \times 7}} = \sqrt{\frac{72}{70}}$$

$$= \sqrt{1.028} = 1.01$$

Table 4.10 Negatively skewed scores: initial computations

	Scores	d	d^2	d^3
	1	−2	4	−8
	3	0	0	0
	4	1	1	1
	4	1	1	1
Sum	12	0	6	−6
Mean	3			

To find out, for example, whether a skewness value of −1.41 for a sample of four differs significantly from normality, we divide this value by 1.01 which gives a figure of −1.40 (−1.41/1.01 = −1.40). We look up this figure in the table in Appendix 6. To use this table, we need to know what the standard normal distribution or curve is.

It is a theoretical distribution which has a mean of zero. Since the distribution is perfectly symmetrical, 50 per cent or 0.5 of the values lie above the mean and 0.5 of the values fall below it. The values given in the table represent that proportion of the distribution which lies between the mean and a cut-off point called z on the horizontal axis. In the left-hand margin of the table are the z values to one decimal place which range from 0.0 to 3.9. Along the top row of the table are the z values given to the second decimal place which vary from 0.00 to 0.09. In the extreme case where the z value is zero (0.00), the proportion of the area between z and the mean is zero which makes the proportion beyond z 0.5 (0.5 − 0.0 = 0.5). The value of z becomes larger as it moves away from the centre of the distribution towards either tail. As it does so, the proportion of the area between it and the mean increases while the proportion beyond it decreases. For example, the proportion of area between a z value of 4.0 and the mean is 0.49997 while the proportion beyond it is 0.00003 (0.50000 − 0.49997 = 0.00003). Since the tails of the standard normal curve never touch the horizontal axis, z increases to infinity.

In effect, dividing skewness by its standard error provides a statistic which can be seen to be comparable to z. When this statistic has a value of zero, the distribution will be perfectly symmetrical. The further this statistic departs from zero, the more asymmetrical the distribution will be. To look up how far a z value of −1.40 is from the midpoint of a distribution, we ignore its negative sign since the z values describe either the left- or the right-hand side of the distribution. In the table of Appendix 6, the relevant portion of which has been reproduced in Table 4.11, we see that the proportion of the area between a z value of 1.40 and the mean is 0.4192 of the distribution. This indicates that the proportion of the area beyond z is 0.0808 (0.5000 − 0.4192 = 0.0808).

Table 4.11 Part of the table of the standard normal distribution

z	0.00	0.01	0.02	...
:				
1.3	0.4032	0.4049	0.4066	
1.4	*0.4192*	0.4207	0.4222	
1.5	0.4332	0.4345	0.4357	
:				

Now, the proportion of the area beyond z can be interpreted as representing the probability of an outcome occurring at the one-tailed level so that a z of -1.40 indicates a one-tailed probability of 0.0808. However, to determine whether a distribution is asymmetrical, we have to use a two-tailed probability level since the asymmetry can be either positive or negative. As the two-tailed probability level reflects the possibility that the value of 1.40 may have been either positive or negative, it is simply twice the one-tailed level which makes it 0.1616 ($2 \times 0.0808 = 0.1616$). Since this figure is larger than 0.05, we would conclude that this distribution was not significantly asymmetrical. On the other hand, the z value for the example of the positively skewed distribution is 1.98 ($2.00/1.01 = 1.98$). From the table in Appendix 6, it can be seen that this value has a one-tailed probability of 0.0239 which may be converted into a two-tailed one of 0.0478 ($0.0239 \times 2 = 0.0478$) by doubling it. As the two-tailed probability level of this value is less than 0.05, we would assume that this distribution is significantly asymmetrical.

Skewness and its standard error (**S.E. Skew**) is produced when **statistic 8** is specified on the SPSS **descriptives** command. The following SPSS commands will provide these statistics for the example above of the negatively skewed distribution.

data list/no 1.
begin data.
1
3
4
4
end data.
descriptives no
 /statistic 8.

The relevant output for this command is

Variable Skewness S.E. Skew N Label
NO   −1.41   1.01   4

As SPSS does not give the probability level for skewness this has to be worked out.

KURTOSIS

Distributions can be symmetrical but not normal if there are either too many or too few cases in the middle of the distribution. A normal distribution may be called *mesokurtic* ('meso' meaning middle) and has a kurtosis value of zero. A distribution with too many cases in the centre of the distribution is known as *leptokurtic* ('lepto' meaning narrow) and has a positive kurtosis value, while a distribution with too few cases at its centre is referred to as *platykurtic* ('platy' meaning flat) and has a negative kurtosis value. The formula for kurtosis is

$$\text{kurtosis} = \frac{[(d^4 \text{ summed})(N)(N+1)] - [(d^2 \text{ summed})(d^2 \text{ summed})(3)(N-1)]}{(SD^4)(N-1)(N-2)(N-3)}$$

where d is the difference of each score from the mean, SD is the standard deviation, N is the total number of cases and values in adjacent parentheses are multiplied by each other (e.g. $(3)(N-1)$).

To work out kurtosis, carry out the following steps (Bliss 1967).

Step 1   Calculate the mean.

Step 2   Subtract the mean from each score.

Step 3   Square each of these differences and sum them (d^2 summed).

Step 4   Raise each of these differences to the power of 4 (i.e. multiply them by themselves four times) and sum them (d^4 summed).

Step 5   Calculate the standard deviation by dividing the sum of squared differences in Step 3 by 1 less the number of cases and then take the square root of the result.

Step 6   Multiply the standard deviation by itself four times (SD^4).

Step 7   Multiply the sum of differences to the power of 4 (d^4 summed) by the number of cases (N) and the number of cases plus 1 ($N+1$).

Step 8   Multiply the sum of squared differences (d^2 summed) by itself, by 3 and by the number of cases minus 1 ($N-1$).

Step 9   Multiply the standard deviation to the power of 4 (SD^4) by the number of cases minus 1 ($N-1$), the number of cases minus 2 ($N-2$) and the number of cases minus 3 ($N-3$).

Step 10   Subtract the result of Step 8 from that of Step 7 and divide the difference by the result of Step 9.

We will illustrate the process of calculating kurtosis for the three kinds of curves. The following set of six scores approximates a mesokurtic distribution:

1 2 3 3 4 5

To clarify the computations, we will arrange these scores in a column with
the relevant difference indices in adjacent columns as presented in Table
4.12. The standard deviation is 1.41 ($\sqrt{(10/5)}$ = 1.41). Substituting the
appropriate figures in the above formula, we obtain a kurtosis of −0.30:

$$\frac{[(34)(6)(6+1)] - [(10)(10)(3)(6-1)]}{(1.41^4)(6-1)(6-2)(6-3)} = \frac{1428 - 1500}{237}$$

$$= \frac{-72}{237} = -0.30$$

Kurtosis for this set of scores is slightly negative.

In the second example a set of five scores, which are arranged in the
column shown in Table 4.13, represents a leptokurtic curve. The standard
deviation is 0.71 ($\sqrt{(2/4)}$ = 0.71). Placing the relevant numbers in the
formula produces a kurtosis of 2:

Table 4.12 A mesokurtic distribution: initial computations

	Scores	d	d^2	d^4
	1	−2	4	16
	2	−1	1	1
	3	0	0	0
	3	0	0	0
	4	1	1	1
	5	2	4	16
Sum	18	0	10	34
Mean	3			

Table 4.13 A leptokurtic distribution: initial computations

	Scores	d	d^2	d^4
	1	−1	1	1
	2	0	0	0
	2	0	0	0
	2	0	0	0
	3	1	1	1
Sum	10	0	2	2
Mean	2			

$$\frac{[(2)(5)(6)] - [(2)(2)(3)(4)]}{(0.71^4)(4)(3)(2)} = \frac{60 - 48}{6} = \frac{12}{6} = 2$$

Kurtosis for this group of scores is positive, indicating a leptokurtic curve.

In the third example, presented in Table 4.14, the five scores characterise a platykurtic distribution. The standard deviation is 1.00 ($\sqrt{(4/4)} = 1.00$). Inserting the pertinent values in the same formula gives a kurtosis of -3.00:

$$\frac{[(4)(5)(6)] - [(4)(4)(3)(4)]}{(1^4)(4)(3)(2)} = \frac{120 - 192}{24} = \frac{-72}{24} = -3.00$$

The negative value for kurtosis signifies that the distribution is platykurtic.

To determine whether a distribution differs significantly from a mesokurtic curve, we divide the kurtosis value by its standard error and look up in the table of the standard normal distribution in Appendix 6 how probable the resulting figure is (Bliss 1967). The standard error of kurtosis is most conveniently described in terms of the following formula:

$$\text{standard error of kurtosis} = \sqrt{\frac{(\text{variance of skewness})(4)(N^2 - 1)}{(N - 3)(N + 5)}}$$

The use of this formula can be illustrated by calculating the standard error of kurtosis for the example of the mesokurtic distribution. First, we need to work out the variance of skewness, which by inserting the appropriate figures in the relevant formula is 0.71:

$$\frac{(6)(6)(5)}{(4)(7)(9)} = \frac{180}{252} = 0.71$$

Putting the variance of skewness in the formula for calculating the standard error of kurtosis gives a standard error of 1.74:

Table 4.14 A platykurtic distribution: initial computations

	Scores	d	d^2	d^3	d^4
	1	−1	1	−1	1
	1	−1	1	−1	1
	2	0	0	0	0
	3	1	1	1	1
	3	1	1	1	1
Sum	10	0	4	0	4
Mean	2				

$$\sqrt{\frac{(0.71)(4)(6^2-1)}{(6-3)(6+5)}} = \sqrt{\frac{99.4}{33}} = \sqrt{3.01} = 1.74$$

Dividing the kurtosis by its standard error results in a value of -0.17 ($-0.30/1.74 = -0.17$) which, looked up in the table in Appendix 6, has a one-tailed probability of 0.4325 and a two-tailed one of 0.8650 (2×0.4325). Consequently, we would conclude that this distribution is mesokurtic.

Kurtosis and its standard error (**S.E. Kurt**) is provided when **statistic 7** is requested on the SPSS **descriptives** command. To produce these statistics for this example, run the following SPSS commands:

data list/no 1.
begin data.
1
2
3
3
4
5
end data.
descriptives no
 /statistic 7.

The relevant output will read

Variable   Kurtosis   S.E. Kurt N Label
NO   −.30   1.74 6

The probability level for kurtosis needs to be calculated as SPSS does not provide this.

PLOTTING FREQUENCY DISTRIBUTIONS

The shape of a distribution can be visualised more clearly if it is displayed graphically as either a *histogram* or a *polygon*. A histogram contains a horizontal line or *axis* (called the *abscissa*) and a vertical line (called the *ordinate*). The values of the distribution are shown on the horizontal axis while the frequencies of the values are depicted on the vertical axis. The frequency of each value is represented by a vertical bar or box which is centred on the midpoint of the value. The height of the box corresponds to the frequency of the value. A histogram of the above example of a mesokurtic distribution is shown in Figure 4.4. In a polygon, on the other hand, the frequency of each value is represented by a point which lies directly above its value and whose height corresponds to its frequency. Adjacent points are connected by straight lines. The line extends to meet

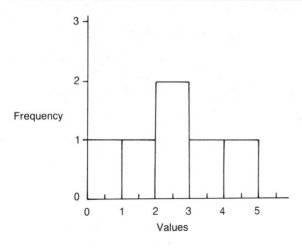

Figure 4.4 A histogram

the horizontal axis where the frequency of the adjacent value is zero so that the whole area of the distribution is bounded by straight lines. Figure 4.5 presents a polygon of the mesokurtic distribution. One advantage of the polygon over the histogram is that it is easier to read when two distributions are plotted along the same axis for comparison. For instance, in Figure 4.6 the polygon for a mesokurtic and a leptokurtic distribution is shown. In both histograms and polygons the frequency of each value can also be plotted as a percentage or proportion of the total number of values. This has the advantage that, where the sizes of two samples differ, the area covered by the two distributions will be the same.

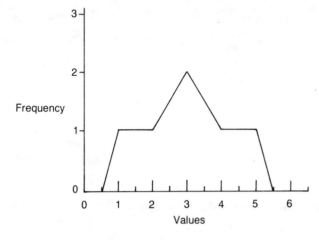

Figure 4.5 A polygon

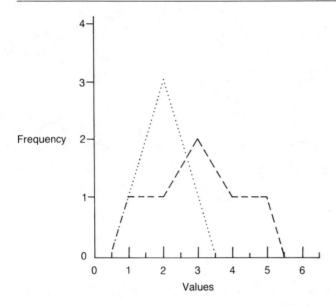

Figure 4.6 Two polygons

Histograms can be plotted with SPSS using the **frequencies** command with the **histogram** subcommand. Adding the keyword **normal** will super-impose a standard normal curve on the histogram which will show how similar the distribution is to the standard normal curve. In addition, the **statistics** subcommand will give various descriptive statistics on request, such as the mean, skewness and kurtosis. As an illustration, the following commands will produce this information for the above example of a mesokurtic distribution.

data list/no 1.
begin data.
1
2
3
3
4
5
end data.
frequencies no
 /histogram normal
 /statistics mean median mode stddev skewness seskew
 kurtosis sekurt.

The relevant output of these commands is shown in Figure 4.7. In the

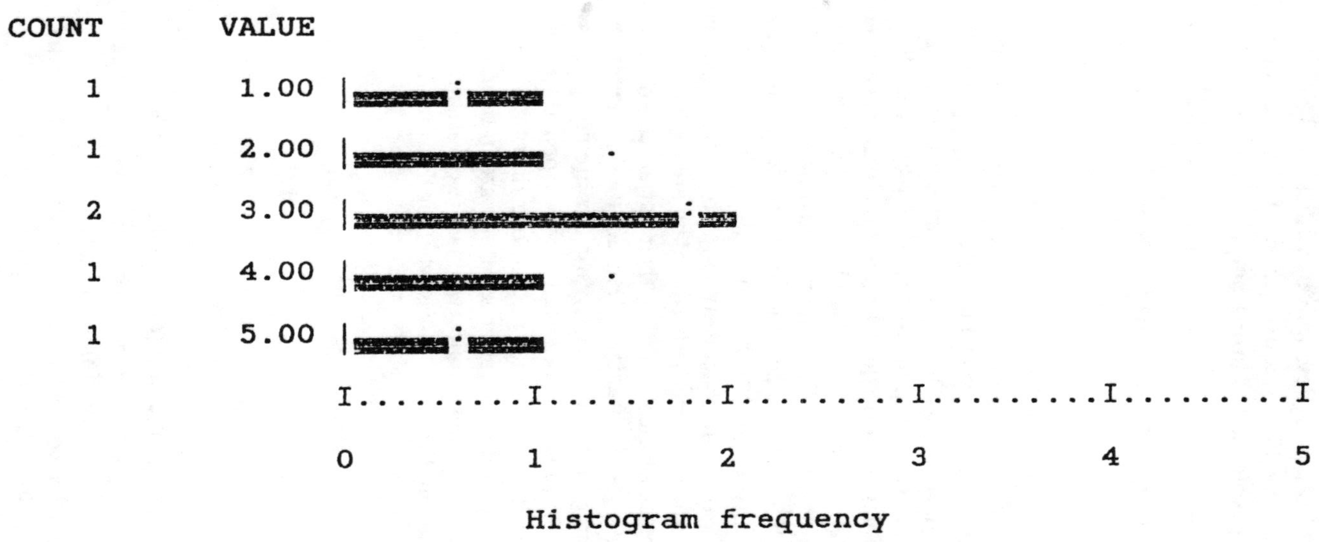

```
COUNT    VALUE

  1       1.00  |
  1       2.00  |
  2       3.00  |
  1       4.00  |
  1       5.00  |
                I.........I.........I.........I.........I.........I
                0         1         2         3         4         5

                          Histogram frequency


Mean        3.000    Median      3.000    Mode        3.000

Std dev     1.414    Kurtosis    -.300    S E Kurt    1.741

Skewness    .000     S E Skew    .845
```

Figure 4.7 Output of a frequency histogram with a superimposed normal curve

histogram presented by SPSS, the horizontal axis represents the frequencies while the vertical axis reflects the values. The output also contains a count of the frequency of each value which is displayed in the left-hand column. Below the histogram are the requested descriptive statistics.

To produce a histogram in which frequencies are presented in percentages, add the keyword **percent** to the **histogram** subcommand.

/**histogram normal percent**

This addition will generate the histogram in Figure 4.8.

SUMMARY

One of the principal uses of statistics in the social sciences is to determine the probability of a finding occurring by chance. Results having a probability of happening less than 0.05 (i.e. 1 out of 20) are considered to be statistically significant and are thought to be unlikely due to chance. Where the direction of the results has been predicted before the data have been analysed a one-tailed probability level is used and where the direction of the results has not been predicted beforehand a two-tailed probability level is employed. A number of different statistical tests exist for determining the size and often the probability of an association between two or more variables and the probability of a difference between two or more groups. Which test to use depends primarily on whether the data are categorical or not, and if the data are not categorical whether their variances are equal and their distributions normal. Non-parametric tests are used for analysing categorical data and non-categorical data whose variances are unequal and whose distributions are non-normal. Parametric tests are applied to non-categorical data whose variances are equal and whose distributions are normal. The F test, which is the greater variance of one group divided by the smaller variance of the other, determines whether two variances are unequal and tests of skewness and kurtosis assess whether distributions are normal.

EXERCISES

1   Toss a coin six times. What is the probability of finding the particular outcome obtained?
2   There are 10 women and 10 men in a room. The first 3 people selected are women. What is the probability of this outcome?
3   There are 15 women and 5 men in a room. The first 3 people selected are women. What is the probability of this outcome?
4   A test of general knowledge consists of 50 statements, half of which are true and half of which are false. One point is awarded for each

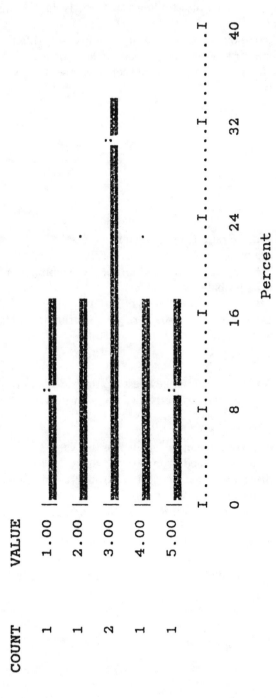

Figure 4.8 Output of percentage histogram with superimposed normal curve

correct answer. What is the most likely score on this test for someone who has no general knowledge?

5   The probability value of a finding was 0.15. Is the finding statistically significant?

6   It is predicted that two groups in a study will differ significantly. Should a one- or a two-tailed probability level be used?

7   Determine for these two groups of scores whether their variances differ significantly.

Group A	Group B
2	1
3	9
2	2
2	8
3	7
4	1
3	

(a) What is the F ratio (to two decimal places)?
(b) What are the degrees of freedom for the numerator?
(c) What are the degrees of freedom for the denominator?
(d) What is its probability level?
(e) Do the two variances differ significantly?

8   Does the skewness and kurtosis of this distribution of scores differ from normality?

5 3 1 2 1 2 3 4 2

(a) What is the value of its skewness (to three decimal places)?
(b) What is the standard error of its skewness (to three decimal places)?
(c) What is its z value?
(d) What is the one-tailed probability of this value?
(e) What is the two-tailed probability of this value?
(f) Is the distribution symmetrical or positively or negatively skewed?
(g) What is the value of its kurtosis?
(h) What is the standard error of its kurtosis?
(i) What is its z value?
(j) What is the one-tailed probability of this value?
(k) What is the two-tailed probability of this value?
(l) Is the kurtosis mesokurtic, leptokurtic or platykurtic?

Chapter 5

Tests of difference for categorical data

The statistical tests covered in this chapter only apply to data in which the number of cases falling into various categories is simply counted. The tests determine whether the frequency of cases in the different categories varies across two or more groups or from some expected distribution. We would use these tests to answer the following kinds of questions. Is the number of women who went on to higher education this year significantly less than the number of men who did so? Has there been an increase this year in the number of women entering higher education compared with last year? Does the academic performance of students generally increase from their first to their second year in terms of the number of students who receive the highest overall grade?

BINOMIAL TEST FOR TWO UNRELATED SAMPLES

The binomial test determines whether the number of cases that fall into one of only two categories differs significantly from some expected number or proportion. Suppose, for instance, that there are only five places on a highly select course and that equal numbers of women and men applied for this course. This year the five places were all taken by women. On the basis of these figures, can we conclude that women are generally more likely than men to be accepted for this course? The binomial test can be used to answer this question, the only two categories being women and men.

The formula for calculating the probability of obtaining a particular number of cases in one category is a little too complicated for our purposes but can be found elsewhere (Siegel 1956). For the present, we need simply to know that, if the size of the sample is less than 26 and the probability of obtaining either outcome is 0.5, then we can look up the probability of finding a particular outcome in the table in Appendix 7. To use the table we need to know the size of the sample (which is represented by N and which in this case is 5) and the smaller of the two frequencies (which is indicated by n and which is 0 for men). The size of the sample being investigated is given in the left-hand column of the table and varies from 1 to 25, while the smaller frequency is presented along the top row of the table and ranges from 0 to 15.

Reading from the table, the relevant part of which has been reproduced in Table 5.1, we can see that the probability of obtaining five women and no men is 0.031. Incidentally, this figure is identical to that worked out in the previous chapter for the same problem. The probability values in this table are one-tailed which is what we need since we have specified the direction of the results we expect to find, namely that women were more likely than men to be accepted for the course. Since this figure of 0.031 is less than 0.05, we can conclude that having all five places filled by women is significantly greater than that expected by chance. If we wished to determine what the probability is of finding a sample containing either all women or all men, then we would require a two-tailed probability level which is simply the one-tailed level doubled (i.e. $0.031 \times 2 = 0.062$).

If the size of our sample is larger than 25 and the probability of obtaining either outcome is near to 0.5, then the binomial distribution tends to be similar to the normal distribution. So, to determine the probability of a particular outcome under these circumstances, we calculate the z value of finding this result by using the following formula:

$$z = \frac{\text{smaller frequency} - (\text{number of cases} \times \text{expected probability of one category})}{\sqrt{(\text{number of cases} \times \text{expected probability of one category} \times \text{expected probability of other category})}}$$

Suppose that 30 of the 40 students admitted onto a course were female. On the basis of these figures, could we argue that women are significantly more likely than men to be accepted on this course? To work out whether this is the case, we need to substitute the following numbers into the formula:

$$\frac{10 - (40 \times 0.5)}{\sqrt{40 \times 0.5 \times 0.5}} = \frac{-10}{3.162} = -3.16$$

Table 5.1 Part of the binomial test one-tailed probabilities table

N	0	1	2	...	15
			n		
5	0.031	0.188	0.500		
6	0.016	0.109	0.344		
7	0.008	0.062	0.227		
.					
.					
.					
25					

The category with the smaller frequency is men, of which there are 10. The expected probability of admitting either a man or a woman onto the course is 0.5 and the total number of students on the course is 40. To determine the statistical significance of this z value, we ignore its sign and look it up in the table in Appendix 6 where we see that the probability of this value occurring by chance is 0.0008.

The normal distribution is based on a continuous variable (consisting of non-whole numbers) whereas the binomial distribution assumes a discrete variable (comprising whole numbers). The binomial distribution can be made more similar to the normal distribution when a correction for continuity is included. This is done by presupposing that the frequency of cases in the smaller category (e.g. 10) occupies an interval, the lower limit of which is half a unit (0.5) below its observed value (e.g. $10 - 0.5 = 9.5$) while its upper limit is half a unit (0.5) above it (e.g. $10 + 0.5 = 10.5$). The correction for continuity consists of reducing by 0.5 the difference between the observed value of the smaller category (e.g. 10) and its expected value (e.g. $40 \times 0.5 = 20$). So, in this case, where the observed frequency (10) is less than the expected frequency (20), we would add 0.5 to 10. If we substitute this new value in the formula for calculating z, we obtain a z value of -3.00:

$$\frac{10.5 - 20}{3.162} = \frac{-9.5}{3.162} = -3.00$$

Looking up this figure in the table in Appendix 6, we see that the probability of obtaining this result at the one-tailed level is slightly higher at 0.0013 which when doubled gives a two-tailed level of 0.0026. Consequently, we can conclude that significantly more women than men gained a place on the course.

The binomial test can be calculated with the following SPSS procedures command:

npar tests/binomial(proportion of value 1)=variable name(lowest value, highest value).

Npar stands for non-parametric. The name of the categorical variable is inserted after the equals sign. If this variable has only two categories, then it is not necessary to specify what these two numerical codes are. The proportion of cases which are expected to fall within the first category is placed in brackets after the keyword **binomial**.

We would first need to file our data to compute the probability of filling all five places on the course with women when the probability of women and men being offered a place was equal. In this example the variable name for the gender of the students is **gen** which is located in column 3. Women are coded as **1** and men as **2**. If we wanted to determine whether women had an equal probability of being offered a place on the course as men, then the expected proportion of women on the course would be 0.5, which is the figure inserted into the procedures command. Consequently, the SPSS command file would look like this:

data list/cno 1 gen 3.
begin data.
1 1
2 1
3 1
4 1
5 1
end data.
npar tests/binomial(.5)=gen(1,2).

The relevant part of the output produced by running this file is presented in Table 5.2. Five cases have a value of 1. The test or expected proportion of cases having a 1 is **.5000**, while the observed proportion is **1.0000**. In other words, all cases were women. The two-tailed probability of finding this result is **0.0625**, which is the figure we obtained earlier.

The following SPSS command file could be created to work out whether the probability of finding that 30 of the 40 places were taken by women was greater than that expected if the probability of being given a place was equal for women and men.

data list/cno 1-2 gen 4.
begin data.
01 1
02 1
03 1
.
.
.
38 2

Table 5.2 Binomial test output with all five places filled by women

– – – – – Binomial Test	
GEN	**Test Prop. = .5000**
Cases	
5 = 1	**Obs. Prop. = 1.0000**
0 = 2	
—	**Exact Binomial**
5 Total	**2-tailed P = .0625**

39 2
40 2
end data.
npar tests/binomial(.5)=gen(1,2).

The pertinent section of the output is shown in Table 5.3 where it can be seen that 30 of the 40 cases were coded as 1 and 10 as 2. The observed proportion of **.7500** women was tested against an expected one of **.5000**. The two-tailed probability of attaining this result is **.0027**, which is slightly higher than the figure calculated above (0.0026) due to the fact that the proportions in the table in Appendix 6 are restricted to four decimal places. The one-tailed probability of finding a z value of 3.0 when the probabilities are presented to five decimal places is 0.00135, which doubled is 0.0027.

CHI-SQUARE TEST FOR TWO OR MORE UNRELATED SAMPLES

The Pearson chi-square (pronounced 'ky-square' and symbolised as χ^2) test compares the observed frequency of cases against the expected frequency for two or more unrelated samples on a variable which may have two or more categories. For example, we may wish to determine whether the number of women and men taking the same course in three consecutive years differs as illustrated with the set of figures shown in Table 5.4. In this

Table 5.3 Binomial test output with 30 of 40 places filled by women

– – – – – Binomial Test	
GEN	**Test Prop. = .5000**
Cases	
30 = 1	**Obs. Prop. = .7500**
10 = 2	
—	**Z Approximation**
40 Total	**2-tailed P = .0027**

Table 5.4 Number of women and men taking the same course in three consecutive years

	1991	1992	1993
Women	19	27	24
Men	11	18	13

case, gender has only two categories ('women' and 'men') and year of study has three categories ('1991', '1992' and '1993').

In calculating chi-square it is useful to display the figures in what is known as a *contingency* table as presented in Table 5.5. This table is known as a *2 × 3* contingency table since the first variable has two categories (*2*) and the second three (*3*). It has six *cells*. The number of women is displayed in the upper left-hand cell for 1991 (i.e. 19), the upper middle cell for 1992 (i.e. 27) and the upper right-hand cell for 1993 (i.e. 24). The number of men, on the other hand, is shown in the lower left-hand cell for 1991 (i.e. 11), the lower middle cell for 1992 (i.e. 18) and the lower right-hand cell for 1993 (i.e. 13). The total number of cases in each row is shown in the right-hand column which is 70 for women and 42 for men, and the total number of cases in each column is presented in the bottom row which is 30 for 1991, 45 for 1992 and 37 for 1993. Row and column totals are sometimes referred to as *marginals*. Finally, the total number of cases in the sample is given in the bottom right-hand corner of the table, 112.

The chi-square test compares the observed number of cases in each cell with the expected number for that cell for all cells. The closer the expected number is to the observed number across all cells, the less likelihood there is of any difference being statistically significant. To work out the expected number of cases in each cell, we multiply the row total by the column total and divide the product by the overall number of cases or *grand total*.

$$\text{expected frequency} = \frac{\text{row total} \times \text{column total}}{\text{grand total}}$$

For example, to calculate the expected number of women in 1991 assuming there were no differences between women and men and between the three years, we note that the total number of women for the three years is 70 while the total number of students in 1991 is 30. Consequently, the expected number of women in 1991 would be 18.8 ((70 × 30)/112 = 18.75). The expected frequency for each of the six cells is presented in parentheses in Table 5.6.

Table 5.5 Contingency table of number of women and men taking the same course in three consecutive years

	Year			Total
	1991	*1992*	*1993*	
Women	19	27	24	70
Men	11	18	13	42
Total	30	45	37	112

Table 5.6 Observed and expected frequencies of women and men taking the same course in three consecutive years

	Year			Total
	1991	*1992*	*1993*	
Women	19	27	24	70
	(18.8)	(28.1)	(23.1)	
Men	11	18	13	42
	(11.3)	(16.9)	(13.9)	
Total	30	45	37	112

The general formula for calculating chi-square is

$$\text{chi-square} = \text{sum of } \frac{(\text{observed frequency} - \text{expected frequency})^2}{\text{expected frequency}} \text{ for each cell}$$

Calculating chi-square involves the following four steps.

Step 1   Subtract the expected frequency from the observed frequency for each cell.

Step 2   Square the difference (to remove any minus values).

Step 3   Divide the squared difference by the expected frequency of that cell (to take account of the expected size of that cell).

Step 4   Add together the results for all the cells.

Applying these steps, we see that chi-square is 0.218:

$$\frac{(19 - 18.8)^2}{18.8} + \frac{(27 - 28.1)^2}{28.1} + \frac{(24 - 23.1)^2}{23.1} + \frac{(11 - 11.3)^2}{11.3} +$$

$$\frac{(18 - 16.9)^2}{16.9} + \frac{(13 - 13.9)^2}{13.9} = 0.002 + 0.043 + 0.035 + 0.008 +$$

$$0.072 + 0.058 = 0.218$$

To determine the probability of obtaining this value, we look it up in the table in Appendix 8. However, before doing this, we need to calculate the degrees of freedom for chi-square which is given by the following formula:

$df = (\text{number of rows} - 1) \times (\text{number of columns} - 1)$

Since we have two rows and three columns of data, the appropriate degrees of freedom are 2 $((2 - 1) \times (3 - 1) = 2)$. To be statistically significant with 2 degrees of freedom, chi-square has to be larger than 5.99 at the 0.05 two-tailed level. As the chi-square value of 0.218 is smaller than 5.99, we can conclude that there is no difference in the number of women and men attending the course in the three years. Except for a 2 × 2 table, the two-tailed level is needed for chi-square.

In chi-square, degrees of freedom refer to the number of cells whose values are free to vary assuming that we know the total values for the rows and columns. In a 2 × 2 contingency table, there is only one degree of freedom $((2 - 1) \times (2 - 1) = 1)$, since if we know one of the cell frequencies we can work out the other three. Take, for instance, the 2 × 2 contingency table presented in Table 5.7. If we know, for example, that cell A is 5, then we can work out that cell B is 5, cell C 25 and cell D 15 as shown in Table 5.8.

In a 2 × 3 contingency table, there are two degrees of freedom $((2 - 1) \times (3 - 1) = 2)$, since we need to know two of the cell frequencies which are free to vary before we can work out the other four. Take the 2 × 3 contingency table displayed in Table 5.9. If we know that cell A is 10, then cell D is fixed at 20. If we also know that cell E is 5, then we can calculate that cell B is 15, cell C 35 and cell F 15 as shown in Table 5.10.

Table 5.7 Row and column totals of a 2 × 2 contingency table

	Column		Total
	1	*2*	
Row 1	A	B	10
Row 2	C	D	40
Total	30	20	50

Table 5.8 Cell totals of the 2 × 2 contingency table

	Column		Total
	1	*2*	
Row 1	5	5	10
Row 2	25	15	40
Total	30	20	50

Table 5.9 Row and column totals of a 2 × 3 contingency table

	Column			Total
	1	*2*	*3*	
Row 1	A	B	C	60
Row 2	D	E	F	40
Total	30	20	50	100

Table 5.10 Cell counts of the 2 × 3 contingency table

	Column			Total
	1	*2*	*3*	
Row 1	10	15	35	60
Row 2	20	5	15	40
Total	30	20	50	100

The use of chi-square is governed by certain restrictions. This general formula can only be used where the following three conditions are met: (1) one variable has more than two categories; (2) fewer than 20 per cent of the cells have an expected frequency of less than 5; and (3) no cell has an expected frequency of less than 1. Where expected frequencies are too small, these categories may have to be dropped from the analysis or combined with other categories to obtain the necessary expected frequency. Suppose, for instance, that we wished to compare the proportion of women to men on the course over four years (1990–3) rather than the original three years (1991–3) and that the intake in 1990 consisted of only seven women and four men. These data are shown in Table 5.11. If there was no difference between women and men in 1990, then the expected frequency would be 4.4 women and 2.6 men. Including this year would mean that more than 20 per cent (2/8 × 100 = 25 per cent) of the cells have an expected frequency of less than 5. Consequently, chi-square could not be used to analyse this table unless the data for 1990 were excluded or were combined with those for the following year 1991.

This general formula has to be corrected for continuity when each variable has only two categories (i.e. a 2 × 2 contingency table) and when the number of cases is greater than 40 or when the number of cases is between 20 and 40 and all four expected frequencies are 5 or more. This

Table 5.11 Observed and expected frequency of women and men taking the same course in four consecutive years

	Year				Total
	1990	*1991*	*1992*	*1993*	
Women	4 (4.4)	19 (18.7)	27 (28.0)	24 (23.0)	74
Men	3 (2.6)	11 (11.3)	18 (17.0)	13 (14.0)	45
Total	7	30	45	37	119

correction, known as *Yates's correction*, consists of subtracting 0.5 from each of the absolute differences (i.e. ignoring the sign of the differences) between the observed and expected frequencies before squaring them. If, for example, we wished to compare the frequency of women and men on the same course for two rather than three years, we would have to apply chi-square with Yates's correction.

Take the figures for 1992 and 1993 in the above example which have been reproduced in Table 5.12. We first calculate the expected frequency for each cell and these are presented in Table 5.13. To calculate chi-square corrected for continuity, carry out the following steps.

Step 1   Subtract the expected from the observed frequency for each cell.

Step 2   Subtract 0.5 from their absolute difference.

Step 3   Square this difference.

Step 4   Divide this squared difference by the expected frequency for that cell.

Step 5   Sum the results for all four cells.

Applying these steps to these data, we find that chi-square is 0.053:

$$\frac{(|28-27|-0.5)^2}{28} + \frac{(|23-24|-0.5)^2}{23} + \frac{(|17-18|-0.5)^2}{17} +$$

$$\frac{(|14-13|-0.5)^2}{14} = \frac{(0.5)^2}{28} + \frac{(0.5)^2}{23} + \frac{(0.5)^2}{17} + \frac{(0.5)^2}{14} =$$

$$0.009 + 0.011 + 0.015 + 0.018 = 0.053$$

Table 5.12 Observed frequency of women and men taking the same course in two consecutive years

	Year		Total
	1992	1993	
Women	27	24	51
Men	18	13	31
Total	45	37	82

Table 5.13 Observed and expected frequency of women and men taking the same course in two consecutive years

	Year		Total
	1992	1993	
Women	27 (28.0)	24 (23.0)	51
Men	18 (17.0)	13 (14.0)	31
Total	45	37	82

The absolute difference is indicated by enclosing the expected and observed frequency between two vertical lines (e.g. |28 − 27|). Looking up this figure in the table in Appendix 8, we see that, at the 0.05 two-tailed level and with one degree of freedom, it is smaller than 3.84 and so is not statistically significant. In other words, the number of women and men do not differ significantly in the two years.

When each variable has only two categories, when the number of cases is less than 40 and when one of the expected frequencies is less than 5, then *Fisher's exact test* has to be used to analyse the data. The procedure for working out this test can be found elsewhere (Siegel 1956) and will not be described here as it involves lengthy calculations.

Chi-square can be computed by SPSS with the following general command called **crosstabs**.

crosstabs table=first variable name **by** second variable name
  /cells=count expected
  /statistics=chisq.

Crosstabs is short for cross-tabulations which is another term for contingency tables. To calculate chi-square for the example of whether there was a difference in the number of women and men taking the same course over three years, we would first have to specify with a **data list** command where the data were and what the variable names were. As we did previously, we will give each case a number which will go in columns **1-3** and we will call the gender variable **gen**, code women as **1** and men as **2**, and locate these data in column **5**. We will call the year variable **year**, code 1991 as **1**, 1992 as **2** and 1993 as **3**, and place these data in column **7**. Consequently, our SPSS command would look like this:

data list/cno 1-3 gen 5 year 7.
begin data.
001 2 3
002 1 1
003 2 1
.
.
.
112 1 2
end data.
crosstabs tables=gen by year
 /cells=count expected
 /statistics=chisq.

The cases, of course, do not have to be arranged in any particular order.

It is also possible to carry out a chi-square test on data already available in a contingency table as is the case with the present example. To do this, you need to indicate the number of cases in each of the cells by using the **weight** command and to include another variable on the **data list** command which provides the appropriate frequencies. In terms of this example, the SPSS command file would take the following form:

data list/gen 1 year 3 wt 5-7.
weight by wt.
begin data.
1 1 19
1 2 27
1 3 24
2 1 11
2 2 18
2 3 13
end data.
crosstabs table=gen by year
 /cells=count expected
 /statistics=chisq.

Since the data no longer consist of rows of cases, we omit the variable specifying the case number but add a new variable which we have called **wt** to indicate the number of cases in each of the six cells. The data for this variable have been placed in columns **5-7**. The six cells are defined by the location and code of the two variables so that gender is indicated by the numbers in the first column with **1** for women and **2** for men, and the year of study is displayed in the third column with **1** for 1991, **2** for 1992 and **3** for 1993. After the **data list** command, we insert the **weight** command which states that we will weight the cells by the variable called **wt**.

Regardless of how we specify the data, the output produced by this **crosstabs** command is shown in Table 5.14. The frequencies for gender are displayed in two of the rows of the table and those for the year of study in three of its columns. The first line in each cell gives the observed number of cases for that cell and the second line the expected number. In addition, the number and percentage of cases in each row and column are presented together with the grand total. SPSS produces three different measures of chi-square. The value of chi-square is shown together with the appropriate degrees of freedom and the statistical significance of this value. As we can see, the value of the Pearson chi-square is **.21718**, which when rounded to three decimal places is 0.217 and is similar to that previously calculated. This value is not statistically significant and so the numbers of women and men in the three years do not differ.

The likelihood ratio chi-square is twice the sum of the observed frequency of each cell multiplied by the natural logarithm of its observed frequency divided by its expected frequency:

$$L^2 = 2 \times \text{sum} \left[\text{observed frequency} \times \text{natural logarithm} \left(\frac{\text{observed frequency}}{\text{expected frequency}} \right) \right] \text{for each cell}$$

Because of the small values of the numbers involved in these calculations, it is necessary to work to five decimal places. Substituting the appropriate values in the formula, we see that the likelihood ratio chi-square is 0.21698 which is almost identical to the figure reported in Table 5.12:

$$2 \times \{[19 \times \ln(19/18.75)] + [27 \times \ln(27/28.125)] + [24 \times \ln(24/23.125)]$$
$$+ [11 \times \ln(11/11.25)] + [18 \times \ln(18/16.875)] + [13 \times \ln(13/13.875)]\}$$
$$= 2 \times [(19 \times \ln 1.01333) + (27 \times \ln 0.96000) + (24 \times \ln 1.03784) +$$
$$(11 \times \ln 0.97778) + (18 \times \ln 1.06667) + (13 \times \ln 0.93694)]$$
$$= 2 \times [(19 \times 0.01325) + (27 \times -0.04082) + (24 \times 0.03714) +$$
$$(11 \times -0.02247) + (18 \times 0.06454) + (13 \times -0.06514)]$$
$$= 2 \times [0.25166 + -1.1022 + 0.89135 + -0.24720 + 1.16169 + -0.84681]$$
$$= 2 \times 0.10849$$
$$= 0.21698$$

The Mantel–Haenszel chi-square of linear association will be discussed in Chapter 9.

Table 5.14 Chi-square output

GEN by YEAR

	YEAR			Page 1 of 1
Count Exp Val Exp Val	1	2	3	Row Total
GEN				
1	19 18.8	27 28.1	24 23.1	70 62.5%
2	11 11.3	18 16.9	13 13.9	42 37.5%
Column Total	30 26.8%	45 40.2%	37 33.0%	112 100.0%

Chi-Square	Value	DF	Significance
Pearson	.21718	2	.89710
Likelihood Ratio	.21699	2	.89718
Mantel–Haenszel test for linear association	.02482	1	.87483

Minimum Expected Frequency – 11.250
Number of Missing Observations: 0

The output also gives the smallest or minimum expected frequency for any cell which is **11.250** for the men in 1991. This information is useful for drawing to our attention whether the expected frequencies fall above the minimum required for applying chi-square. In this case, this condition is met since all six cells have an expected frequency of 5 or more. However, if we carried out an analysis on the previous example of data for the four years where only seven students were enrolled in the first year and where the conditions for a chi-square test were not met, the relevant output shown in Table 5.15 would state that (in addition to the minimum expected frequency) two of the eight cells (25 per cent) had expected frequencies of less than 5.

SPSS gives Yates's correction for continuity for all 2×2 contingency tables. This is shown in Table 5.16 which presents the relevant output for the analysis which concerned only the two years of 1992 and 1993. The value of **.04984** for Yates's corrected chi-square is slightly smaller than the previously calculated value of 0.053. This discrepancy is due to differences in rounding decimal places, particularly those of the expected frequencies. SPSS, for example, does not use the figures displayed in its table whereas the manual calculation did. The minimum expected frequency of **13.988** is for men in 1992.

The value for Fisher's exact test is given for 2×2 contingency tables when one or more of the four cells have an expected frequency of less than 5. For example, it would be produced if we analysed the data in our example for the first two years of 1990 and 1991. The relevant output for these data is shown in Table 5.17. In this case, a significance level greater than 0.05 indicates that there is no difference in the numbers of women and men taking the course in the two years.

McNEMAR TEST FOR TWO RELATED SAMPLES

The McNemar test compares the frequencies of a dichotomous variable from two related samples of cases. These two samples may consist of the same or *matched* cases tested on two occasions or receiving two treatments. Matching involves selecting samples of cases to be the same in certain respects such as age, gender and socio-economic status and is used to make the samples as similar as possible. We could employ the McNemar test, for example, to determine whether the same students are more likely to obtain the overall highest grade in the second rather than the first year of their course. The dichotomous variable in this instance would be whether the overall grade was the highest or not and the two related samples would be the first and second year of the course.

Suppose that, of a class of 40 students, 6 received the highest grade in both their first and second years, 12 obtained lower grades in both years, 4 attained the highest grade in their first but not their second year and 8

Table 5.15 Chi-square output with expected frequencies of less than 5

GEN by YEAR

		YEAR				Page 1 of 1
Count		1	2	3	4	Row Total
Exp Val						
Exp Val						
GEN						
1		4	19	27	24	74
		4.4	18.7	28.0	23.0	62.2%
2		3	11	18	13	45
		2.6	11.3	17.0	14.0	37.8%
Column		7	30	45	37	119
Total		5.9%	25.2%	37.8%	31.1%	100.0%

Chi-Square

	Value	DF	Significance
Pearson	.29686	3	.96062
Likelihood Ratio	.29625	3	.96073
Mantel–Haenszel test for linear association	.08160	1	.77514

Minimum Expected Frequency – 2.647
Cells with Expected Frequency < 5 – 2 OF 8 (25.0%)
Number of Missing Observations: 0

Table 5.16 Chi-square output with Yates's continuity correction

GEN by YEAR

	YEAR	Page 1 of 1	

Count Exp Val Exp Val	1	2	Row Total
GEN			
1	27 28.0	24 23.0	51 62.2%
2	18 17.0	13 14.0	31 37.8%
Column Total	45 54.9%	37 45.1%	82 100.0%

Chi-Square	Value	DF	Significance
Pearson	.20438	1	.65121
Continuity Correction	.04984	1	.82334
Likelihood Ratio	.20482	1	.65085
Mantel–Haenszel test for linear association	.20189	1	.65320

Minimum Expected Frequency – 13.988
Number of Missing Observations: 0

Table 5.17 Chi-square output with Fisher's exact test

GEN by YEAR

Page 1 of 1

Count	YEAR		
Exp Val	1	2	Row Total
GEN			
1	4	19	23
	4.4	18.6	62.2%
2	3	11	14
	2.6	11.4	37.8%
Column	7	30	37
Total	18.9%	81.1%	100.0%

Chi-Square	Value	DF	Significance
Pearson	.09247	1	.76106
Continuity Correction	.00000	1	1.00000
Likelihood Ratio	.09141	1	.76240
Mantel–Haenszel test for linear association	.08997	1	.76421
Fisher's Exact Test: One-Tail			.54150
Two-Tail			1.00000

Minimum Expected Frequency – 2.649
Cells with Expected Frequency < 5 –   4 (50.0%)
Number of Missing Observations: 0

achieved the highest grade in their second but not their first year. Do these results suggest that students in this sample are more likely to obtain the highest grade in their second year? To visualise the data, it may be helpful to arrange it in the form of a table as displayed in Table 5.18. With the McNemar test, we are only interested in whether the number of cases who have changed in one direction on the two occasions (say, those dropping the highest grade in their second year) are different from the number who have changed in the other direction (say, those gaining the highest grade in their second year). In other words, we are only concerned with the number of cases who have changed from one occasion to the next (i.e. those in the top left and bottom right cell). If there was no difference between the number of cases who dropped the highest grade in their second year and those who achieved the highest grade in that year, then the expected frequency of cases in each of these two cells should be 6 (i.e. $(4 + 8)/2 = 6$). If the expected frequency is less than 5, the binomial test should be used.

The McNemar test is like the chi-square test in that it compares the observed with the expected frequency of cases and the statistic that is computed is chi-square but, unlike the chi-square test, it only does this for the cases who have changed from one occasion (or condition) to the next. The formula for the McNemar test is

$$\text{chi-square} = \frac{(\mid \text{cell}_1 \text{ frequency} - \text{cell}_2 \text{ frequency} \mid - 1)^2}{\text{cell}_1 \text{ frequency} + \text{cell}_2 \text{ frequency}}$$

where the two cells (cell_1 and cell_2) refer to the two cells which indicate change. This test has one degree of freedom.

The steps involved in calculating chi-square for the McNemar test are as follows.

Step 1   Subtract the observed frequency of cases for the two cells representing a change from one occasion or condition to the next from each other.

Table 5.18 Number of students receiving the highest grades in their first and second years

		Second year	
		Lower	Highest
First year	Highest	4	6
	Lower	12	8

Step 2   Subtract 1 from their absolute difference to correct for continuity.

Step 3   Square this difference.

Step 4   Divide this squared difference by the sum of the observed frequencies in the two cells reflecting change.

Carrying out these steps on the data from this example, we find that chi-square is 0.75:

$$\frac{(|8 - 4| - 1)^2}{4 + 8} = \frac{9}{12} = 0.75$$

We look up the statistical significance of this value in the table in Appendix 8. Because we specified the direction of the results we expected to find, we can use the one-tailed level of significance which simply involves halving the significance value. When we do this, we see that with one degree of freedom this value is less than 2.71 at the 0.05 one-tailed level, indicating that students were not significantly more likely to obtain the highest overall grade in the second rather than the first year of their course.

The McNemar test can be computed with the following SPSS **npar tests** procedures command.

npar tests mcnemar=first variable second variable

We could use the following SPSS commands to calculate the significance level of the McNemar test for the data in our example.

data list/cno 1-2 yr1 yr2 3-6.
begin data.
01 1 0
.
05 1 1
.
11 0 0
.
23 0 1
.
30 0 1
end data.
npar tests mcnemar=**yr1 yr2.**

In the data the highest grade is coded as **1** and the other grades as **0**. First year grades are given in column 4 and second year grades in column 6. Since there were four cases who received the highest grade in the first year but not their second year, there will be 4 cases in the data who will be coded **1 0**. There will be 6 cases coded as **1 1**, 12 cases as **0 0** and 8 cases as **0 1**.

The relevant output for these commands is reproduced in Table 5.19. The output shows that the results have a two-tailed probability of **.3877**, which when halved gives a one-tailed probability of 0.1938. Since 0.1938 is greater than 0.05, the number of cases gaining the highest grade in the second year is not statistically greater than the number who dropped the highest grade in that year. SPSS automatically gives the binomial value when the number of cases changing values from the first to the second occasion (or variable) is less than 10.

COCHRAN Q FOR THREE OR MORE RELATED SAMPLES

If we wanted to compare the frequencies of a dichotomous variable from three or more related samples of cases, we would use the Cochran Q test. We would apply this test if we wished to determine, for example, whether the number of students who obtained the highest overall grade varied across the three years of their course. Suppose the grades for eight students were as in Table 5.20 where 1 represents the highest grade and 0 the other grades.

Table 5.19 McNemar test output

```
- - - - - McNemar Test
    YR1
with YR2

                        YR2
                    1           0       Cases              30
            0  |    8    |    12   |
YR1         1  |    6    |     4   |    (Binomial)
                                        2-tailed P        .3877
```

Table 5.20 Number of students receiving the highest grades in their first, second and third years

Cases	Year 1	Year 2	Year 3
1	1	0	1
2	1	0	0
3	1	0	0
4	0	1	0
5	0	0	0
6	0	0	0
7	0	1	1
8	0	0	0

The values of the Q test approximate those of chi-square when the number of rows is not too small, although Cochran does not specify what the minimum number is. To calculate Q, we first need to sum each of the rows (RT) and columns (CT) and then square them (RT^2 and CT^2) as shown in Table 5.21. So, from this table we can see that the number of highest grades across all students is 3 in the first year, 2 in the second and 2 in the third, giving a total number of 7 over all three years. The number of highest overall grades attained over all three years is 2 for the first student, 1 for the next three students and so on, giving a total of 7 across all eight students.

The formula for computing Q is

$$Q = \frac{[(\text{number of groups} \times \text{sum of CT}^2) - \text{squared sum of RT}] \times (\text{number of groups} - 1)}{(\text{number of groups} \times \text{sum of RT}) - \text{sum of RT}^2}$$

To compute the Q value, we carry out the following steps.

Step 1 Take the sum of the row totals (which is 7 and which is the total number of 1s in this example) and square this to give the squared sum of row totals (i.e. 49).

Step 2 Multiply the sum of the squared column totals (i.e. 17) by the number of groups (i.e. 3).

Step 3 Subtract from this figure (i.e. $17 \times 3 = 51$) the squared sum of row totals (i.e. 49).

Step 4 Multiply this difference (i.e. $51 - 49 = 2$) by the number of groups minus 1 (i.e. $3 - 1 = 2$). This figure (i.e. $2 \times 2 = 4$) which we will

Table 5.21 Cochran Q test: initial computations

Cases	Year 1	Year 2	Year 3	RT	RT^2
1	1	0	1	2	4
2	1	0	0	1	1
3	1	0	0	1	1
4	0	1	0	1	1
5	0	0	0	0	0
6	0	0	0	0	0
7	0	1	1	2	4
8	0	0	0	0	0
CT	3	2	2	7	11
CT^2	9	4	4	17	

call the numerator is divided by another figure which we shall call the denominator and which is calculated in the following way.

Step 5   Multiply the sum of row totals (i.e. 7) by the number of groups (i.e. 3) and subtract from this the sum of the squared row totals (i.e. 11) to give the denominator (i.e. $21 - 11 = 10$).

Step 6   Divide the numerator (i.e. 4) by the denominator (i.e. 10) to produce the Q value (i.e. 0.4).

Substituting the appropriate values in the formula, we see that Q is 0.4:

$$\frac{[(3 \times 17) - 49] \times 2}{(3 \times 7) - 11} = \frac{(51 - 49) \times 2}{21 - 11} = \frac{4}{10} = 0.4$$

To check the statistical significance of this value, we look it up in the table in Appendix 8. Since, with 2 degrees of freedom, the value of 0.4 is smaller than that of 5.99 at the two-tailed 0.05 level, we would conclude that there was no significant difference in the number of highest grades achieved by the same students across the three years.

To compute the Cochran Q test with SPSS, we would use the following **npar tests** command:

npar tests cochran=variables

So, we could work out the Q value for our example with the following SPSS commands:

data list/cno 1 yr1 yr2 yr3 2-7.
begin data.
1 1 0 1
2 1 0 0
3 1 0 0
4 0 1 0
5 0 0 0
6 0 0 0
7 0 1 1
8 0 0 0
end data.
npar tests cochran=yr1 yr2 yr3.

The output produced by these commands is shown in Table 5.22. As we can see, the Q value of 0.4 has a probability of **.8187** of occurring by chance which is greater than 0.05, indicating that the results are not statistically significant.

Table 5.22 Cochran Q test output

–––––Cochran Q test			
Cases			
= 0 = 1 Variable			
5 3 YR1			
6 2 YR2			
6 2 YR3			
Cases	Cochran Q	D.F.	Significance
8	.4000	2	.8187

SUMMARY

The computation of non-parametric tests for assessing whether the number of cases in different categories varies across two or more groups or from some expected distribution is described. The binomial test determines whether the number of cases falling into one of only two categories differs significantly from some expected number or proportion. The Pearson chi-square test compares the observed frequency of cases against the expected frequency for two or more unrelated samples on a variable with two or more categories. Yates's correction is applied when each variable has only two categories and when the number of cases is greater than 40 or when the number of cases is between 20 and 40 and all four expected frequencies are 5 or more. Fisher's exact test is used when each variable has only two categories, when the number of cases is less than 40 and when one of the expected frequencies is less than 5. The McNemar test compares the frequencies of a dichotomous variable which have changed values in two related samples of cases whereas the Cochran Q test compares them in three or more related samples.

EXERCISES

1   Of 90 married couples, 10 of the women compared with 25 of the men said that they fell in love with their partner at first sight.
    (a) What test would you use to determine whether this difference was significant?
    (b) What is the value of this test?
    (c) What are the degrees of freedom?
    (d) Would you use a one- or two-tailed probability level to evaluate the significance of this value?
    (e) What is the probability value of the test?
    (f) Do significantly more men than women fall in love with their future spouse at first sight?

2   Of 30 members who are supposed to meet twice, 5 attend both
    meetings, 5 attend neither meeting, 15 attend the first but not the
    second meeting and 5 attend the second but not the first meeting.
    (a) What test would you use to determine whether of the people
        attending the first meeting significantly fewer were present at the
        second meeting?
    (b) What is the value of this test?
    (c) What are the degrees of freedom?
    (d) Would you use a one- or two-tailed probability level to evaluate
        the significance of this value?
    (e) What is the probability value of the test?
    (f) Of the people attending the first meeting did significantly fewer
        attend the second?

Chapter 6

Tests of difference for ordinal data

The statistical tests described in this chapter are used to analyse ordinal data from two or more groups of cases. These tests determine whether the distribution of cases differs significantly from chance across the groups. Suppose we are interested in finding out which method is most effective in reducing exam anxiety. To measure how anxious people are we ask them to rate their anxiety on a four-point scale where 1 indicates 'not at all anxious', 2 'slightly anxious', 3 'moderately anxious' and 4 'very anxious'. This measure is an ordinal scale since the intervals between the four points do not necessarily represent equal increments or intervals in the level of anxiety. We could use some of the tests discussed in this chapter to find out whether one method for reducing exam anxiety was significantly more effective than one or more other methods in terms of how anxious people rated themselves as being after trying these methods. We could use the other tests contained in this chapter to see whether there was a significant decrease in how anxious people judged themselves to be after, compared with before, using a particular method and whether any decrease which occurred was maintained over, say, the next three months.

In this example, which we will use throughout this chapter, people who are anxious about sitting exams volunteer to take part in a study which is designed to determine which of two methods is more effective in alleviating exam anxiety. Six participants each are randomly assigned to one of three conditions. One condition involves learning muscular relaxation (relaxation training), while another consists of changing negative beliefs about sitting exams (cognitive training). The third condition is a control condition in which participants are not taught to reduce their anxiety. The purpose of this control condition is to find out whether one or both of the methods being tested are better than no treatment. Participants rate their anxiety on the four-point scale immediately before receiving treatment (pre-test), immediately after treatment has ended (post-test) and three months later (follow-up). The results for the three conditions are shown in Table 6.1.

Table 6.1 Pre-test, post-test and follow-up anxiety ratings for relaxation, cognitive and control conditions

Condition	Pre-test	Post-test	Follow-up
Relaxation training	3	2	2
	4	3	4
	3	3	3
	3	3	2
	4	2	1
	4	3	3
Cognitive training	4	3	2
	4	3	3
	3	2	2
	3	2	1
	4	2	2
	3	2	2
Control	3	3	3
	4	4	3
	3	2	3
	3	3	2
	4	3	2
	4	3	3

KOLMOGOROV–SMIRNOV TEST FOR TWO UNRELATED SAMPLES

The Kolmogorov–Smirnov test determines whether the distribution of an ordinal variable differs significantly between two unrelated samples. We could apply this test if we wanted to compare the distribution of anxiety ratings for any two of the three conditions, such as follow-up anxiety for the relaxation and cognitive training conditions. To do this, we would carry out the following steps.

Step 1   Draw up a cumulative frequency table for the two conditions in which the frequency of the previous category is added to the frequency of the subsequent category as shown in Table 6.2. For example, in the relaxation training condition one person has a rating of 1 and two have a rating of 2 so that the cumulative frequency of people having a rating of 1 and 2 is 3.

Step 2   Calculate the cumulative frequency proportion for each rating by dividing each cumulative frequency by the total number of cases in each sample as illustrated in Table 6.3.

Step 3   Compute the absolute difference between the cumulative proportions within each rating as displayed in Table 6.3.

Table 6.2 Cumulative frequency table of follow-up anxiety ratings for the relaxation and cognitive conditions

	1	2	3	4
Relaxation training	1	3	5	6
Cognitive training	1	5	6	6

Table 6.3 Cumulative frequency proportions of follow-up anxiety ratings for the relaxation and cognitive conditions

	1	2	3	4
Relaxation training	1/6	3/6	5/6	6/6
Cognitive training	1/6	5/6	6/6	6/6
Absolute difference	0	2/6	1/6	0

Step 4 for small samples   When both samples are equal in size and 40 or less, look up the numerator of the largest absolute difference (i.e. 2 of 2/6) in the table in Appendix 9. As we did not predict the direction of any difference, we would use a two-tailed test. Since a numerator of 2 with 6 cases is smaller than the 0.05 level of 5, we would conclude that there is no significant difference in the distribution of follow-up anxiety between the relaxation and cognitive training conditions.

Step 4: Two-tailed level for large samples   When both samples are larger than 40 (where it is not necessary that the two samples are equal in size), we would look to the table in Appendix 10 to determine the two-tailed significance level. If we multiplied the numbers within each rating by 10, we would have 60 cases in each sample. To determine the value which an absolute difference of 0.33 from 60 cases would have to be larger than to be significant, we would carry out the computation shown in this table. We have to add the two sample sizes together ($60 + 60 = 120$), divide by the product of the two sample sizes [$120/(60 \times 60) = 0.033$], take the square root of the resulting figure ($\sqrt{0.033} = 0.18$) and multiply by 1.36 which gives a value of 0.24.

Since the absolute difference of 0.33 is larger than 0.24, we would conclude in this instance that the two distributions differed significantly at less than the 0.05 two-tailed level and that the cognitive training condition had significantly lower follow-up anxiety ratings than the relaxation training condition. We could go on to calculate that the absolute difference of 0.33 was larger than the 0.005 two-tailed value (i.e. $0.18 \times 1.73 = 0.31$)

but smaller than the 0.001 two-tailed value (i.e. $0.18 \times 1.95 = 0.35$). In other words, the cognitive training condition had significantly lower follow-up anxiety ratings than the relaxation training condition at less than the 0.005 two-tailed level.

Step 4: One-tailed level for large samples   To calculate the one-tailed probability level when both samples are larger than 60, we compute a chi-square according to the following formula where n_1 is the number of cases in one sample and n_2 is the number of cases in the other sample:

$$\text{chi-square} = \frac{n_1 \times n_2}{n_1 + n_2} \times 4 \times \text{largest absolute difference squared}$$

If we substitute the appropriate figures into this formula we see that chi-square is 13.2:

$$\frac{3600}{120} \times 4 \times 0.33^2 = 30 \times 4 \times 0.11 = 13.2$$

We look up this figure in the table in Appendix 8. Since this test has two degrees of freedom and since a chi-square of 13.2 is larger than 9.21 at the 0.01 two-tailed level, we can conclude that the cognitive training condition had significantly lower follow-up anxiety ratings than the relaxation training condition at less than 0.005 one-tailed level.

The Kolmogorov–Smirnov test can be calculated with the following SPSS **npar tests** procedure command:

npar tests k-s=ordinal variable **by** grouping variable(value of one group,value of other group).

To compute the Kolmogorov–Smirnov test for a difference in follow-up anxiety between the relaxation and cognitive training conditions for our original example, we would first have to access the data which we could do with the following kinds of commands:

data list/cno 1-2 con 4 pre pos fol 5-10.
begin data.
01 1 3 2 2
02 1 4 3 4
03 1 3 3 3
.
.
.
12 3 4 3 3
end data.

The variable specifying the three conditions is called **con** and is located in column **4**. The relaxation training, cognitive training and control conditions are coded respectively **1**, **2** and **3**. Pre-test, post-test and follow-up anxiety ratings are respectively referred to as **pre**, **pos** and **fol** and placed in columns **6**, **8** and **10**. Consequently, the **npar tests** command would take the following form:

npar tests k-s=fol by con(1,2).

The relevant output for this command is presented in Table 6.4. The output shows the largest absolute difference (**.3333**) and the Kolmogorov–Smirnov Z value which is based on the Smirnov (1948) formula. To obtain the Z value, we multiply the two sample sizes together ($6 \times 6 = 12$), divide by the sum of the two sample sizes ($36/(6 + 6) = 3$), take the square root of the resulting figure ($\sqrt{3} = 1.732$) and multiply by the absolute difference of 0.333 to give **.577**.

MANN–WHITNEY U TEST FOR TWO UNRELATED SAMPLES

The Mann–Whitney U test determines the number of times a score from one of the samples is ranked higher than a score from the other sample. If the two sets of scores are similar, then the number of times this happens should be similar for the two samples. To calculate the Mann–Whitney test to find out if the sum of ranked scores for follow-up anxiety ratings is different for the relaxation and cognitive training conditions, we would carry out the following steps.

Table 6.4 Kolmogorov–Smirnov test output

- - - - - **Kolmogorov–Smirnov 2-Sample Test**

FOL
by CON
    Cases

      6 CON = 1
      6 CON = 2
      ———
    12 Total

WARNING – Due to small sample size, probability tables should be consulted.
      Most Extreme Differences

Absolute	Positive	Negative	K-S Z	2-tailed P
.33333	.00000	−.33333	.577	.893

Step 1   Rank the scores of both the samples together, using rank 1 for the lowest score, rank 2 for the next lowest score and so on. If two or more scores have the same value, each of the tied scores has the same rank which is equal to the average rank of those scores for the combined samples. For example, if two scores are equal and would have occupied first and second place, the two positions are added together $(1 + 2 = 3)$ and divided by the number of scores (2) to give a ranking of 1.5 (3/2), which is then assigned to the two scores. The ranking of the follow-up anxiety ratings for the two conditions is shown in Table 6.5.

Step 2   Sum the ranks for the smaller sample. Since in our example both samples are the same size, it does not matter with which sample we work. We will use the first sample (the relaxation training group) as indicated in Table 6.6.

Table 6.5 Ranking of follow-up anxiety ratings for the relaxation and cognitive conditions

Scores			
Original	Reordered	Position	Ranked
2	1	1	1.5
4	1	2	1.5
3	2	3	5.5
2	2	4	5.5
1	2	5	5.5
3	2	6	5.5
2	2	7	5.5
3	2	8	5.5
2	3	9	10.0
1	3	10	10.0
2	3	11	10.0
2	4	12	12.0

Table 6.6 Ranked anxiety ratings for the relaxation condition

2	5.5
4	12.0
3	10.0
2	5.5
1	1.5
3	10.0
Total	44.5

Step 3   The Mann–Whitney U is calculated by the following formula where n_1 represents the smaller sample and n_2 the larger sample:

$$U = (n_1 \times n_2) + \frac{n_1 \times (n_1 + 1)}{2} - \text{summed ranks of } n_1$$

Substituting the appropriate values into this formula, we find that U is 12.5:

$$(6 \times 6) + \frac{6 \times (6 + 1)}{2} - 44.5 = 36 + \frac{42}{2} - 44.5 = 12.5$$

Step 4   Calculate the U value for the second sample using the following formula:

U of second sample $= n_1 \times n_2 - U$ of first sample

Putting the relevant figures into this formula, we see that the U of the second sample is 23.5:

$$(6 \times 6) - 12.5 = 23.5$$

Note that if we know the U value of one sample (e.g. 23.5) and the two sample sizes (i.e. 6 and 6), we can work out the U value for the other sample ($36 - 23.5 = 12.5$) since the two U values combined equal the product of the number of cases in the two samples.

Step 5 for samples up to 20   If the samples are 20 or less, as they are in this case, we look up the significance of the smaller of the two U values (i.e. 12.5) in the appropriate table in Appendix 11 or 12. If the value of the smaller U is greater than the critical value of U in the table, we conclude that there is no significant difference between the summed ranks of the two samples. Since we did not specify the direction of any difference we might find, we would use the 0.05 two-tailed level shown in the table in Appendix 12. As the U value of 12.5 is greater than the critical value of 7 when the size of both samples is 6, we would argue that there is no significant difference in follow-up anxiety between the two conditions.

Step 5 for samples larger than 20   If the samples are greater than 20, we convert our U value into an approximate z value by using the following formula:

$$z = \frac{U - (n_1 \times n_2)/2}{\sqrt{[(n_1 \times n_2)(n_1 + n_2 + 1)]/12}}$$

We can change our U value into a z value by substituting the appropriate numbers into the formula which gives a z of -0.88:

$$\frac{12.5 - [(6 \times 6)/2]}{\sqrt{[(6 \times 6)(6 + 6 + 1)]/12}} = \frac{12.5 - 18}{\sqrt{468/12}} = \frac{-5.5}{6.24} = -0.88$$

Since we ignore the sign of the U value, it does not matter which U value is put into the formula. If we subtracted 18 from 23.5 instead of 12.5 the absolute difference is still 5.5.

We look up the significance of this z value in the table in Appendix 6. The area between the middle of the curve and a z value of 0.88 is 0.3106, indicating that the area beyond the z value on one side of the curve is 0.1894 (0.5000 − 0.3106 = 0.1894). We need to double this figure to give the two-tailed probability level which is 0.3788 (0.1894 × 2 = 0.3788). Since 0.3788 is larger than 0.05, we would conclude that there is no significant difference in follow-up anxiety between the relaxation and cognitive training conditions.

When ties occur between the scores of the two samples, the U value is affected although this effect is usually slight. To correct for tied ranks in calculating z, we carry out the following steps.

Step 1   Count the number of ties for each score. So, in our example, we have two scores or ties of 1, six ties of 2 and three ties of 3.

Step 2   For each tied score, subtract the number of ties from the number of ties cubed and divide by 12. So, two ties becomes 0.5 ($(2^3 - 2)/12 = 0.5$).

Step 3   Sum these values for each tied score, which in our example would give a figure of 20:

$$\frac{2^3 - 2}{12} + \frac{6^3 - 6}{12} + \frac{3^3 - 3}{12} = \frac{8 - 2}{12} + \frac{216 - 6}{12} + \frac{27 - 3}{12}$$

$$= \frac{6}{12} + \frac{210}{12} + \frac{24}{12}$$

$$= 0.5 + 17.5 + 2$$

$$= 20$$

Step 4   This value (which we shall call ST for sum of ties) is used in the following formula to calculate z, where N stands for the total number of cases in both samples:

$$z = \frac{U - [(n_1 \times n_2)/2]}{\sqrt{\{(n_1 \times n_2)/[N \times (N - 1)]\} \times \{[(N^3 - N)/12] - ST\}}}$$

Inserting the values of our example, we find that z is 0.9496:

$$\frac{12.5 - [(6 \times 6)/2]}{\sqrt{\{(6 \times 6)/[12 \times (12 - 1)]\} \times \{[(12^3 - 12)/12] - 20\}}}$$

$$= \frac{12.5 - 18}{\sqrt{(36/132) \times [(1716/12) - 20]}}$$

$$= \frac{-5.5}{\sqrt{0.2727 \times 123}}$$

$$= \frac{-5.5}{5.792}$$

$$= 0.9496$$

Looking up the significance of this value of 0.95 in the table in Appendix 6, we find that we obtain a two-tailed probability value of 0.3422 ((0.5000 − 0.3289) × 2 = 0.3422). Since this value is larger than 0.05, we would conclude that there was no significant difference in follow-up anxiety between the relaxation and cognitive training conditions.

The Mann–Whitney U test, also sometimes called the Wilcoxon Rank Sum W test, can be computed with the following SPSS **npar tests** procedure command:

npar tests m-w=ordinal variable **by** grouping variable(value of one group,value of other group).

To obtain the Mann–Whitney U test for a difference in follow-up anxiety between the relaxation and cognitive training conditions for our example, we would use the following kind of command:

npar tests m-w=fol by con(1,2).

The output for this command is shown in Table 6.7. As can be seen, the mean rank for the two conditions is given as well as the U and W values. The U and W values of the smaller group are presented, unless as in this case the two groups are of equal size when the U and W values of the group with the lowest code (i.e. 1) are shown. The W value is the rank sum of the smaller group (i.e. **7.42 × 6 = 44.5**). For samples with less than 30 cases, the exact two-tailed significance level is calculated using the algorithm of Dinneen and Blakesley (1973) together with the z statistic corrected for ties. For larger samples, only the z statistic is displayed.

Table 6.7 Mann–Whitney *U* test output

––––– **Mann–Whitney U – Wilcoxon Rank Sum W Test**

FOL
by CON

Mean Rank	Cases	
7.42	6	CON = 1
5.58	6	CON = 2
	12	Total

U	W	EXACT 2-tailed P	Corrected for Ties Z	2-tailed P
12.5	44.5	.3939	−.9496	.3423

KRUSKAL–WALLIS ONE-WAY ANALYSIS OF VARIANCE OR *H* TEST FOR THREE OR MORE UNRELATED SAMPLES

The Kruskal–Wallis *H* test is similar to the Mann–Whitney *U* test in that the cases in the different samples are ranked together in one series except that this test can be used with more than two unrelated samples. If there is little difference between the sets of scores, then their mean ranks should be similar. We would use the Kruskal–Wallis *H* test to determine if follow-up anxiety differed between the three conditions of relaxation training, cognitive training and the no-treatment control. To apply this test to these data, we would carry out the following steps.

Step 1   Rank the scores of the conditions taken together, giving rank 1 to the lowest score. Where two or more scores are tied, allocate the average rank to those scores. The follow-up anxiety ratings for the three conditions are presented in Table 6.8 where they have been rearranged in three parallel columns. The ranking of these data is shown in Table 6.9.

Step 2   Sum the ranks for each group which, in this example, gives 60.5, 41.5 and 69 respectively.

Step 3   For each group, square the sum of ranks and divide by the number of cases. This in turn yields 610.04 (3660.25/6 = 610.04), 287.04 (1722.25/6 = 287.04) and 793.5 (4761/6 = 793.5).

Step 4   Sum these values which, in this case, is 1690.5.

Step 5   Place this figure (which we shall call SR for sum of ranks) in the following formula which gives *H*:

Table 6.8 Follow-up anxiety ratings for the relaxation, cognitive and control
conditions

Relaxation training	Cognitive training	Control
2	2	3
4	3	3
3	2	3
2	1	2
1	2	2
3	2	3

Table 6.9 Ranking of follow-up anxiety ratings for the relaxation, cognitive and
control conditions

Relaxation training	Cognitive training	Control
6.5	6.5	14
18	14	14
14	6.5	14
6.5	1.5	6.5
1.5	6.5	6.5
14	6.5	14

$$H = \frac{12 \times SR}{N \times (N+1)} - [3 \times (N+1)]$$

Substituting the appropriate values, H is 2.32:

$$\frac{12 \times 1690.58}{18 \times (18+1)} - [3 \times (18+1)] = \frac{20286.96}{342} - 57 = 2.32$$

When there are more than five cases in each of the conditions, the
significance of H may be determined from the chi-square table in
Appendix 8. The degree of freedom is one less than the number of samples
which in this case is 2 $(3 - 1 = 2)$. Since with 2 degrees of freedom an H
value of 2.32 is not greater than 5.99 at the two-tailed 0.05 level, we would
conclude that there was no significant difference in follow-up anxiety
between the three conditions.

To correct for tied scores, we carry out the following steps.

Step 1   Count the number of ties for each score. In this example, we have
two ties of 1, eight ties of 2 and seven ties of 3.

Step 2   For each tied score, subtract the number of ties from the number of ties cubed. So, two ties becomes 6 ($2^3 - 2 = 6$).

Step 3   Sum these values for each tied score, which in this case gives 846:

$$(2^3 - 2) + (8^3 - 8) + (7^3 - 7) = 6 + 504 + 336 = 846.$$

Step 4   Divide this value by the total number of cases subtracted from the total number of cases cubed, which in this instance produces a figure of 0.145:

$$\frac{846}{18^3 - 18} = \frac{846}{5832} = 0.145$$

Step 5   Subtract this number from 1, which gives 0.855 ($1 - 0.145 = 0.855$).

Step 6   Divide the uncorrected value of H by this figure to give the value corrected for ties, which in this example is 2.71 ($2.32/0.855 = 2.71$). We look up this value in the chi-square table in Appendix 8. Since with 2 degrees of freedom this figure is greater than 5.99 at the two-tailed 0.05 level, we would conclude that there was no significant difference in follow-up anxiety between the three conditions.

The Kruskal–Wallis H test can be computed with the following SPSS **npar tests** procedure command:

npar tests k-w=ordinal variable **by** grouping variable(value of first group,value of last group).

To obtain the Kruskal–Wallis H test for a difference in follow-up anxiety between the three conditions in our example, we would use the following kind of command.

npar tests k-w=**fol by con(1,3).**

The output for this command is shown in Table 6.10. The mean rank for the three conditions is given, which is simply the sum of ranks for each group divided by the number of cases in that group. For example, the sum of ranks for the relaxation condition is 60.5 which divided by 6 gives **10.08**. The chi-square test, uncorrected and corrected for ties, with its associated significance level is also depicted.

SIGN TEST FOR TWO RELATED SAMPLES

The sign test compares the number of positive and negative differences between scores from the same or matched samples. If the two samples do

Table 6.10 Kruskal–Wallis *H* test output

----- **Kruskal–Wallis 1-way ANOVA**

FOL
by CON

Mean Rank Cases

10.08	6	CON = 1
6.92	6	CON = 2
11.50	6	CON = 3
18	**Total**	

			Corrected for Ties	
CASES	**Chi-Square**	**Significance**	**Chi-Square**	**Significance**
18	2.3187	.3137	2.7136	.2575

not differ, then the number of positive and negative differences should be similar. We could use the sign test to determine whether there had been for one or more conditions any change in anxiety between any two occasions when anxiety had been measured such as at pre-test and post-test.

To apply the sign test to determine whether anxiety had decreased from pre-test to post-test for people receiving cognitive training, we would carry out the following steps.

Step 1   Record the direction of change between the two occasions, giving a plus (+) if the second score is larger than the first, a minus (−) if it is smaller and a zero (0) if there is no difference. These differences have been noted in Table 6.11 for the pre-test and post-test anxiety scores for the cognitive training sample.

Step 2   Count the number of pluses and minuses. Let n represent the less frequent sign and N the total number of pluses and minuses. In this example, n is 0 since there are no pluses and N is 6.

Step 3 for less than 26 differences   For samples containing less than 26 differences (number of pluses and minuses), look up the significance of the results in the binomial table in Appendix 7. The one-tailed probability of obtaining this value is 0.016 which is less than the 0.05 criterion. In other words, anxiety decreased significantly from pre-test to post-test for the cognitive training condition.

Step 3 for greater than 25 differences   For samples having more than 25 differences, the less frequent difference can be converted into a z value using the following formula:

Table 6.11 Pre-test and post-test anxiety ratings for the cognitive condition

Pre-test	Post-test	Sign of Difference
4	3	−
4	3	−
3	2	−
3	2	−
4	2	−
3	2	−

$$z = \frac{(n + 0.5) - (N/2)}{0.5 \times \sqrt{N}}$$

where n and N have the same meaning as before. Substituting the appropriate values in this formula, z is -2.05:

$$\frac{(0 + 0.5) - (6/2)}{0.5 \times \sqrt{6}} = \frac{-2.5}{1.22} = -2.05$$

We look up the significance of this z value of 2.05 in the normal distribution table in Appendix 6, where we see that it has a one-tailed probability value of less than 0.0202 ($0.5000 - 0.4798 = 0.0202$).

The following SPSS **npar tests** procedure command is used to compute a sign test:

npar tests sign=first variable second variable

So to compare pre-test and post-test anxiety in our example, we would run the following command:

npar tests sign=pre pos.

Since we only want to compare pre-test and post-test anxiety for the cognitive training condition, we first have to select these cases by preceding the **npar tests** command with the following **select if** command:

select if (con eq 2).

The output for these commands is presented in Table 6.12. The numbers of negative, positive and zero differences are shown. The two-tailed binomial level is used with fewer than 26 differences (as in this instance) and the two-tailed z level with more than 25 differences.

Table 6.12 Sign test output

```
----- Sign Test
      PRE
   with POS
          Cases
            6  - Diffs    (POS Lt PRE)
            0  + Diffs    (POS Gt PRE)    (Binomial)
            0    Ties                     2-tailed P =      .0313
           ___
            6    Total
```

WILCOXON MATCHED-PAIRS SIGNED-RANKS TEST FOR TWO RELATED SAMPLES

Whereas the sign test only makes use of the sign of the difference between the two samples, the Wilcoxon matched-pairs signed-ranks test (or Wilcoxon test for short) takes some account of the size of the difference by ranking the size of the differences and summing ranks of the same sign.

To conduct a Wilcoxon test to determine whether anxiety had decreased from pre-test to post-test for people receiving cognitive training, we would carry out the following steps.

Step 1   Calculate the difference between each pair of scores and rank these in size, ignoring the sign of the difference. Give a rank of 1 to the smallest difference (regardless of its sign) and omit pairs where there is no difference. For example, 2 would receive a higher rank than either 1 or −1, which would be given the same rank. The size and rank of the differences between pre-test and post-test anxiety scores for the cognitive training sample are presented in Table 6.13. Where two or more differences are the same size, they are given the average of the ranks they would have received if they had differed. The smallest difference in our data is 1 so it is assigned a rank of 1. Five of the differences have a rank of 1, so we sum their ranks which is 15 (1 + 2 + 3 + 4 + 5 = 15) and then divide this sum by the number of differences to give an average rank of 3 (15/5 = 3).

Step 2   Sum the ranks of the difference with the less frequent sign. In this case, the less frequent sign is minus. Since there are no minus differences, the sum of ranks is zero.

Step 3 for less than 26 differences   For data having fewer than 26 differences, look up the significance of the smaller sum of ranks with the same sign in the table in Appendix 13. We can use the one-tailed significance level as we are testing for a decrease rather than a change in

Table 6.13 Ranked differences between pre-test and post-test anxiety ratings for the cognitive condition

Pre-test	Post-test	Difference	Rank
4	3	+1	3
4	3	+1	3
3	2	+1	3
3	2	+1	3
4	2	+2	6
3	2	+1	3

anxiety. Since a sum of ranks of 0 for a sample of 6 is smaller than 2 at the two-tailed 0.10 level (and therefore at the one-tailed 0.05 level), we can conclude that anxiety has decreased significantly from pre-test to post-test for the cognitive training condition.

Step 3 for more than 25 differences   For data with more than 25 differences, the following formula is used to transform the smaller sum of ranks (denoted as SR) into a z score where N stands for the number of differences:

$$z = \frac{SR - \{[N \times (N+1)]/4\}}{\sqrt{\{N \times (N+1) \times [(2 \times N) + 1]/24\}}}$$

To illustrate the use of this formula, we will substitute the values of our example which gives a z of -2.2014:

$$\frac{0 - \{[6 \times (6+1)]/4\}}{\sqrt{\{6 \times (6+1) \times [(2 \times 6) + 1]\}/24}}$$

$$= \frac{0 - 42/4}{\sqrt{(42 \times 13)/24}} = \frac{-10.5}{4.7696} = -2.2014$$

We look up the significance of this z value of 2.2014 in the normal distribution table in Appendix 6, where we see that it has a one-tailed probability of less than 0.0139 ($0.5000 - 0.4861 = 0.0139$).

We compute the Wilcoxon test with the following SPSS **npar tests** procedure command:

npar tests wilcoxon=first variable second variable.

So to compare pre-test and post-test anxiety in our example, we would run the following command:

npar tests wilcoxon=pre pos.

Since we only want to compare pre-test and post-test anxiety for the cognitive training condition, we once again first have to select these cases by preceding the **npar tests** command with the following **select if** command:

select if (con eq 2).

The output for these commands is shown in Table 6.14. The mean negative and positive rank is displayed together with the number of negative, positive and tied ranks, the Z statistic and its two-tailed probability. SPSS also uses the Z statistic for samples with fewer than 25 differences which in this case has a one-tailed probability of 0.01385 (**.0277**/2 = 0.01385).

FRIEDMAN TWO-WAY ANALYSIS OF VARIANCE TEST FOR THREE OR MORE RELATED SAMPLES

The Friedman two-way analysis of variance test (or Friedman test for short) compares the mean ranks of three or more related samples. If the samples do not differ, the mean ranks should be similar. The Friedman test approximates a chi-square distribution.

To calculate the Friedman test to determine whether pre-test, post-test and follow-up anxiety differ for the cognitive training group, we would carry out the following steps.

Step 1   Arrange the scores in a table where the columns represent the conditions and the rows the cases. This has been done for the pre-test, post-test and follow-up anxiety scores for the cognitive training group in Table 6.15.

Step 2   Rank the scores in each row across all the conditions, ranking the

Table 6.14 Wilcoxon test output

-----Wilcoxon Matched-pairs Signed-ranks Test

 PRE
with POS

Mean Rank	Cases		
3.50	6	– Ranks	(POS Lt PRE)
.00	0	+ Ranks	(POS Gt PRE)
	0	Ties	(POS Eq PRE)
	—		
	6	Total	

 Z = –2.2014   2-tailed P = .0277

Table 6.15 Pre-test, post-test and follow-up anxiety ratings for the cognitive condition

Pre-test	Post-test	Follow-up
4	3	2
4	3	3
3	2	2
3	2	1
4	2	2
3	2	2

lowest score as 1. Where two or more scores are tied, allocate the average rank to those scores. The scores in Table 6.15 have been ranked in this way in Table 6.16.

Step 3   Sum the ranks for each condition, as shown in Table 6.16.

Step 4   Square the sum of ranks for each condition, as indicated in Table 6.16.

Step 5   Add together the squared sum of ranks to form the total squared sum of ranks (which we shall abbreviate as TSSR).

Step 6   Insert this value into the following formula where C represents the number of columns and N the number of rows or cases:

$$\chi^2_r = \frac{12 \times \text{TSSR}}{N \times C \times (C+1)} - [3 \times N \times (C+1)]$$

Substituting the appropriate figures in our example, we find that χ^2_r is 9.33:

$$\frac{12 \times 488}{6 \times 3 \times (3+1)} - [3 \times 6 \times (3+1)] = \frac{5856}{72} - 72 = 9.33$$

We look up the significance of this value in the table in Appendix 14. With three conditions ($C = 3$) and six cases ($N = 6$), χ^2_r has to be larger than 9.000 to be statistically significant at less than the 0.01 two-tailed level, which it is. Consequently, we would conclude that there is a significant difference in pre-test, post-test and follow-up anxiety for the cognitive training condition.

The Friedman test is computed with the following SPSS **npar tests** procedures command:

Table 6.16 Ranked pre-test, post-test and follow-up anxiety ratings for the cognitive condition and initial computations

	Pre-test	Post-test	Follow-up
	3	2	1
	3	1.5	1.5
	3	1.5	1.5
	3	2	1
	3	1.5	1.5
	3	1.5	1.5
Sum	18	10	8
Sum^2	324	100	64

npar tests friedman=variables.

To compare pre-test, post-test and follow-up anxiety for the cognitive training condition we would use the following command having selected the cases in the cognitive training condition with the appropriate **select if** command:

npar tests friedman=pre pos fol.

The output for these commands is presented in Table 6.17 which displays the mean rank for each variable, the chi-square statistic, its degrees of freedom and probability. The degrees of freedom are the number of conditions minus one while the probability is based on the χ^2 rather than the χ^2_r distribution.

SUMMARY

The computation of non-parametric tests for assessing whether the distribution of ordinal data from two or more samples differs significantly across the samples is described. The Kolmogorov–Smirnov test determines whether the largest absolute difference between two unrelated samples is significant. The Mann–Whitney U test ascertains the number of times a score from one of the samples is ranked higher than a score from the other sample whereas the Kruskal–Wallis H test does this for three or more unrelated samples. If the different sets of scores are similar, then the number of times this happens should be similar for the samples being compared. The sign test compares the number of positive and negative differences between scores from two related samples. If the two samples do not differ, then the number of positive and negative differences should be similar. The Wilcoxon test takes account of the size of the difference between the two unrelated samples by ranking the size of the differences and summing ranks of the same sign. The Friedman test compares the

Table 6.17 Friedman test output

– – – – – Friedman Two-way ANOVA			
Mean Rank	**Variable**		
3.00	PRE		
1.67	POS		
1.33	FOL		
Cases	**Chi-Square**	**D.F.**	**Significance**
6	9.3333	2	.0094

mean ranks of three or more related samples. If the samples do not differ, the mean ranks should be similar.

EXERCISES

The data presented in Table 6.18 will be used for the exercises in Chapters 6–11. The data consist of type of school (with single-sex schools coded as 1 and mixed-sex schools as 2), gender of pupil (with girls coded as 1 and boys as 2), socio-economic status (with higher status coded as 1, middle as 2 and lower as 3) and educational interest rated on a four-point scale (with 1 for 'not interested', 2 for 'slightly interested', 3 for 'fairly interested' and 4 for 'very interested') at ages 9, 12 and 15 for the same pupils.

1   Use the Mann–Whitney U test to compare educational interest at 12 between single- and mixed-sex schools.
    (a) What is the value of this test?
    (b) What is the two-tailed probability level?
    (c) Is educational interest at 12 significantly greater at single- than at mixed-sex schools?
2   Use the Kruskal–Wallis H test to compare educational interest at 12 for pupils of different socio-economic status.
    (a) What is the value of this test?
    (b) What are the degrees of freedom?
    (c) What is the two-tailed probability level?
    (d) Does educational interest at 12 differ significantly between pupils of different socio-economic status?
3   Use the sign test to compare educational interest at 12 and 15 for pupils from mixed-sex schools.
    (a) What is the two-tailed probability level?
    (b) Is educational interest significantly greater at 12 than at 15 for pupils from mixed-sex schools?
4   Use the Wilcoxon test to compare educational interest at 12 and 15 for pupils from mixed-sex schools.

Table 6.18 Type of school, gender, socio-economic status and educational
interest at 9, 12 and 15

Case	School	Gender	SES	Age 9	Age 12	Age 15
1	1	1	3	2	4	3
2	1	1	2	2	3	4
3	1	2	1	2	3	4
4	1	2	1	3	4	2
5	1	2	2	1	2	3
6	2	1	2	2	2	2
7	2	1	2	2	2	3
8	2	1	3	2	1	3
9	2	1	3	1	1	2
10	2	1	3	1	1	3
11	2	2	2	2	2	1
12	2	2	3	1	1	2
13	2	2	3	2	1	1
14	2	2	3	2	1	2

(a) What is the two-tailed probability level?
(b) Is educational interest significantly greater at 12 than at 15 for
pupils from mixed-sex schools?
5   Use the Friedman test to compare educational interest at 9, 12 and 15
for pupils from single-sex schools.
(a) What is the value of this test?
(b) What are the degrees of freedom?
(c) What is the two-tailed probability level?
(d) Does educational interest differ significantly between 9, 12 and 15
for pupils from single-sex schools?

Chapter 7

Tests of difference for interval/ratio data in unrelated samples

The statistical tests covered in this chapter determine whether the means and variances of interval or ratio measures differ between two or more unrelated samples of cases. However, as discussed in Chapter 4, these tests can also be employed with ordinal data and the example used in the previous chapter of the effect of different treatments on reducing exam anxiety will also be used in this chapter to illustrate the way in which these parametric tests are calculated. In addition, some of the tests discussed in this chapter can examine the effect of more than one variable. So, for example, the effect of gender as well as the effect of different treatments can be looked at in the same analysis. For instance, it is possible that cognitive training may be more effective for, say, men than women while relaxation training is more effective for women than men.

t TEST FOR TWO UNRELATED SAMPLES

The *t* test for unrelated or independent samples determines whether the means of two such samples differ. For example, we may wish to find out if mean anxiety at follow-up differs significantly between the relaxation training and cognitive training conditions. The *t* test compares the difference between the means of the two samples with the probability of those two means differing by chance. To determine the probability of two means differing by chance, we would draw a large number of samples from some given population, subtract the means of these samples from each other and plot the distribution of these differences. If we did this, these differences would be normally distributed. Since the means of most of the samples will be close to the mean of the population and therefore similar to one another, most of the differences will be close to zero. The *t* test compares the means of the two samples with what is known as the *standard error of the difference in means* which is the standard deviation of the sampling distribution of differences between pairs of means:

$$t = \frac{\text{mean of one sample} - \text{mean of other sample}}{\text{standard error of the difference in means}}$$

Before applying the t test, we need to know whether the variances of the two samples differ significantly since the way in which the standard error of the difference in means is calculated varies slightly according to whether the variances are equal or not. If the variances are equal, they are pooled together for the two samples according to the following formula:

$$\sqrt{\left\{ \frac{[\text{variance}_1 \times (n_1 - 1)] + [\text{variance}_2 \times (n_2 - 1)]}{n_1 + n_2 - 2} \right\} \times \left(\frac{1}{n_1} + \frac{1}{n_2} \right)}$$

where variance_1 and variance_2 are the variances of the two samples 1 and 2 and n_1 and n_2 are the numbers of cases in each sample. If, on the other hand, they are unequal, they are treated separately according to the following formula:

$$\sqrt{\frac{\text{variance}_1}{n_1} + \frac{\text{variance}_2}{n_2}}$$

To determine whether the variances of two samples differ, we apply the F test described in Chapter 4, which is simply the greater variance of one group divided by the smaller variance of the other.

Consequently, to apply the t test to determine whether the mean follow-up anxiety differs between the relaxation and cognitive training conditions we would carry out the following steps.

Step 1   Calculate the means of the two samples by adding the scores for each sample and dividing by the number of cases in that sample. The individual follow-up anxiety scores for the relaxation and cognitive training conditions as well as their means are shown in Table 7.1

Step 2   Calculate the variance for each of the samples by subtracting each score from the mean score for the sample, squaring these differences, adding the squared differences together and dividing this total by the number of scores minus 1.

If we do this, we obtain a variance of 1.1 for the relaxation training condition and 0.4 for the cognitive training condition.

Step 3   To apply the F test, we divide the larger by the smaller variance and look up the significance of the resulting F value in the table in Appendix 5.

Dividing 1.1 by 0.4 gives an F value of 2.75 which, with 5 degrees of freedom for both samples, needs to be greater than 5.0503 to be statis-

Table 7.1 Follow-up anxiety ratings in the relaxation and cognitive conditions and initial computations for the unrelated *t* test

	Relaxation training			Cognitive training		
	Original	*Difference*	*Squared*	*Original*	*Difference*	*Squared*
	2	0.5	0.25	2	0	0
	4	−1.5	2.25	3	−1	1
	3	−0.5	0.25	2	0	0
	2	0.5	0.25	1	1	1
	1	1.5	2.25	2	0	0
	3	−0.5	0.25	2	0	0
Total	15		5.5	12		2
Mean	2.5			2		
Variance			1.1			0.4

tically significant at the 0.05 level, which it is not. Consequently, the variances of the two samples in this instance do not differ significantly and the variances need to be pooled.

Step 4 for pooled variances Substitute the appropriate values in the formula for calculating the standard error of the difference in the means for pooled variances, which in our example is 0.5:

$$\sqrt{\left\{ \frac{[1.1 \times (6-1)] + [0.4 \times (6-1)]}{6+6-2} \right\} \times \left(\frac{1}{6} + \frac{1}{6} \right)}$$

$$= \sqrt{\frac{5.5 + 2.0}{10} \times 0.3333}$$

$$= \sqrt{0.75 \times 0.3333}$$

$$= \sqrt{0.25}$$

$$= 0.5$$

Step 5 for pooled variances To calculate *t*, subtract the mean of one sample from that of the other and divide by the standard error of the difference in the means. Substituting the relevant values from our example, *t* is 1.0:

$$\frac{2.5 - 2}{0.5} = \frac{0.5}{0.5} = 1.0$$

Step 6 for pooled variances   The degrees of freedom is found by using the following formula:

$$df = (n_1 - 1) + (n_2 - 1) = n_1 + n_2 - 2$$

Consequently, the degrees of freedom for this example is 10.

Step 7 for pooled variances   To determine the significance of this t value, look it up in the table in Appendix 15. Since we did not specify the direction of any difference in anxiety between the two groups, we would use a two-tailed test. With 10 degrees of freedom, the t value would have to be greater than 2.228 to be statistically significant at less than the 0.05 two-tailed level. As a t value of 1.0 is smaller than 2.228, we would conclude that there was no significant difference in follow-up anxiety between the two conditions.

Step 4 for separate variances   Substitute the appropriate values in the formula for calculating the standard error of the difference in means for separate variances, which for our example would be 0.5:

$$\sqrt{\frac{1.1}{6} + \frac{0.4}{6}} = \sqrt{0.1833 + 0.0666} = \sqrt{0.25} = 0.5$$

Step 5 for separate variances   To calculate t, subtract the mean of one sample from that of the other and divide by the standard error of the difference in the means. Substituting the relevant values from our example, t is 1.0:

$$\frac{2.5 - 2}{0.5} = \frac{0.5}{0.5} = 1.0$$

Step 6 for separate variances   The degrees of freedom are calculated using the following formula:

$$df = \frac{(\text{variance}_1/n_1 + \text{variance}_2/n_2)^2}{(\text{variance}_1/n_1)^2/(N_1 - 1) + (\text{variance}_2/n_2)^2/(N_2 - 1)}$$

Substituting the appropriate figures from our example, the degrees of freedom is 8 when rounded to the nearest whole number which needs to be done:

$$\frac{(1.1/6 + 0.4/6)^2}{(1.1/6)^2/5 + (0.4/6)^2/5} = \frac{(0.1833 + 0.0666)^2}{0.0336/5 + 0.0044/5} = \frac{0.0625}{0.0076} = 8.22$$

Step 7 for separate variances   Look up the significance of the t value in the table in Appendix 5. With 8 degrees of freedom, a t value of 1.0 would have to be greater than 2.306 to be statistically significant at less than the 0.05 two-tailed level which it is not.

It should be clear that if we know the means, standard deviations (the square root of the variances) and numbers of cases of any two samples, we should be able to compute t tests by inserting the relevant information in the appropriate formulae.

The unrelated t test is computed with the following SPSS **t-test** procedures command:

t-test groups=grouping variable(value of one group, value of other group)/**variables**=variable names

To carry out a t test on follow-up anxiety between the relaxation and the cognitive training condition, we could use the following command:

t-test groups=con(1,2)/variables=fol.

The output for this command is presented in Table 7.2. For each group, the number of cases, mean, standard deviation and standard error are shown, followed by the F test and the t test for pooled and separate variances. One-tailed probabilities are obtained by dividing the two-tailed levels by 2 so that the one-tailed levels for the pooled and separate tests would be 0.170 (**.341**/2 = 0.170) and 0.173 (**.346**/2 = 0.173) respectively.

Standard error refers to *standard error of the mean* which is the standard deviation of the mean divided by the square root of the number of cases:

$$\text{standard error of the mean} = \frac{\text{std deviation}}{\sqrt{\text{no. of cases}}}$$

Table 7.2 Unrelated **t-test** output

Independent samples of CON

Group 1: CON EQ 1   **Group 2: CON EQ 2**

t-test for: FOL

	Number of cases	Mean	Standard Deviation	Standard Error
Group 1	6	2.5000	1.049	.428
Group 2	6	2.0000	.632	.258

		Pooled Variance Estimate			Separate Variance Estimate		
F Value	**2-Tail Prob.**	**t Value**	**Degrees of Freedom**	**2-Tail Prob.**	**t Value**	**Degrees of Freedom**	**2-Tail Prob.**
2.75	.291	1.00	10	.341	1.00	8.21	.346

For example, the standard error of the mean of the relaxation training group is its standard deviation (**1.049**) divided by the square root of 6 (2.449) which gives **.428**. If we draw a number of samples from a population, the means of those samples are likely to differ and will form a distribution of means. The smaller the sample is the more likely that the mean will differ from the mean of the samples. The standard error of the mean provides an estimate of the extent to which the sample mean is likely to differ from the mean of the samples and takes into account the size of the sample.

Means, standard deviations and numbers of cases are often presented in social science papers. Having this information enables you to determine whether the means and variances differ. SPSS, however, does not compute *t* tests with these descriptive statistics as data. However, if you wish to carry out a number of these tests, then you might find it quicker to write a program using SPSS commands which will allow you to do this.

First, we need to define and enter the data which we do with the following SPSS commands:

data list/ cf 1 m1 3-7 s1 9-13 n1 15-16 m2 18-22 s2 24-28 n2 30-31.
begin data.
1 2.500 1.049 6 2.000 0.632 6
end data.

If we wished to carry out a number of *t* tests, it may be useful to identify the test by giving it a number. This we have done with a variable called **cf** which is the abbreviation for comparison. The mean, standard deviation and number of cases for the group entered first have been called **m1, s1** and **n1** respectively and **m2, s2** and **n2** for the group entered second.

Since we have to know whether we need to use pooled or separate variances, the next step will be to compute the *F* test which involves dividing the greater variance by the smaller variance. Consequently, we calculate the variance by squaring the standard deviation using the following commands where the symbols ** refer to exponentiation which in this case is to the power of 2:

compute v1=s1**2.
compute v2=s2**2.

To ensure that the larger variance is always divided by the smaller variance, we will use the following **if** command which specifies that, if the first variance (**v1**) is greater than or equal to (**ge**) the second variance (**v2**), the value of **f** will be **v1** divided by **v2** whereas if the second variance (**v2**) is greater than (**gt**) the first variance (**v1**), the value of **f** will be **v2** divided by **v1**:

if (v1 ge v2) f=v1/v2.
if (v2 gt v1) f=v2/v1.

To display the results of this computation, we need to use the **list** command, specifying the variables we want to see which in this case will be **cf, v1, v2** and **f**.

list cf v1 v2 f.

If we do this, the following output will be presented:

CF	V1	V2	F
1	1.10	.40	2.75

We need to look up the statistical significance of this F value in the appropriate tables. Where the number of cases in each group differs, it would be useful if we also calculated and listed the degrees of freedom which can be done with the following SPSS commands:

if (v1 ge v2) df1=n1-1.
if (v1 ge v2) df2=n2-1.
if (v2 gt v1) df1=n2-1.
if (v2 gt v1) df2=n1-1.
list cf v1 v2 df1 df2 f.

When writing a command for a fairly complex computation such as the pooled variances t test, it might be advisable to begin by breaking down the computation into a series of simpler steps to ensure that the correct sequence of calculations is carried out. Each step in the calculation can be checked by listing the relevant values. Without any further information, SPSS will perform the following mathematical operations in order of priority: (1) square root (**sqrt**); (2) exponentiation (******); (3) multiplication (*****) and division (**/**); and (4) addition (**+**) and subtraction (**−**). However, you can control the order in which operations are carried out by enclosing in brackets the operation you first want to perform. So, for example, if you want to add or subtract two variables before multiplying or dividing them by another variable, you would bracket the first operation.

Since the calculation for the separate variance t test is simpler than that for the pooled variance one, we will begin by showing the commands that can be used for working out this test. The computation can be broken down into two steps, the first which calculates the standard error for separate variances (**ses**) and the second which gives the t value for separate variances (**ts**):

compute ses=sqrt((v1/n1)+(v2/n2)).
compute ts=(m1-m2)/ses.

The operations in brackets will be performed before those outside them so, for example, **m2** will be subtracted from **m1** before being divided by **ses**. These two commands could be collapsed into one as follows:

compute ts=(m1-m2)/(sqrt((v1/n1)+(v2/n2))).

To calculate the appropriate degrees of freedom for separate variances (**dfs**), we could use the following two commands where the first command computes the denominator of the formula:

compute dfs=(((v1/n1)**2)/(n1-1))+(((v2/n2)**2)/(n2-1)).
compute dfs=(((v1/n1)+(v2/n2))**2)/dfs.

These two commands could be reduced to one as follows:

compute dfs=(((v1/n1)+(v2/n2))**2)/(((((v1/n1)**2)/(n1-1))
+(((v2/n2)**2)/(n2-1))).

The obvious disadvantage of doing this is that the command is difficult to read.

If we run these commands and list **cf**, **ts** and **dfs**, the following output is produced:

CF	TS	DFS
1	1.00	8.21

For the pooled variance test, we could break down the computation into the following five steps:

compute sep=(v1*(n1-1))+(v2*(n2-1)).
compute sep=sep/(n1+n2-2).
compute sep=sep*(1/n1+1/n2).
compute sep=sqrt(sep).
compute tp=(m1-m2)/sep.

If we wished, we could collapse these steps into a single one as follows:

compute tp=(m1-m2)/(sqrt(((((v1*(n1-1))+(v2*(n2-1)))/(n1+n2-2))*
(1/n1+1/n2))).

Calculating the degrees of freedom for the pooled variance t test can be done with this simple command:

compute dfp=n1+n2-2.

The following output is displayed if we run these commands and list **cf**, **dfp** and **tp**:

CF	DFP	TP
1	10.00	1.00

Once we have checked that this set of commands for calculating the F test, t test and degrees of freedom for pooled and separate variances from means, standard deviations and number of cases is accurate, we can store it as a file for future use.

ONE-WAY ANALYSIS OF VARIANCE FOR TWO OR MORE UNRELATED SAMPLES

One-way analysis of variance compares the means of two or more unrelated samples such as the mean follow-up anxiety ratings of the three treatment conditions in our example. Analysis of variance (often abbreviated and referred to as ANOVA) is essentially an F test in which an estimate of the variance between the groups (i.e. the between-groups estimated variance) is compared with an estimate of the variance within the groups (i.e. the within-groups estimated variance) by dividing the former by the latter:

$$F = \frac{\text{between-groups estimated variance}}{\text{within-groups estimated variance}}$$

The between-groups estimated variance is based on the extent to which the means of the groups vary from the overall or total mean of the groups, while the within-groups estimated variance reflects the degree to which the scores within each group differ from the mean of that group for all the groups. If the variance between the groups is considerably greater than the overall variance within the groups, then this implies that the differences between the means are less likely to be due to chance. The between-groups estimated variance is often referred to as the *explained* variance and the within-groups estimated variance as the *error* (or sometimes as the *residual*) variance since the between-groups estimated variance is more likely to represent the variance of the variable being investigated whereas the within-groups estimated variance is more likely to correspond to the variance of other factors which have not been measured or controlled.

The procedures described in this book for calculating analysis of variance will be based on the *fixed model* where the results apply only to the particular categories of the variables chosen by the investigator. The fixed model is distinguished from the *random model* where the categories of the variables have been randomly selected to represent those variables and where, therefore, the results can be generalised to the variables as a whole.

To compute a one-way analysis of variance we carry out the following steps which we can illustrate with the follow-up anxiety ratings of the individuals in the three treatment conditions.

Step 1   To compute the between-groups estimated variance: (1) calculate the mean of each group; (2) subtract the overall (or *grand*) mean from the group mean; (3) square this difference; (4) multiply this squared difference by the number of cases within that group; (5) sum these products for all the groups (giving what is known as the between-groups *sum of squares*); and (6) divide by the degrees of freedom which is the number of groups minus

1 (forming what is known as the between-groups *mean square*).

The individual follow-up anxiety scores for the three treatments are shown in Table 7.3 together with the group and overall (or grand) sum and mean. All means have been rounded to one decimal place. The between-groups sum of squares is 1.56:

$$[(2.5 - 2.4)^2 \times 6] + [(2 - 2.4)^2 \times 6] + [(2.7 - 2.4)^2 \times 6]$$
$$= 0.06 + 0.96 + 0.54$$
$$= 1.56$$

which divided by the within-groups degrees of freedom $(3 - 1 = 2)$ is 0.78.

Step 2   To calculate the within-groups estimated variance, compute the total sum of squares, subtract from it the between-groups sum of squares and divide the result by the within-groups degrees of freedom. To compute the within-groups degrees of freedom subtract 1 from the number of cases in each group and sum the results across all the groups:

$$\text{within-groups estimated variance} = \frac{\text{total sum of squares} - \text{between-groups sum of squares}}{\text{within-groups df}}$$

To calculate the total sum of squares subtract each score from the grand mean, square them, and add them together. The total sum of squares is 10.28:

$$(2.4 - 2)^2 + (2.4 - 4)^2 + (2.4 - 3)^2 + (2.4 - 2)^2 + (2.4 - 1)^2$$
$$+ (2.4 - 3)^2 + (2.4 - 2)^2 + (2.4 - 3)^2 + (2.4 - 2)^2 + (2.4 - 1)^2$$
$$+ (2.4 - 2)^2 + (2.4 - 2)^2 + (2.4 - 3)^2 + (2.4 - 3)^2 + (2.4 - 3)^2$$
$$+ (2.4 - 2)^2 + (2.4 - 2)^2 + (2.4 - 3)^2$$
$$= 0.16 + 2.56 + 0.36 + 0.16 + 1.96 + 0.36 + 0.16 + 0.36 + 0.16$$

Table 7.3 Follow-up anxiety ratings for the relaxation, cognitive and control conditions

	Relaxation training	Cognitive training	Control		
	2	2	3		
	4	3	3		
	3	2	3		
	2	1	2		
	1	2	2		
	3	2	3		
Sum	15	12	16	Grand sum	43
Mean	2.5	2	2.7	Grand mean	2.4

$$+ 1.96 + 0.16 + 0.16 + 0.36 + 0.36 + 0.36 + 0.16 + 0.16 + 0.36$$
$$= 10.28$$

For our example, the within-groups estimated variance is 0.58:

$$\frac{10.28 - 1.56}{(6-1)+(6-1)+(6-1)} = \frac{8.72}{15} = 0.58$$

Step 3 To calculate the F ratio, simply divide the between-groups estimated variance (or mean square) by the within-groups estimated variance (or mean square). In this case the F ratio is 1.34 ($0.78/0.58 = 1.34$).

Step 4 Look up the statistical significance of this F ratio in the table in Appendix 5. The degrees of freedom for the between-groups estimated variance is the number of groups minus 1 while for the within-groups estimated variance it is the sum of the number of cases within each group minus 1. So, the degrees of freedom is 2 for the between-groups estimated variance (or the numerator of the F ratio) and 15 for the within-groups estimated variance (or the denominator of the F ratio). With these degrees of freedom the F value has to be greater than 3.6823 to be significant at the 0.05 level which it is not. Consequently, we would conclude that there were no significant differences in follow-up anxiety between the three conditions.

However, before we can draw such a conclusion we need to know whether the variances are homogeneous. If the variances are unequal, then depending on the exact conditions there is a greater or lesser possibility that the F ratio will be significant. When the number of cases in each group is the same or nearly the same, there is a greater tendency for F to be significant. In these circumstances *Hartley's* and *Cochran's* test can be used for comparing variances.

Hartley's test (F_{max}) is simply the largest of the group variances divided by the smallest. In our example the variances for the relaxation, cognitive and control conditions are 1.1, 0.4 and 0.27 respectively. So F_{max} is 4.07 ($1.1/0.27 = 4.07$). We check the significance of F_{max} in the table in Appendix 16 where the parameters of the distribution are the number of conditions in the numerator and the number of cases in a group minus 1 in the denominator (or where the numbers of cases in each group vary slightly, the number of cases in the largest group minus 1). The parameters for our example are 3 and 5 respectively. For the variances to be significantly different at the 0.05 level, F_{max} would have to be larger than 10.8 which it is not. Consequently, we would conclude that the variances were equal.

In Cochran's C test the largest variance is divided by the sum of the variances. In this case, C is 0.62 (1.1/(1.1 + 0.4 + 0.27) = 0.62). We look up the C value in the table in Appendix 17 where the parameters of the distribution are the number of groups in the numerator and the number of cases in a group minus 1 in the denominator (or where the numbers of cases in each group vary slightly, the number of cases in the largest group minus 1). For the variances to be significantly different at the 0.05 level, C has to be bigger than 0.7071 which it is not. Therefore, we would conclude that the variances are homogeneous.

Where the numbers of cases vary considerably and where no group is smaller than 3 and most groups are larger than 5, the *Bartlett–Box F* test can be used for comparing variances. The procedure for computing this test will be illustrated with our example and is as follows:

Step 1   Calculate the value called M based on the following formula:

$M = (N -$ no. of groups$) \times \log[(n_1 - 1 \times$ variance$_1)$
$+ (n_2 - 1 \times$ variance$_2) + \ldots/(N -$ no. of groups$)] - [(n_1 - 1 \times \log$ of variance$_1) + (n_2 - 1 \times \log$ of variance$_2) + \ldots]$

where log is the natural logarithm, N is the total number of cases, n_1, n_2 and so on are the number of cases in each of the groups in the analysis and variance$_1$, variance$_2$ the variances.

For our example, M is 2.75:

$(18 - 3) \times \log[(6 - 1 \times 1.1) + (6 - 1 \times 0.4) + (6 - 1 \times 0.27)/$
$(18 - 3)] - [(6 - 1 \times \log 1.1) + (6 - 1 \times \log 0.4)$
$+ (6 - 1 \times \log 0.27)]$
$= 15 \times \log[(5.5 + 2.0 + 1.35)/15] - [(5 \times 0.1) + (5 \times -0.92)$
$+ (5 \times -1.32)]$
$= (15 \times -0.53) - -10.7$
$= 2.75$

Step 2   Calculate the value called A based on the following formula:

$$A = \frac{1}{3 \times (\text{no. of groups} - 1)} \times \left(\frac{1}{n_1 - 1} + \frac{1}{n_2 - 1} + \ldots - \frac{1}{N - \text{no. of groups}} \right)$$

where n_1, n_2 and so on are the number of cases in each of the groups in the analysis.

For our example, A is 0.09:

$$\frac{1}{3 \times (3 - 1)} \times \left(\frac{1}{5} + \frac{1}{5} + \frac{1}{5} - \frac{1}{15} \right) = 0.167 \times 0.53 = 0.09$$

Step 3   Calculate the value f_2 from the following formula:

$$f_2 = \frac{\text{no. of groups} + 1}{A^2}$$

For our example, f_2 is

$$\frac{3+1}{0.09^2} = 500$$

Step 4   Calculate the value f_1 from the following formula:

$$f_1 = \frac{1 - A + 2}{f_2}$$

For our example, f_1 is 0.914:

$$\frac{1 - 0.09 + 2}{500} = 0.914$$

Step 5   Calculate the Bartlett–Box F from the following formula:

$$F = \frac{f_2 \times M}{(\text{no. of groups} - 1) \times (f_2/f_1 - M)}$$

For our example, F is 1.26:

$$\frac{500 \times 2.75}{(3-1) \times (500/0.914 - 2.75)} = \frac{1375}{1088.6} = 1.26$$

Step 6   We look up the significance of this F value in the table in Appendix 5 where the degrees of freedom is the number of groups minus 1 in the numerator and f_2 in the denominator. With 3 and 500 degrees of freedom respectively, F would have to be larger than 3.0718 to be statistically significant which it is not. Consequently, we would conclude that the variances did not differ significantly among the three groups. If the variances were found to be unequal, then it may be possible to make them similar through transforming the scores by, for example, taking their log or square root. Alternatively, a non-parametric test could be used for analysing the data.

One-way analysis of variance is computed by the following SPSS **oneway** command:

oneway variable names **by** grouping variable (value of first group,value of last group).

So, to compute a one-way analysis of variance on follow-up anxiety for the three treatment conditions, we could use the following command:

oneway fol by con(1,3).

The relevant output from this command is presented in Table 7.4 which shows the sum of squares and degrees of freedom for the between-groups, within-groups and total variances, as well as the mean squares for the between- and within-groups variances, the F ratio and its probability. The total sum of squares is simply the between- and within-groups sums of squares added together. The F ratio shown (**1.2264**) differs slightly from the one we calculated (1.34) due to rounding differences in the way the between-groups sum of squares was calculated.

To display descriptive statistics for the groups such as their means and standard deviations, we need to add the following subcommand:

/statistics=1.

So, the **oneway** command for providing the descriptive statistics for follow-up anxiety for the three conditions is

oneway fol by con(1,3)
/statistics=1.

The output provided by this command for our example is shown in Table 7.5 which for each group gives the number of cases or count, the mean, the standard deviation, the standard error, the 95 per cent confidence interval for the mean, the minimum and the maximum value.

The 95 per cent confidence interval for the mean indicates the interval in which the mean has a 95 per cent chance of falling. For example, for group 1 (the relaxation training condition), the mean has a 95 per cent

Table 7.4 **Oneway** analysis of variance output

```
----- ONEWAY -----
```

Variable   FOL
By Variable   CON

Analysis of Variance

Source	D.F.	Sum of Squares	Mean Squares	F Ratio	F Prob.
Between Groups	2	1.4444	.7222	1.2264	.3211
Within Groups	15	8.8333	.5889		
Total	17	10.2778			

Table 7.5 **Oneway** descriptive statistics output

Group	Count	Mean	Standard Deviation	Standard Error	95 Pct Conf Int for Mean		
Grp 1	6	2.5000	1.0488	.4282	1.3994	To	3.6006
Grp 2	6	2.0000	.6325	.2582	1.3363	To	2.6637
Grp 3	6	2.6667	.5164	.2108	2.1247	To	3.2086
Total	18	2.3889	.7775	.1833	2.0022	To	2.7756

Group	Minimum	Maximum
Grp 1	1.0000	4.0000
Grp 2	1.0000	3.0000
Grp 3	2.0000	3.0000
Total	1.0000	4.0000

probability of falling between **1.3994** and **3.6006**. To calculate the 95 per cent confidence interval for the mean of this group, we carry out the following steps.

Step 1   Look up in the table in Appendix 15 the *t* value at the 0.05 per cent level for the appropriate degrees of freedom for the sample which is the number of cases minus 1. The *t* value for 5 degrees of freedom is 2.571.

Step 2   Multiply the *t* value by the standard error of the mean, which gives the size of the interval falling either above or below the mean. In this case, the size of this interval is 1.10 (2.571 × 0.4282 = 1.1009022).

Step 3   To find the lower and upper limits of the 95 per cent confidence interval, respectively subtract and add this value to the mean of the sample. For this group, the lower limit is 1.40 (2.50 − 1.10 = 1.40) and the upper limit 3.60 (2.5 + 1.10 = 3.60).

To compute the Hartley, Cochran and Bartlett–Box tests for comparing homogeneity of variance, we add 3 to the **statistics** subcommand of **oneway**:

/**statistics 1 3**.

The output for this command for our example is shown in Table 7.6.

INTERPRETING A SIGNIFICANT ANALYSIS OF VARIANCE *F* RATIO

The *F* ratio in the analysis of variance only tells us whether there is a significant difference between one or more of the means. It does not let us know where that difference lies. To find this out, we have to carry out further statistical tests. Which tests we use depends on whether we

Table 7.6 **Oneway** tests for homogeneity of variance

----- ONEWAY -----

Tests for Homogeneity of Variances
Cochrans C = Max. Variance/Sum (Variances) = .6226,   P = .153 (Approx.)
Bartlett–Box F =   1.274 ,   P = .281
Maximum Variance / Minimum Variance   4.125

predicted where the differences would be. If we had predicted, for example, that mean follow-up anxiety would be higher in the control condition than in either the relaxation or the cognitive training condition and had the F ratio been significant, then we would have employed unrelated t tests to determine whether these predictions were confirmed. If, on the other hand, we had not anticipated any differences but discovered that the F ratio was significant, we could use one of a number of *post hoc* or *a posteriori* tests to find out where any differences lay. These tests take into account the fact that, the more comparisons we make, the more likely we are to find that some of these comparisons will differ significantly by chance. For example, at the 5 per cent level of significance, of twenty comparisons one would be expected to differ significantly by chance, while this figure would rise to five if a hundred comparisons had been made. The *Scheffé* test will be described as it provides an exact value for groups of unequal size and is more conservative in the sense that the probability of a type I error is less (i.e. accepting a difference when there is no difference).

SCHEFFÉ TEST

The formula for the Scheffé test is

$$\sqrt{\text{within-groups mean square} \times (\text{no. of groups} - 1) \times F \times \left(\frac{1}{n_1} + \frac{1}{n_2}\right)}$$

where n_1 and n_2 are the number of cases in the two groups being compared and F refers to the desired probability level (e.g. 0.05) with the appropriate degrees of freedom (i.e. those for the between-groups variance as the numerator and those for the within-groups variance as the denominator).

However, in order to compare the results of our manual computation with the output given by SPSS, we shall use the following modified formula where the multiplier 0.5×2 has been added:

$$\sqrt{\text{within-groups mean square} \times 0.5 \times 2 \times (\text{no. of groups} - 1) \times F}$$

$$\times \left(\frac{1}{n_1} + \frac{1}{n_2}\right)$$

Both formulae give the same result since 0.5×2 is 1.

If the difference between the two means being compared is greater than the value given by the Scheffé test, then the two means differ significantly at the specified probability level.

To calculate the Scheffé test for our example, we substitute into the formula the following values, which will be the same for all three comparisons as the number of subjects in each of the three groups is the same, giving a figure of 1.20:

$$\sqrt{0.589 \times 0.5 \times 2 \times (3-1) \times 3.68 \times (1/6 + 1/6)}$$
$$= \sqrt{0.589 \times 0.5 \times 2 \times 2 \times 3.68 \times 0.333}$$
$$= \sqrt{1.44}$$
$$= 1.20$$

According to the table in Appendix 5, the F value at the 0.05 per cent level with 2 and 15 degrees respectively as the numerator and denominator is 3.68.

The differences in means for the three comparisons are as follows.

Group 1 (relaxation) vs Group 2 (cognitive)
$2.5 - 2.0 = 0.25$
Group 1 (relaxation) vs Group 3 (control)
$2.5 - 2.7 = 0.04$
Group 2 (cognitive) vs Group 3 (control)
$2.0 - 2.7 = 0.49$

Since none of these differences is greater than the Scheffé test value of 1.20, none of the group means differs significantly from each other.

To compute the Scheffé test with SPSS, we need to add the following subcommand to the **oneway** command:

/ranges=scheffe

The complete **oneway** command for carrying out the Scheffé test on follow-up anxiety for the three conditions reads

oneway fol by con(1,3)
/ranges=scheffe.

The output generated by this command is shown in Table 7.7. The table ranges are calculated by taking the square root of the product of 2, the number of groups minus 1 and the appropriate F value:

$$\sqrt{2 \times (\text{no. of groups} - 1) \times F}$$

Its value in this case is 3.84:

$$\sqrt{2 \times (3-1) \times 3.68} = \sqrt{14.72} = \mathbf{3.84}$$

The value of **.5426** is derived by taking the square root of the within-groups mean square divided by 2 (i.e. multiplied by 0.5):

$$\sqrt{0.5889 \times 0.5} = \sqrt{0.294} = \mathbf{.5426}$$

The range for comparing any two means (**Mean(J)** and **Mean(I)**) is worked out for this example as follows:

Table 7.7 **Oneway** Scheffé test output

Variable FOL
By Variable CON

Multiple Range Test

Scheffé Procedure
Ranges for the .050 level –
        3.84   3.84

The ranges above are table ranges.
The value actually compared with Mean(J) – Mean(I) is. .
        .5426 * Range * Sqrt (1/N(I) + 1/N(J))

No two groups are significantly different at the   .050 level

Homogeneous Subsets   (Subsets of groups, whose highest and lowest
                            means do not differ by more than the shortest
                            significant range for a subset of that size)

SUBSET 1

Group	Grp 2	Grp 1	Grp 3
Mean	2.0000	2.5000	2.6667

$$.5426 \times 3.84 \times \sqrt{1/6 + 1/6} = 1.20$$

None of the three means differs from each other and so they are arranged in a single subset of increasing values.

To illustrate the output produced when some of the means do differ, we will create another data set which we will assume also consists of anxiety ratings at pre-test, post-test and follow-up for the same three treatments. However, to distinguish the two sets of data, we will say that the first set has come from women and the second set from men. The second set of data is presented in Table 7.8 and is listed as it might appear in an SPSS file with the following **data list** command:

data list/cno 1-2 gen 4 con 6 pre pos fol 7-12.

To distinguish the two data sets we have to add to both sets of data the variable **gen** which refers to gender and which has been placed in column 4. Women are coded as 1 and men as 2.

To select the data for just the men, we use the **select if** command followed by the **oneway** command:

select if (gen eq 2).
oneway fol by con(1,3)
 /ranges=scheffe
 /sta=1.

Table 7.8 Pre-test, post-test and follow-up anxiety ratings in men for the relaxation, cognitive and control conditions

19	2	1	3	1	1
20	2	1	3	1	1
21	2	1	4	2	1
22	2	1	4	2	1
23	2	1	4	3	2
24	2	1	4	3	2
25	2	2	3	2	1
26	2	2	3	2	1
27	2	2	2	2	1
28	2	2	2	1	1
29	2	2	2	1	2
30	2	2	2	1	2
31	2	3	3	3	3
32	2	3	3	3	3
33	2	3	4	3	3
34	2	3	4	4	4
35	2	3	4	4	4
36	2	3	4	4	4

The output for the analysis of variance is presented in Table 7.9, the descriptive statistics in Table 7.10 and the Scheffé test in Table 7.11. As can be seen from the results in Table 7.9, the F ratio is statistically significant at less than the **.0000(5)** level. To determine which of the means differ significantly we turn to the output shown in Table 7.11 which tells us that the means of group 1 (relaxation) and 2 (cognitive) do not differ from each other but that both differ significantly from the mean of group 3 (control).

To calculate how big the difference between any two means must be in this example for them to differ significantly, we work out the value for the expression

$$0.3727 \times 3.84 \times \text{sqrt}[1/N(I) + 1/N(J)]$$

which is 0.826:

$$0.3727 \times 3.84 \times \text{sqrt}(1/6 + 1/6) = 0.826$$

The means of group 1 and 2 do not differ because their difference is 0 and so is less than 0.826. However, the means of these two groups do differ from that of group 3 because this difference is 2.1667 which is larger than 0.826.

TWO-WAY ANALYSIS OF VARIANCE

Two-way analysis of variance compares the means of groups made up of two variables or *factors*. The two factors in our example are gender and

Table 7.9 **Oneway** analysis of variance output (for significant group differences)

$$----\text{ONEWAY}----$$

Variable FOL
By Variable CON

Analysis of Variance

Source	D.F.	Sum of Squares	Mean Squares	F Ratio	F Prob.
Between Groups	2	18.7778	9.3889	33.8000	.0000
Within Groups	15	4.1667	.2778		
Total	17	22.9444			

Table 7.10 **Oneway** descriptive statistics output (for significant group differences)

Group	Count	Mean	Standard Deviation	Standard Error	95 Pct Conf Int for Mean		
Grp 1	6	1.3333	.5164	.2108	.7914	To	1.8753
Grp 2	6	1.3333	.5164	.2108	.7914	To	1.8753
Grp 3	6	3.5000	.5477	.2236	2.9252	To	4.0748
Total	18	2.0556	1.1618	.2738	1.4778	To	2.6333

Group	Minimum	Maximum
Grp 1	1.0000	2.0000
Grp 2	1.0000	2.0000
Grp 3	3.0000	4.0000
Total	1.0000	4.0000

treatment. With two categories or *levels* of gender and three of treatment (relaxation, cognitive and control), we have what is known as a *2 × 3* analysis of variance. If we just had two levels of treatment (e.g. cognitive and control), we would have a *2 × 2* analysis of variance. The variable being compared is often called the *dependent* variable because it is usually assumed that the value of this variable *depends* on, or is affected by, the factors being investigated. As a consequence, the factors being investigated are frequently referred to as *independent* variables since they are not thought to be affected by the dependent variable. Furthermore, their statistical association with the dependent variable is called an *effect.*

There are two main advantages to analysing two factors at a time. The first is that it enables us to determine whether the two factors affect each other or *interact.* An interaction is when the effect of one variable is not the same under all conditions of the other variable. An example of an

Table 7.11 **Oneway** Scheffé test output (for significant group differences)

Variable FOL
By Variable CON

Multiple Range Test

Scheffé Procedure
Ranges for the   .050 level –
**   3.84   3.84**

The ranges above are table ranges.
The value actually compared with Mean (J) – Mean (I) is. .
**   .3727 * Range * Sqrt (1/N(I) + 1/N(J))**

(*) Denotes pairs of groups significantly different at the .050 level
**   Variable FOL**

		G	G	G
		r	r	r
		p	p	p
		1	2	3
Mean	**Group**			
1.3333	Grp 1			
1.3333	Grp 2			
3.5000	Grp 3	*	*	

Homogeneous Subsets   **(Subsets of groups, whose highest and lowest**
means do not differ by more than the shortest
significant range for a subset of that size)

SUBSET 1
Group   Grp 1   Grp 2
Mean   1.3333   1.3333
– –
SUBSET 2
Group   Grp 3
Mean   3.5000

---

interaction would be if follow-up anxiety in the cognitive condition was higher for women than for men while in the control condition there was no difference between women and men. Interactions are often more readily grasped when they are portrayed in the form of a graph. This example is shown in Figure 7.1. The vertical axis represents the mean follow-up anxiety while the horizontal axis can depict either of the other two variables. In this case it is used to show the two treatments. The effects of the other variable are indicated by points on the graph and lines joining them. Women are represented by a circle and a broken line and men by a cross and a continuous line.

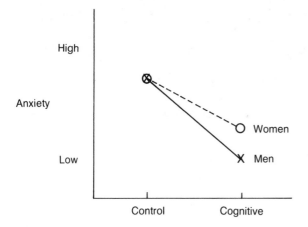

Figure 7.1 An example of an interaction

An interaction is likely when the lines representing the variable are not parallel. Another example of an interaction is illustrated in Figure 7.2 where follow-up anxiety is lower for both women and men in the cognitive treatment than in the control condition but this difference is greater for men than women with men reporting less anxiety than women in the cognitive treatment.

The absence of an interaction is likely when the lines representing the second independent variable are more or less parallel as shown in Figures 7.3 and 7.4. In Figure 7.3 women are less anxious than men in both treatments but the two treatments do not differ from one another. In Figure 7.4 women are also less anxious than men but the two treatments also differ. Although interactions are more easily conveyed graphically, whether an interaction actually exists needs to be determined statistically.

The second advantage of a two-way over a one-way analysis of variance is that it provides a more sensitive or powerful test of the effect of either factor than evaluating them singly, provided that the two factors do not interact substantially. The variance of the dependent variable is made up of variance attributed to the independent variable (explained variance) and variance that is unaccounted for (error or residual variance). When two variables are being analysed separately, the residual error is likely to be greater than when the two variables are being examined together since part of the residual error may be due to the other variable and to their inter-action. Since the F ratio is derived by dividing the explained variance by the error variance, the F ratio is likely to be smaller and hence less likely to be significant when variables are analysed separately. This point will be illustrated after the procedure for computing a two-way analysis of variance has been described.

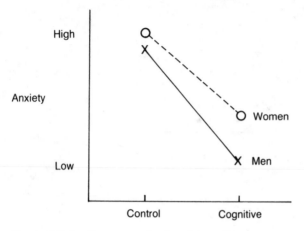

Figure 7.2 Another example of an interaction

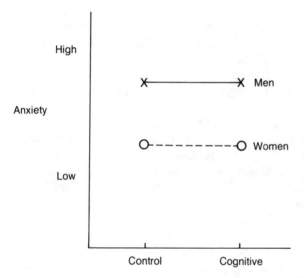

Figure 7.3 An example of no interaction

In a two-way analysis of variance there are four sources of variance: (1) the between-groups variance of the first factor; (2) the between-groups variance of the second factor; (3) the between-groups variance of the interaction of the two factors; and (4) the within-groups variance. Consequently, three main F ratios have to be calculated which respectively compare the variance of the first and second factor and their interaction with the within-groups variance. To simplify matters a little, we will illustrate the computation of a two-way analysis of variance with the follow-up anxiety scores from only two of the three treatment conditions,

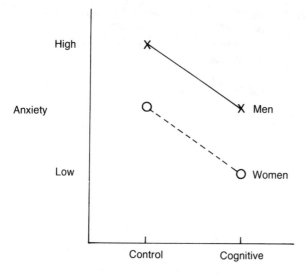

Figure 7.4 Another example of no interaction

namely the cognitive and control conditions. The individual scores together with the group sums and means (rounded to one decimal place) are presented in Table 7.12. In addition, the sum and mean for women and men (across treatments) are shown as the row sum and mean while the sum and mean for the two treatments (ignoring gender) are presented as the column sum and mean, together with the grand sum and mean.

Step 1   To compute the between-groups sum of squares for the first factor: (1) calculate the mean of each group of this factor (ignoring the other factor); (2) subtract the grand mean from the group mean of this factor; (3) square this difference; (4) multiply this squared difference by the number of cases within that group; and (5) sum these products for all the groups of that factor.

The sum of squares for the treatment factor is 11.76:

$$[(1.7 - 2.4)^2 \times 12] + [(3.1 - 2.4)^2 \times 12]$$
$$= 5.88 + 5.88$$
$$= 11.76$$

Step 2   We repeat the same procedure for the second factor except that we use the group means of the second factor (ignoring the first factor).

The sum of squares for the gender factor is 0:

$$[(2.4 - 2.4)^2 \times 12] + [(2.7 - 2.4)^2 \times 12] = 0 + 0 = 0$$

Step 3   To compute the between-groups sum of squares for the inter-

Table 7.12 Follow-up anxiety ratings of women and men in the cognitive and control conditions together with initial computations

Gender	Treatment		Row sum and mean
	Cognitive training	Control	
Women	2	3	
	3	3	
	2	3	
	1	2	
	2	2	
	2	3	
Sum	12	16	28
Mean	2	2.7	2.4
Men	1	3	
	1	3	
	1	3	
	1	4	
	2	4	
	2	4	
Sum	8	21	29
Mean	1.3	3.5	2.4
Column sum	20	37	Grand sum 57
Column mean	1.7	3.1	Grand mean 2.4

action we calculate the overall between-groups sum of squares and subtract from it the sum of squares for the first and second factors.

The overall between-groups sum of squares is calculated using the means of the groups formed by the two factors. We subtract the grand mean from the mean of each of these groups, square this difference, multiply this squared difference by the number of cases within that group and sum these products for all the groups.

In this example, there are four such groups and so the overall between-groups sum of squares is 16.02:

$$[(2.0 - 2.4)^2 \times 6] + [(2.7 - 2.4)^2 \times 6] + [(1.3 - 2.4)^2 \times 6]$$
$$+ [(3.5 - 2.4)^2 \times 6]$$
$$= 0.96 + 0.54 + 7.26 + 7.26$$
$$= 16.02$$

Subtracting the sum of squares for the two factors from the overall between-groups sum of squares gives the sum of squares for the interaction which is 4.26:

$$16.02 - 11.76 - 0 = 4.26$$

Step 4 Calculate the within-groups or residual sum of squares by computing the total sum of squares and subtracting from it the explained sum of squares.

The total sum of squares can be obtained by subtracting each score from the grand mean, squaring them, and adding them together.

The total sum of squares for our example is 21.64:

$$
\begin{aligned}
& (2.4 - 2)^2 + (2.4 - 3)^2 + (2.4 - 2)^2 + (2.4 - 1)^2 + (2.4 - 2)^2 \\
& + (2.4 - 2)^2 + (2.4 - 1)^2 + (2.4 - 1)^2 + (2.4 - 1)^2 + (2.4 - 1)^2 \\
& + (2.4 - 2)^2 + (2.4 - 2)^2 + (2.4 - 3)^2 + (2.4 - 3)^2 + (2.4 - 3)^2 \\
& + (2.4 - 2)^2 + (2.4 - 2)^2 + (2.4 - 3)^2 + (2.4 - 3)^2 + (2.4 - 3)^2 \\
& + (2.4 - 3)^2 + (2.4 - 4)^2 + (2.4 - 4)^2 + (2.4 - 4)^2 \\
& = 0.16 + 0.36 + 0.16 + 1.96 + 0.16 + 0.16 + 1.96 + 1.96 + 1.96 \\
& + 1.96 + 0.16 + 0.16 + 0.36 + 0.36 + 0.36 + 0.16 + 0.16 + 0.36 \\
& + 0.36 + 0.36 + 0.36 + 2.56 + 2.56 + 2.56 \\
& = 21.64
\end{aligned}
$$

The residual sum of squares is the total sum of squares (21.64) minus the explained sum of squares (16.02) which is 5.62.

Step 5 Calculate the residual mean square by dividing the residual sum of squares by its degrees of freedom. To compute the residual degrees of freedom subtract 1 from the number of cases in each group and sum the results across all the groups.

The residual mean square for our example is 0.281:

$$\frac{5.62}{(6-1)+(6-1)+(6-1)+(6-1)} = \frac{5.62}{20} = 0.281$$

Step 6 To derive the mean square for the first factor or main effect, divide the sum of squares for this factor by its degrees of freedom, which is the number of groups making up this factor minus 1.

The mean square for the treatment factor is 11.76:

$$\frac{11.76}{2-1} = \frac{11.76}{1} = 11.76$$

Step 7 To calculate the F ratio for the first main effect, divide its mean square by the residual mean square.

The F ratio for the treatment effect is 41.85:

$$\frac{11.76}{0.281} = 41.85$$

Look up the statistical significance of this F ratio in the table in Appendix 5. With 1 degree of freedom in the numerator and 20 degrees in the denominator, the F ratio has to be larger than 4.3512 to be statistically significant at the 0.05 level which it is. Since there are only two conditions in this factor, we would conclude that follow-up anxiety was significantly higher in the control condition than in the cognitive training condition. If there were more than two conditions in this factor and if the F ratio were significant, we would have to use tests such as the unrelated t or the Schaffé to determine where this significant difference lay.

Step 8   Repeat this procedure for working out the mean square and F ratio for the second main effect.

The mean square for the gender effect is 0:

$$\frac{0}{2-1} = 0$$

The F ratio for the gender effect is 0:

$$\frac{0}{0.281} = 0$$

Since this F ratio is smaller than 4.3512, we would conclude that follow-up anxiety did not differ significantly between women and men.

Step 9   Repeat this procedure for calculating the mean square and F ratio for the interaction effect. The degrees of freedom for the interaction effect is calculated by subtracting 1 from the number of groups in each factor and multiplying the resulting values.

The mean square for the interaction effect is 4.26:

$$\frac{4,26}{(2-1) \times (2-1)} = \frac{4.26}{1} = 4.26$$

The F ratio for the interaction effect is 15.16:

$$\frac{4.26}{0.281} = 15.16$$

Since this F ratio is larger than 4.3512, we would conclude that there was a significant interaction between treatment and gender on follow-up anxiety. If we had predicted an interaction effect, we could use the t tests for unrelated samples to determine whether our predictions were confirmed. If, on the other hand, we had not anticipated an interaction effect, we could use a *post hoc* test such as the Scheffé test.

The formula for computing the Scheffé test for a two-way analysis of variance is modified by multiplying the degrees of freedom for the first factor by the degrees of freedom for the second:

$$\sqrt{\text{within-groups mean square} \times (\text{no. of groups in factor A} - 1)}$$

$$\times (\text{no. of groups in factor B} - 1) \times F \times \left(\frac{1}{n_1} + \frac{1}{n_2}\right)$$

where n_1 and n_2 are the number of cases in the two groups being compared and F refers to the desired probability level (e.g. 0.05). The appropriate degrees of freedom for F in the numerator is the product of the number of groups in the first factor (A) minus 1 times the number of groups in the second factor (B) minus 1, and in the denominator the total number of cases minus the product of the number of groups in the first and second factors.

With four groups, as in our example, we would have to make six comparisons:

1 women in cognitive group vs women in control group;
2 men in cognitive group vs men in control group;
3 women in cognitive group vs men in cognitive group;
4 women in control group vs men in control group;
5 women in cognitive group vs men in control group;
6 men in cognitive group vs women in control group.

We shall illustrate the computation of this Scheffé test with the first comparison which has the smallest difference between two group means $(2.7 - 2.0 = 0.7)$. The 0.05 F ratio with 1 degree of freedom in the numerator $((2 - 1) \times (2 - 1) = 1)$ and 20 in the denominator $(24 - 4 = 20)$ is 4.3512. Substituting the appropriate values in the formula for the Scheffé test, this difference would have to exceed 0.64 to be statistically significant which it does:

$$\sqrt{0.281 \times 1 \times 1 \times 4.3512 \times (1/6 + 1/6)} = 0.64$$

Since this is the smallest group difference and as the Scheffé value is 0.64 for all the comparisons, all the six differences between the four groups are statistically significant.

The proportion of variance in the dependent variable that is explained by the independent variables can be described by a statistic called *eta squared*. Eta squared is defined as the ratio of the between-groups variance to the total variance:

$$\text{eta squared} = \frac{\text{between-groups variance (sum of squares)}}{\text{total variance (sum of squares)}}$$

To calculate the amount of variance explained by the treatment factor we divide the between-groups sum of squares for this factor by the total sum of squares which gives 0.54:

$$\frac{11.76}{21.64} = 0.54$$

In this instance, 54 per cent of the variance in follow-up anxiety is explained by the treatment factor. To work out the proportion of variance explained by two factors, we would add together the two eta squared values. Since the between-groups sum of squares for gender is zero, the amount of variance explained by both treatment and gender is 0.54 $(0.54 + 0 = 0.54)$.

Two-way analysis of variance is computed by the following SPSS **anova** command:

anova dependent variable names **by** first grouping variable (value of first group, value of last group) second grouping variable (value of first group, value of last group).

So, to compute a two-way analysis of variance on follow-up anxiety with treatment and gender as the two factors and where treatment consisted of the cognitive and the control conditions, we would use the following command:

anova fol by con(2,3) gen(1,2).

The relevant output from this command is presented in Table 7.13 which shows the sums of squares, degrees of freedom and mean squares for the sources of variation together with F ratios and their probability levels. The differences in values between the manual calculations and the SPSS output are due to rounding differences.

SPSS will display the means and numbers of cases for groups or cells defined by the two factors and their combination (as well as the mean and number of cases for the total sample) if the following **statistics** subcommand is added to the **anova** command:

/statistics=3.

The output produced by this command for this example is shown in Table 7.14.

Eta values are produced for the two factors singly and together when **1** is placed after the = sign on the **statistics** subcommand, either on its own if

Table 7.13 **Anova** output

* * * ANALYSIS OF VARIANCE * * *

FOL
By CON
GEN

Source of Variation	Sum of Squares	DF	Mean Square	F	Signif of F
Main Effects	12.083	2	6.042	19.595	.000
CON	12.042	1	12.042	39.054	.000
GEN	.042	1	.042	.135	.717
2-Way Interactions	3.375	1	3.375	10.946	.004
CON GEN	3.375	1	3.375	10.946	.004
Explained	15.458	3	5.153	16.712	.000
Residual	6.167	20	.308		
Total	21.625	23	.940		

Table 7.14 **Anova** descriptive statistics output

* * * CELL MEANS * * *

FOL
By CON
GEN

TOTAL POPULATION
         2.38
    (24)

CON
         2   3
       1.67   3.08
    (12)   (12)

GEN
         1   2
       2.33   2.42
    (12)   (12)

GEN
                     1   2

CON
       2   2.00   1.33
                (6)   (6)
       3   2.67   3.50
                (6)   (6)

the group means are not required or in conjunction with the **3** if the group means are also wanted.

The output produced by this subcommand is shown in Table 7.15 in what is known as a *multiple classification table*. The grand mean, the categories of the two factors and the number of cases in those categories are presented. The column labelled **Unadjusted Dev'n** shows the amount of deviation of the mean of that group from the grand mean. For example, the mean of the cognitive condition as shown in Table 7.14 is **1.67**. Subtracting the grand mean from this value gives −0.71. Since eta squared is the between-groups sum of squares for that factor divided by the total sum of squares, eta (also known as the *correlation ratio*) is the square root of eta squared. As displayed in Table 7.13 the between-groups sum of squares for the treatment factor is **12.042** while the total sum of squares is **21.625**. Consequently, unadjusted eta for the treatment factor is **.75** ($\sqrt{12.042/21.625} = 0.75$).

The column called **Adjusted for Independents Dev'n** presents what the deviation would be if adjusted for the effects of the other variable. Since the other variable has no effect in this case, the adjusted deviations are the same as the unadjusted ones. Beta is actually partial beta and will be discussed in the chapter on regression. **Multiple R squared** is the combined sum of squares for the two main effects divided by the total sum of squares (**12.083/21.625** = **.559**) while **Multiple R** is the square root of this value

Table 7.15 **Anova** multiple classification analysis output

*** MULTIPLE CLASSIFICATION ANALYSIS ***

FOL
By CON
GEN

Grand Mean =   2.375

Variable + Category	N	Unadjusted Dev'n	Eta	Adjusted for Independents Dev'n	Beta	Adjusted for Independents + Covariates Dev'n	Beta
CON							
2	12	−.71		−.71			
3	12	.71		.71			
			.75		.75		
GEN							
1	12	−.04		−.04			
2	12	.04		.04			
			.04		.04		
Multiple R Squared					.559		
Multiple R					.748		

($\sqrt{0.559} = .748$). Because there were no covariates in this analysis, the final columns are empty.

To illustrate that a two-way analysis is a more sensitive test of the effect of a variable than a one-way analysis of variance, we will run a one-way analysis on follow-up anxiety for the cognitive and control conditions for the whole sample using the following **anova** command:

anova fol by con(2,3).

The output for this command is displayed in Table 7.16. As we can see from comparing the information in the table with that of Table 7.13, while the mean square for the treatment factor is the same in the two analyses **(12.042)**, the residual mean square is smaller in the two-way analysis **(.308)** than in the one-way analysis **(.436)**. Consequently, the F ratio for the treatment main effect (which is the treatment mean square divided by the residual mean square) is larger for the two-way analysis **(39.054)** than the one-way analysis **(27.643)**. As shown in the two-way analysis in Table 7.13, although the gender effect is not significant the interaction effect between treatment and gender is significant. When this interaction effect is taken into account, the residual error is reduced.

SUMMARY

The computation of parametric tests for assessing whether the means and variances of equal interval or ratio data from two or more unrelated samples differ significantly across the samples is described. The unrelated t test compares the difference between the means of the two samples with the standard error of the difference in means which takes into account the variances of the two samples. The variances are pooled if they are equal and treated separately if they are unequal. The F test, which is the greater

Table 7.16 One-way **anova** output

* * * ANALYSIS OF VARIANCE * * *

FOL
By CON

Source of Variation	Sum of Squares	DF	Mean Square	F	Signif of F
Main Effects	12.042	1	12.042	27.643	.000
CON	12.042	1	12.042	27.643	.000
Explained	12.042	1	12.042	27.643	.000
Residual	9.583	22	.436		
Total	21.625	23	.940		

variance of one group divided by the smaller variance of the other, determines whether the variances differ. The two means differ significantly if their difference is substantially larger than the standard error of the difference in means.

One-way analysis of variance compares the means of two or more unrelated samples and is essentially an F test in which the between-groups estimated variance is divided by the within-groups estimated variance. The difference between the means is less likely to be due to chance when the between-groups variance is considerably greater than the within-groups variance provided that the variances are equal. The Hartley, Cochran C and Bartlett–Box F tests assess whether the variances differ. When the F ratio is significant, the t test determines if the predicted differences are significant; otherwise a range test such as the Scheffé test is used. Two-way analysis of variance compares the means of groups made up of two variables or factors and enables the interaction between those two factors to be examined. It is a more sensitive test of the effect of either factor than evaluating them singly provided that the two factors do not interact substantially. The proportion of variance explained by one or more factors is estimated by eta squared.

EXERCISES

The data for these exercises are available in Table 6.18.

1   Use the unrelated t test to compare educational interest at 12 between single- and mixed-sex schools.
    (a) What is the value of the F test?
    (b) What are its degrees of freedom?
    (c) What is its probability level?
    (d) Do the variances differ significantly?
    (e) Should the variances be pooled?
    (f) What is the value of the t test?
    (g) What are its degrees of freedom?
    (h) What is its two-tailed probability level?
    (i) Is educational interest at 12 significantly greater at single- than at mixed-sex schools?
2   Use a one-way analysis of variance to compare educational interest at 12 between single- and mixed-sex schools.
    (a) What is the value of this test?
    (b) What are the degrees of freedom?
    (c) What is the two-tailed probability level?
    (d) Is educational interest at 12 significantly greater at single- than at mixed-sex schools?
    (e) What proportion of variance of educational interest at 12 is explained by type of school?

3   Use a one-way analysis of variance to compare educational interest at 12 for pupils of different socio-economic status.
   (a) What is the value of this test?
   (b) What are the degrees of freedom?
   (c) What is the probability level?
   (d) Does educational interest at 12 differ significantly between pupils of different socio-economic status?
   (e) What is the Scheffé range which the means of the higher and middle socio-economic status groups have to exceed to be significantly different?
   (f) What is the Scheffé range which the means of the higher and lower socio-economic status groups have to exceed to be significantly different?
   (g) What is the Scheffé range which the means of the middle and lower socio-economic status groups have to exceed to be significantly different?
   (h) Which group means differ according to this range?
4   Use a two-way analysis of variance to determine the effect of socio-economic status and type of school on educational interest at 12.
   (a) What is the F ratio for the effect of socio-economic status?
   (b) What are its degrees of freedom?
   (c) What is its probability?
   (d) Does educational interest at 12 differ significantly between pupils of different socio-economic status?
   (e) What is the F ratio for the effect of type of school?
   (f) What are its degrees of freedom?
   (g) What is its probability?
   (h) Is educational interest at 12 significantly greater at single- than at mixed-sex schools?
   (i) What is the F ratio for the interaction between socio-economic status and type of school?
   (j) What are its degrees of freedom?
   (k) What is its probability?
   (l) Is there a significant interaction between socio-economic status and type of school on educational interest at 12?

Chapter 8

Tests of difference for interval/ratio data in related and mixed samples

The statistical tests described in this chapter ascertain whether the means of two or more related samples differ. For example, we may wish to know whether exam anxiety is lower immediately after cognitive training compared with immediately before it and whether any decrease in anxiety is maintained at follow-up. We may also be interested in whether any decrease in anxiety for the cognitive training group is greater than that for the control condition which does not receive any training. Furthermore, we may want to know whether there is any difference in post-test anxiety between the cognitive and control condition when any differences at pre-test have been controlled.

t TEST FOR TWO RELATED SAMPLES

The *t* test for related samples determines whether the means of two such samples differ. The means of related samples are less likely to differ than the means of unrelated samples since the scores come from the same or similar cases. Consequently, the *t* test for related samples takes into account the extent to which the scores of the two samples are correlated by modifying the way the standard error of the difference in means is computed. This standard error can be calculated with the following formula:

$$\sqrt{\frac{\text{variance}_1 + \text{variance}_2 - (2 \times \text{covariance}_{1.2})}{N-1}}$$

where N is the total number of pairs of cases. The covariance is defined as the average cross-product of two sets of deviation scores and is calculated by (1) subtracting each of a pair of scores from their respective means; (2) multiplying the deviations together; (3) summing the product for all pairs of scores; and (4) dividing this sum by the degrees of freedom which is the number of pairs of cases minus 1.

To illustrate the computation of the *t* test for related samples, we will compare pre-test anxiety with post-test anxiety for the women in the cognitive training condition. The individual scores for these women are shown in Table 8.1 together with the results of the computational procedure needed to calculate the variance and covariance of pre-test and post-test anxiety. To calculate a *t* test for related samples, carry out the following steps.

Step 1   Calculate the variance for each of the samples by subtracting each score from the mean score for that sample, squaring these differences, adding the squared differences together and dividing this total by the number of scores minus 1.

When this is done, we obtain variances of 0.3 for pre-test anxiety and 0.27 for post-test anxiety.

Step 2   Compute the covariance for the two samples by subtracting each score from the mean score for that sample, multiplying this difference by the difference from the corresponding score, summing the products for all pairs of scores and dividing this sum by the number of cases minus 1. Ignore the sign of the covariance.

The covariance for these scores is 0.23.

Step 3   Work out the standard error of the difference in means by multiplying the covariance by 2, subtracting this product from the sum of the variances, dividing this result by the number of cases minus 1 and taking the square root of this value.

The standard error of the difference in means for our example is 0.148:

Table 8.1 Pre-test and post-test anxiety ratings for the women in the cognitive condition together with initial computations

Pre-test			Post-test			Pre-test × Post-test Difference
Original	Difference	Squared	Original	Difference	Squared	Difference
4	0.5	0.25	3	−0.7	0.49	−0.35
4	0.5	0.25	3	−0.7	0.49	−0.35
3	−0.5	0.25	2	0.3	0.09	−0.15
3	−0.5	0.25	2	0.3	0.09	−0.15
4	0.5	0.25	2	0.3	0.09	0.15
3	−0.5	0.25	2	0.3	0.09	−0.15
Sum 21		1.50	14		1.34	−1.15
Mean 3.5			2.3			
Variance		0.30			0.27	
Covariance						0.23

$$\sqrt{\frac{0.3 + 0.27 - (2 \times 0.23)}{6 - 1}} = \sqrt{\frac{0.11}{5}} = 0.148$$

Step 4   Subtract one sample mean from the other and divide by the standard error of the difference in the mean to give the *t* value.

In this case, *t* is 8.11:

$$\frac{3.5 - 2.3}{0.148} = 8.11$$

Step 5   Look up the *t* value in the table in Appendix 15 where the degrees of freedom is the number of cases minus 1.

For *t* to be significant at the 0.05 two-tailed level with 5 degrees of freedom it would have to be bigger than 2.571 which it is. Consequently, we would conclude that anxiety in the cognitive training condition is significantly lower at post-test than at pre-test.

A simpler procedure for calculating *t* uses the following formula which is mathematically the same as the previous one:

$$t = \frac{\text{difference between sample means}}{\sqrt{[\text{sum of } D^2 - (\text{sum of } D)^2 / N] / [N \times (N - 1)]}}$$

where D stands for the difference between pairs of scores and N refers to the number of pairs of scores. It is also more accurate since it involves less rounding error.

The pairs of scores for our example are shown in Table 8.2 together with the difference between these pairs (D) and the square of this difference (D^2).

Substituting the appropriate values in the computational formula gives a *t* of 7.19:

Table 8.2 Pre-test and post-test anxiety ratings together with their differences and squared differences

	Pre-test	Post-test	D	D^2
	4	3	1	1
	4	3	1	1
	3	2	1	1
	3	2	1	1
	4	2	2	4
	3	2	1	1
Sum	21	14	7	9
Mean	3.5	2.3		

$$\frac{3.5 - 2.3}{\sqrt{(9 - 7^2/6)/[6 \times (6 - 1)]}} = \frac{1.2}{\sqrt{(9 - 8.167)/30}} = \frac{1.2}{0.167} = 7.19$$

The following SPSS **t-test** command computes a *t* test for related means:

t-test pair=first variable second variable.

To run a *t* test comparing pre-test and post-test anxiety for the women in the cognitive training condition, we first need to select this condition and the women in it which is done with the following **select if** command:

select if (con eq 2 and gen eq 1).

We then add the following **t-test** command:

t-test pair=pre pos.

The output for these commands is displayed in Table 8.3 which gives the number of cases, mean, standard deviation and standard error for the two samples; the mean difference and its standard deviation and error; the correlation (**Corr.**) between the two sets of scores and its probability; and the *t* value, its degrees of freedom and its probability. Any differences in the values of the SPSS and the two manual computations are due to rounding differences. Because the second manual computation involves less rounding, its results are closer to those of SPSS. If we divide the mean difference by the standard error of the difference in the mean, we see that *t* equals 7.00 (**1.1667/.167 = 6.99**). The standard deviation of the difference in the mean is the square root of its standard error ($\sqrt{.167} = .408$).

SINGLE FACTOR REPEATED MEASURES

Analysis of variance also determines whether the means of three or more related samples differ. Since measures from the same or similar cases are taken more than once, this analysis is often known as a *repeated measures* analysis. In this analysis the total variation in the scores consists of three sources of variation: (1) the variation between cases which is usually called the *between-subjects* variation; (2) the variation within the conditions of the factor being investigated; and (3) the residual variation. The sources of variation for a single factor repeated measures analysis of variance are shown in Table 8.4 together with their associated degrees of freedom. The *F* ratio for determining whether the three or more means differ is the mean square for the factor divided by the residual mean square.

The procedure for calculating a single factor repeated measures analysis of variance will be illustrated by comparing the pre-test, post-test and follow-up anxiety scores for the women in the cognitive training condition. The individual scores for these women are shown in Table 8.5. The total and mean score for women are presented in the last two columns of the table

Table 8.3 Related **t-test** output

Paired samples t-test:

Variable	Number of Cases	Mean	Standard Deviation	Standard Error			t Value	Degrees of Freedom	2-Tail Prob.
PRE	6	3.5000	.548	.224			7.00	5	.001
POS	6	2.3333	.516	.211					

(Difference) Mean	Standard Deviation	Standard Error	Corr.	2-Tail Prob.
1.1667	.408	.167	.707	.116

Table 8.4 Sources of variation and degrees of freedom in a single factor repeated
measures analysis

Sources of variation	Degrees of freedom
Between subjects	No. of cases −1
Within subjects	No. of cases × (no. of conditions −1)
Within factor	No. of conditions −1
Residual	(No. of cases −1) × (no. of conditions −1)
Total	(No. of cases × no. of conditions) −1

Table 8.5 Pre-test, post-test and follow-up individual, total and mean anxiety
ratings for the women in the cognitive condition

Pre-test	Post-test	Follow-up	Sum	Mean
4	3	2	9	3.0
4	3	3	10	3.3
3	2	2	7	2.3
3	2	1	6	2.0
4	2	2	8	2.7
3	2	2	7	2.3
Sum 21	14	12	47	
Mean 3.5	2.3	2.0		2.6

while the total and mean score for the three periods are displayed in the
last two rows. The overall total and mean score (grand mean) are in the
bottom right-hand corner of the table. Means have been calculated to one
decimal place.

Step 1 Calculate the total sum of squares by subtracting the grand mean
from each score, squaring them and adding them together.
If we do this for our example, the total sum of squares is 12.28:

$$(4 - 2.6)^2 + (3 - 2.6)^2 + (2 - 2.6)^2 + (4 - 2.6)^2 + (3 - 2.6)^2$$
$$+ (3 - 2.6)^2 + (3 - 2.6)^2 + (2 - 2.6)^2 + (2 - 2.6)^2 + (3 - 2.6)^2$$
$$+ (2 - 2.6)^2 + (1 - 2.6)^2 + (4 - 2.6)^2 + (2 - 2.6)^2 + (2 - 2.6)^2$$
$$+ (3 - 2.6)^2 + (2 - 2.6)^2 + (2 - 2.6)^2$$
$$= 12.28$$

Step 2 Compute the between-subjects sum of squares by subtracting the
grand mean from the mean score for each subject, squaring them, multiplying them by the number of conditions and adding them together.

The between-subjects sum of squares for our example is 3.57:

$$(3.0 - 2.6)^2 + (3.3 - 2.6)^2 + (2.3 - 2.6)^2 + (2.0 - 2.6)^2$$
$$+ (2.7 - 2.6)^2 + (2.3 - 2.6)^2$$
$$= 3.57$$

Step 3   Work out the within-factor sum of squares by subtracting the grand mean from the mean score for each of the conditions, squaring them, multiplying them by the number of cases and summing them.

The within-factor sum of squares for our example is 7.56:

$$(3.5 - 2.6)^2 + (2.3 - 2.6)^2 + (2.0 - 2.6)^2 = 7.56$$

Step 4   Calculate the residual sum of squares by adding together the between-subjects and within-subjects sum of squares and subtracting them from the total sum of squares.

For our example the residual sum of squares is 1.15:

$$12.28 - (3.57 + 7.56) = 1.15$$

Step 5   Calculate the within-factor and residual mean square by dividing their sum of squares by their degrees of freedom.

For our example the within-factor mean square is 3.78 ($7.56/2 = 3.78$) while the residual mean square is 0.115 ($1.15/10 = 0.115$).

Step 6   Divide the within-factor mean square by the residual mean square to give the F ratio for the factor.

This F ratio for our example is 32.87 ($3.78/0.115 = 32.87$).

The results of these steps are presented in Table 8.6 which shows the sums of squares, the degrees of freedom, the mean squares and the F ratio.

Step 7   Look up the significance of the F ratio in the table in Appendix 5.

With 2 degrees of freedom in the numerator and 10 in the denominator, F has to exceed 4.1028 to be significant at less than the 0.05 level which it is. Consequently, we would conclude that the three means differ significantly.

Table 8.6 Single factor repeated measures analysis of variance table

Sources of variation	SS	df	MS	F
Between subjects	3.57	5		
Within subjects				
Within factor	7.56	2	3.78	32.87
Residual	1.15	10	0.115	
Total	12.28	17		

If we had predicted where the significant differences lay, we could use the *t* test for related samples to test whether our predictions were confirmed. If, on the other hand, we had not expected any significant differences, we could use a *post hoc* test such as a modified Scheffé test to find out which differences were significant. The details of this procedure go beyond the scope of this book but can be found in more advanced texts such as Hays (1988).

To compute a single factor repeated measures analysis of variance with SPSS we have to use the following **manova** (multivariate analysis of variance) command:

manova variable names
  /wsfactor=name(number of conditions)
  /print=cellinfo(means) signif(brief).

The **wsfactor** subcommand names the within-subjects (**ws**) factor and specifies in brackets the number of levels it has. The **cellinfo(means)** keyword on the **print** subcommand provides the means and standard deviations for the different levels while the **signif(brief)** keyword produces a table similar to analysis of variance.

To run this test for our example, we would first have to select the women in the cognitive condition which we do with the following **select if** command:

select if (con eq 2 and gen eq 1).

We then add the following **manova** command where we have called the repeated measures or within-subjects factor **time**:

manova pre pos fol
  /wsfactor=time(3)
  /print=cellinfo(means) signif(brief).

The output for the **print=cellinfo(means)** subcommand is shown in Table 8.7 which presents the mean, standard deviation and number of cases for the pre-test, post-test and follow-up scores.

The relevant output for the repeated measures analysis is displayed in Table 8.8 which shows the factor (**TIME**) and residual (**WITHIN CELLS**) sum of squares, degrees of freedom, mean squares, *F* ratio and probability level.

TWO-WAY ANALYSIS OF VARIANCE WITH REPEATED MEASURES ON ONE FACTOR

Two-way analysis of variance with repeated measures on one factor compares the means of groups consisting of two factors, one of which is repeated. For example, we may employ this analysis if we wished to

Table 8.7 **Manova** output of cell means, standard deviations and number of cases

* * ANALYSIS OF VARIANCE * *

Cell Means and Standard Deviations

Variable .. PRE

	Mean	Std. Dev.	N
For entire sample	3.500	.548	6

Variable .. POS

	Mean	Std. Dev.	N
For entire sample	2.333	.516	6

Variable .. FOL

	Mean	Std. Dev.	N
For entire sample	2.000	.632	6

Table 8.8 **Manova** output of the within-subjects effect

* * ANALYSIS OF VARIANCE – DESIGN 1 * *

Tests involving 'TIME' Within-Subject Effect.

AVERAGED Tests of Significance for MEAS. 1 using UNIQUE sums of squares

Source of Variation	SS	DF	MS	F	Sig of F
WITHIN CELLS	1.22	10	.12		
TIME	7.44	2	3.72	30.45	.000

determine whether the decrease in anxiety for the men in the cognitive condition is greater than that in the control condition. In this kind of analysis the total variation in the scores is broken down into five main sources of variation: (1) between-subjects factor (i.e. independent variable); (2) between-subjects error; (3) within-subjects factor (i.e. repeated measures); (4) within-subjects error; and (5) interaction of between- and within-subjects factors. These sources of variation are presented in Table 8.9 together with their associated degrees of freedom. The *F* ratio for determining whether there is a significant effect for the between-subjects factor is the between-subjects mean square divided by the between-subjects error mean square. The *F* ratio for finding out whether the within-subjects factor is significant is the within-subjects factor mean square divided by the within-subjects error mean square, while the *F* ratio for seeing whether the interaction effect is significant is the interaction mean square divided by the within-subjects error mean square.

The procedure for calculating this analysis will be illustrated by

Table 8.9 Sources of variation and degrees of freedom in a two-way analysis of variance with repeated measures on one factor

Sources of variation	Degrees of freedom
Between-subjects factor (A)	No. of conditions in $A - 1$
Between-subjects error	No. of conditions in $A \times$ (no. of cases-1)
Within-subjects factor (B)	No. of conditions in $B - 1$
Within-subjects error	No. of conditions in $A \times$ (no. of cases $-1) \times$ (no. of conditions in $B - 1$)
$A \times B$ interaction	(No. of conditions in $A - 1) \times$ (no. of conditions in $B - 1$)
Total	(No. of cases $\times$ no. of conditions in $A \times$ no. of conditions in B) -1

comparing pre-test and post-test anxiety in the cognitive and control conditions for men. The individual scores for these men are presented in Table 8.10. The total and mean score of the pre-test and post-test are shown in the last two columns of the table while the total and mean score for the two conditions are displayed at the bottom of each condition and in the last two rows. The overall total and mean score (grand mean) are in the bottom right-hand corner of the table. Means have been calculated to one decimal place apart from that for the grand mean which is to two decimal places.

Step 1 Calculate the total sum of squares by subtracting the grand mean from each score, squaring them and adding them together.

If we do this for our example, the total sum of squares is 24.5:

$$(3 - 2.75)^2 + (2 - 2.75)^2 + (3 - 2.75)^2 + (2 - 2.75)^2 + (2 - 2.75)^2$$
$$+ (2 - 2.75)^2 + (2 - 2.75)^2 + (1 - 2.75)^2 + (2 - 2.75)^2$$
$$+ (1 - 2.75)^2 + (2 - 2.75)^2 + (1 - 2.75)^2 + (3 - 2.75)^2$$
$$+ (3 - 2.75)^2 + (3 - 2.75)^2 + (3 - 2.75)^2 + (4 - 2.75)^2$$
$$+ (3 - 2.75)^2 + (4 - 2.75)^2 + (4 - 2.75)^2 + (4 - 2.75)^2$$
$$+ (4 - 2.75)^2 + (4 - 2.75)^2 + (4 - 2.75)^2$$
$$= 24.5$$

Step 2 Compute the sum of squares for the between-subjects factor by subtracting the grand mean from the overall mean score for each condition (ignoring time of testing), squaring them, multiplying them by the number of scores in each condition and adding them together.

The sum of squares for the between-subjects factor for our example is 17.34:

$$[12 \times (1.9 - 2.75)^2] + [12 \times (3.6 - 2.75)^2] = 17.34$$

Table 8.10 Pre-test and post-test anxiety ratings of the men in the cognitive and control conditions together with initial computations

Condition	Pre-test	Post-test	Sum	Mean
Cognitive	3	2	5	2.5
	3	2	5	2.5
	2	2	4	2.0
	2	1	3	1.5
	2	1	3	1.5
	2	1	3	1.5
Sum	14	9	23	
Mean	2.3	1.5	1.9	
Control	3	3	6	3.0
	3	3	6	3.0
	4	3	7	3.5
	4	4	8	4.0
	4	4	8	4.0
	4	4	8	4.0
Sum	22	21	43	
Mean	3.7	3.5	3.6	
Column sum	36	30	Grand sum 66	
Column mean	3.0	2.5	Grand mean 2.75	

Step 3   Work out the sum of squares for the within-subjects factor by subtracting the grand mean from the overall mean score for each of the tests, squaring them, multiplying them by the number of cases and summing them.

The sum of squares for the within-subjects factor for our example is 1.5:

$$[12 \times (3.0 - 2.75)^2] + [12 \times (2.5 - 2.75)^2] = 1.5$$

Step 4   Calculate the sum of squares for the interaction term by subtracting the grand mean from the mean for each of the conditions formed by the two factors, squaring them, multiplying them by the number of cases in each condition, summing them and subtracting from the result the sum of squares for the between-subjects and within-subjects factors.

The sum of squares for the interaction term in our example is 0.54:

$$[6 \times (2.3 - 2.75)^2] + [6 \times (1.5 - 2.75)^2] + [6 \times (3.7 - 2.75)^2]$$
$$+ [6 \times (3.5 - 2.75)^2] - 17.34 - 1.5 = 0.54$$

Step 5   Compute the sum of squares for the between-subjects error by subtracting the grand mean from the mean score for each case, squaring them, multiplying them by the number of scores for each case, summing them and subtracting from the result the sum of squares for the between-subjects factor.

The sum of squares for the between-subjects error for our example is 4.16:

$$[2 \times (2.5 - 2.75)^2] + [2 \times (2.5 - 2.75)^2] + [2 \times (2.0 - 2.75)^2]$$
$$+ [2 \times (1.5 - 2.75)^2] + [2 \times (1.5 - 2.75)^2] + [2 \times (1.5 - 2.75)^2]$$
$$+ [2 \times (3.0 - 2.75)^2] + [2 \times (3.0 - 2.75)^2] + [2 \times (3.5 - 2.75)^2]$$
$$+ [2 \times (4.0 - 2.75)^2] + [2 \times (4.0 - 2.75)^2] + [2 \times (4.0 - 2.75)^2]$$
$$- 17.34 = 4.16$$

Step 6   Calculate the sum of squares for the within-subjects error by subtracting from the total sum of squares the sum of squares for the between-subjects factor, the within-subjects factor, the interaction and the between-subjects error.

The sum of squares for the within-subjects error for our example is 0.96:

$$24.5 - 17.34 - 1.5 - 0.54 - 4.16 = 0.96$$

The sums of squares for these six sources of variation are presented in Table 8.11 together with the degrees of freedom, mean squares and F ratios.

Step 7   The F ratio for the between-subjects factor is the mean square of that factor divided by the mean square of the between-subjects error.

For our example the F ratio for the between-subjects factor of treatment is 41.29 ($17.34/0.42 = 41.29$). If we look up the significance of this value in the table in Appendix 5 with 1 and 10 degrees of freedom in the numerator and denominator respectively, the F ratio has to be bigger than 4.9646 to be significant at the 0.05 level, which it is. Accordingly, we would conclude that there is a significant treatment effect. In this instance we would not be interested in this effect since it collapses the pre-test and

Table 8.11 Two-way analysis of variance table with repeated measures on one factor

Sources of variation	SS	df	MS	F
Between-subjects factor	17.34	1	17.34	41.29
Between-subjects error	4.16	10	0.42	
Within-subjects factor	1.50	1	1.50	15.00
Within-subjects error	0.96	10	0.10	
Interaction	0.54	1	0.54	5.40
Total	24.50	23		

post-test scores and so does not provide any evidence as to whether the post-test scores differ among the treatments. To determine this we would have to carry out a one-way analysis of variance as described in Chapter 7.

Step 8   The F ratio for the within-subjects factor is the mean square of that factor divided by the mean square of the within-subjects error.

The F ratio for the within-subjects factor of time of testing is 15.00 ($1.50/0.10 = 15.00$). From the table in Appendix 5, we can see that with 1 and 10 degrees of freedom in the numerator and denominator respectively the F ratio has to exceed 4.9646 to be statistically significant at less than the 0.05 level, which it is. Therefore, we would conclude that there was a significant time of testing effect across the two treatments. Since one of the treatments was a control condition, we would not be primarily concerned with this effect since we would wish to compare the two treatments.

Step 9   The F ratio for the interaction effect is the mean square of that effect divided by the mean square of the within-subjects error.

The F ratio for the interaction between treatment and time of testing is 5.4 ($0.54/0.10 = 5.4$). With 1 and 10 degrees of freedom in the numerator and denominator respectively, the F value has to be larger than 4.9646 to be statistically significant at less than the 0.05 level which it is. So, we would conclude that there was a statistically significant interaction effect between treatment and time of testing. If a significant interaction was predicted, t tests could be used to determine where the significant differences lay. If a significant interaction was not expected, then a *post hoc* test such as the Scheffé test could be applied to comparing the pre-test and post-test means for the two conditions.

To compute with SPSS a two-way analysis of variance with repeated measure on one factor we need to use the following **manova** command:

manova names of dependent variables **by** grouping variable name (value of
   first group, value of last group)
   /wsfactor=name(number of conditions)
   /print=cellinfo(means) signif(brief)
   /design.

The **design** subcommand specifies a between-subjects analysis of variance.

To conduct this test for our example, we first have to select the men in the sample with the following **select if** command:

select if (gen eq 2).

We then add the following **manova** command where the repeated measures factor is **time** and the cognitive and control conditions are specified by their values **2** and **3**:

manova pre pos by con(2,3)
  /wsfactor=time(2)
  /print=cellinfo(means) signif(brief)
  /design.

The output for the **print=cellinfo(means)** subcommand is shown in Table 8.12 which presents the mean, standard deviation and number of cases for the pre-test and post-test scores for the two conditions separately and combined.

The relevant output for the between-subjects factor is displayed in Table 8.13 where the between-subjects error is called the **(Between-Subjects) WITHIN CELLS** source of variation. The **CONSTANT** source of variation is the total score squared and divided by the number of scores and is not normally used in the interpretation of the output.

The requisite output for the within-subjects factor and the interaction effect has been reproduced in Table 8.14 where the within-subjects error is called the **(Within-Subject) WITHIN CELLS** source of variation, the within-subjects factor **TIME** and the interaction effect **CON BY TIME**.

ONE-WAY ANALYSIS OF COVARIANCE

One-way analysis of covariance compares the means of two or more groups controlling for the effects of a second factor which is known to be associated with the first factor. The variable which is controlled is called a *covariate*. Suppose, for example, that we found as shown in Figure 8.1 that the pre-test anxiety of the men in the cognitive condition was lower than

Table 8.12 **Manova** output of cell means, standard deviations and number of cases

---

** ANALYSIS OF VARIANCE **

Cell Means and Standard Deviations

Variable .. PRE

FACTOR	CODE	Mean	Std. Dev.	N
CON	2	2.333	.516	6
CON	3	3.667	.516	6
For entire sample		3.000	.853	12

Variable .. POS

FACTOR	CODE	Mean	Std. Dev.	N
CON	2	1.500	.548	6
CON	3	3.500	.548	6
For entire sample		2.500	1.168	12

Table 8.13 **Manova** output for between-subjects effects

* * ANALYSIS OF VARIANCE – DESIGN 1 * *

Tests of Between-Subjects Effects.
Tests of Significance for T1 using UNIQUE sums of squares

Source of Variation	SS	DF	MS	F	Sig of F
WITHIN CELLS	4.83	10	.48		
CONSTANT	181.50	1	181.50	375.52	.000
CON	16.67	1	16.67	34.48	.000

Table 8.14 **Manova** output of the within-subjects and interaction effects

* * ANALYSIS OF VARIANCE – DESIGN 1 * *

Tests involving 'TIME' Within-Subject Effect.
Tests of Significance for T2 using UNIQUE sums of squares

Source of Variation	SS	DF	MS	F	Sig of F
WITHIN CELLS	.83	10	.08		
TIME	1.50	1	1.50	18.00	.002
CON BY TIME	.67	1	.67	8.00	.018

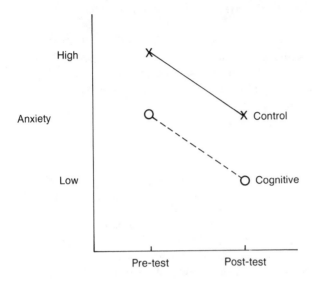

High

Anxiety

Low

Pre-test   Post-test

Figure 8.1 Example of pre-test and post-test differences

that in the control condition and that we knew that pre-test anxiety was positively correlated with post-test anxiety so that the more anxious people were at pre-test the more anxious they were at post-test. If we observed that post-test anxiety was lower in the cognitive condition than in the control condition, then this difference may be due not to the result of the cognitive training but to the fact that anxiety in these men was initially lower. One way of taking into account these pre-test differences is to conduct a one-way analysis of covariance on the post-test scores covarying out the pre-test scores.

In an analysis of covariance the variations in the scores of the dependent variable are adjusted in accordance with the differences in the covariate and the correlation between the dependent variable and the covariate. The adjusted between-groups sum of squares ($BG\text{-}SS_{adj}$) is a function of (1) the (unadjusted) between-groups sum of squares for the dependent variable ($BG\text{-}SS_{dep}$); (2) added to the within-groups sum of products for the dependent variable and the covariate (WG-SP) squared and divided by the covariate within-groups sum of squares ($WG\text{-}SS_{cov}$); (3) minus the total sum of products for the dependent variable and the covariate (T-SP) squared and divided by the covariate total sum of squares ($T\text{-}SS_{cov}$):

$$BG\text{-}SS_{adj} = BG\text{-}SS_{dep} + \frac{WG\text{-}SP^2}{WG\text{-}SS_{cov}} - \frac{T\text{-}SP^2}{T\text{-}SS_{cov}}$$

The sum of products is simply the deviation of the dependent variable multiplied by the deviation of the covariate for each pair of scores summed across all scores.

The adjusted within-groups sum of squares ($WG\text{-}SS_{adj}$) is a function of (1) the (unadjusted) within-groups sum of squares for the dependent factor ($WG\text{-}SS_{dep}$); (2) minus the within-groups sum of products for the dependent variable and the covariate (WG-SP) squared and divided by the within-groups sum of squares for the covariate:

$$WG\text{-}SS_{adj} = WG\text{-}SS_{dep} - \frac{WG\text{-}SP^2}{WG\text{-}SS_{cov}}$$

The sources of variation and their associated degrees of freedom are shown in Table 8.15. The between-groups mean square is simply the between-groups sum of squares divided by its degrees of freedom while the within-groups mean square is the within-groups sum of squares divided by its degrees of freedom. The F ratio is the between-groups mean square divided by the within-groups mean square.

The procedure for carrying out a one-way analysis of covariance will be illustrated by comparing post-test anxiety in men in the cognitive and control conditions while covarying pre-test anxiety (see Table 8.10). To increase the accuracy of the computation, means will be calculated to three decimal places.

Step 1   Calculate the total sum of squares for the covariate by subtracting its grand mean from each of its scores, squaring them and adding them together.

The total sum of squares for pre-test anxiety is 8:

$$(3-3)^2 + (3-3)^2 + (2-3)^2 + (2-3)^2 + (2-3)^2 + (2-3)^2$$
$$+ (3-3)^2 + (3-3)^2 + (4-3)^2 + (4-3)^2 + (4-3)^2 + (4-3)^2$$
$$= 8$$

Step 2   Calculate the between-groups sum of squares for the covariate by subtracting its grand mean from its mean for each group, squaring these differences, multiplying them by the number of cases in each of the groups and summing the products for all the groups.

Table 8.15 Sources of variation and degrees of freedom in a one-way analysis of covariance

Sources of variation	Degrees of freedom
Between groups	No. of groups −1
Within groups	No. of cases − no. of groups −1
Total	No. of cases −1

The between-groups sum of squares for pre-test anxiety is 5.34:

$$[(2.333 - 3)^2 \times 6] + [(3.667 - 3)^2 \times 6] = 5.34$$

Step 3 Calculate the within-groups sum of squares for the covariate by subtracting its between-groups sum of squares from its total sum of squares.

The within-groups sum of squares for pre-test anxiety is 2.66:

$$8 - 5.34 = 2.66$$

Step 4 Calculate the total sum of squares for the dependent variable by subtracting its grand mean from each of its scores, squaring them and adding them together.

The total sum of squares for post-test anxiety is 15:

$$(2 - 2.5)^2 + (2 - 2.5)^2 + (2 - 2.5)^2 + (1 - 2.5)^2 + (1 - 2.5)^2$$
$$+ (1 - 2.5)^2 + (3 - 2.5)^2 + (3 - 2.5)^2 + (3 - 2.5)^2 + (4 - 2.5)^2$$
$$+ (4 - 2.5)^2 + (4 - 2.5)^2$$
$$= 15$$

Step 5 Calculate the between-groups sum of squares for the dependent variable by subtracting its grand mean from its mean for each group, squaring these differences, multiplying them by the number of cases in each of the groups and summing the products for all the groups.

The between-groups sum of squares for post-test anxiety is 12:

$$[(1.5 - 2.5)^2 \times 6] + [(3.5 - 2.5)^2 \times 6] = 12$$

Step 6 Calculate the within-groups sum of squares for the dependent variable by subtracting its between-groups sum of squares from its total sum of squares.

The within-groups sum of squares for post-test anxiety is 3:

$$15 - 12 = 3$$

Step 7 Calculate the total sum of products for the covariate and dependent variable by (1) subtracting the covariate grand mean from each covariate score; (2) subtracting the dependent variable grand mean from each of the dependent variable scores; (3) multiplying the deviations for each pair of scores containing one covariate and one dependent variable score; and (4) summing the product for all pairs of these scores.

The total sum of products for pre-test and post-test anxiety is 10:

$$[(3 - 3) \times (2 - 2.5)] + [(3 - 3) \times (2 - 2.5)] + [(2 - 3) \times (2 - 2.5)]$$
$$+ [(2 - 3) \times (1 - 2.5)] + [(2 - 3) \times (1 - 2.5)] + [(2 - 3) \times (1 - 2.5)]$$
$$+ [(3 - 3) \times (3 - 2.5)] + [(3 - 3) \times (3 - 2.5)] + [(4 - 3) \times (3 - 2.5)]$$

$$+ [(4 - 3) \times (4 - 2.5)] + [(4 - 3) \times (4 - 2.5)] + [(4 - 3) \times (4 - 2.5)]$$
$$= 10$$

Step 8   Calculate the between-groups sum of products for the covariate and dependent variable by (1) subtracting the covariate grand mean from each of its group means; (2) subtracting the dependent variable grand mean from each of its group means; (3) multiplying the deviation for each pair of group means of the covariate and dependent variable; (4) multiplying them by the number of pairs in each of the groups; and (5) summing the products for all the groups.

The between-groups sum of products for pre-test and post-test anxiety is 8.0:

$$[(2.333 - 3) \times (1.5 - 2.5) \times 6] + [(3.667 - 3) \times (3.5 - 2.5) \times 6]$$
$$= 8.0$$

Step 9   Calculate the within-groups sum of products for the covariate and dependent variable by subtracting its between-groups sum of products from its total sum of products.

The within-groups sum of products for pre-test and post-test anxiety is 2.0:

$$10 - 8.0 = 2.0$$

The between-groups, within-groups and total sum of squares and sum of products for the covariate and dependent variable are presented in Table 8.16.

Step 10   Calculate the adjusted between-groups sum of squares for the dependent variable by inserting the appropriate values into the following formula:

$$\text{BG-SS}_{adj} = \text{BG-SS}_{dep} + \frac{\text{WG-SP}^2}{\text{WG-SS}_{cov}} - \frac{\text{T-SP}^2}{\text{T-SS}_{cov}}$$

Table 8.16 One-way analysis of covariance table

Source of variation	Covariate SS	Dependent variable SS	SP
Between groups	5.34	12	8.0
Within groups	2.66	3	2.0
Total	8	15	10

The adjusted between-groups sum of squares for post-test anxiety is 1.00:

$$12 + \frac{2.0^2}{2.66} - \frac{10^2}{8} = 12 + 1.50 - 12.5 = 1.00$$

Step 11 Calculate the adjusted within-groups sum of squares for the dependent variable by substituting the pertinent values in the following formula:

$$\text{WG-SS}_{\text{adj}} = \text{WG-SS}_{\text{dep}} - \frac{\text{WG-SP}^2}{\text{WG-SS}_{\text{cov}}}$$

The adjusted within-groups sum of squares for post-test anxiety is 1.50:

$$3 - \frac{2.0^2}{2.66} = 3 - 1.50 = 1.50$$

Step 12 Calculate the adjusted between-groups mean square by dividing the adjusted between-groups sum of squares by its degrees of freedom which is the number of groups minus 1.

The adjusted between-groups mean square for post-test anxiety is 1.00 $(1.00/(2 - 1) = 1.00)$.

Step 13 Calculate the adjusted within-groups mean square by dividing the adjusted within-groups sum of squares by its degrees of freedom which is the total number of cases minus the number of groups minus 1.

The adjusted within-groups mean square for post-test anxiety is 0.17 $(1.50/(12 - 2 - 1) = 0.17)$.

Step 14 Calculate the F ratio for the between-groups effect by dividing the adjusted between-groups mean square by the adjusted within-groups mean square.

The F ratio for the between-groups effect of treatment is 5.88 $(1.00/0.17 = 5.88)$.

Step 15 Look up the F ratio in the table in Appendix 5.

With 1 and 9 degrees of freedom in the numerator and denominator respectively, F has to exceed 5.1174 to be significant at less than the 0.05 level which it is. Consequently, we would conclude that there is a significant difference in post-test anxiety between the cognitive and control conditions when pre-test anxiety is covaried.

Since the means have been adjusted for the influence of the covariate, the adjusted means may differ from the unadjusted ones. Consequently, when interpreting the between-groups treatment effect, we should look at the adjusted means. The group means for the dependent variable can be adjusted according to the following formula:

adjusted group mean = unadjusted group mean

$$- \left[\frac{\text{WG-SP}}{\text{WG-SS}_{\text{cov}}} \times (\text{covariate group mean} - \text{covariate grand mean}) \right]$$

Substituting the pertinent values into this formula, the adjusted group mean for the cognitive condition is 2.0:

$$1.5 - \left[\frac{2.0}{2.66} \times (2.33 - 3.00) \right] = 1.5 - -0.5 = 2.0$$

For the control condition it is 3.0:

$$3.5 - \left[\frac{2.0}{2.66} \times (3.67 - 3.00) \right] = 3.5 - 0.5 = 3.0$$

Although the difference for the adjusted means for post-test anxiety is smaller than that for the unadjusted means, post-test anxiety in the cognitive condition is still higher than that in the control condition.

One condition that has to be met before a significant between-groups effect can be interpreted is that the statistical association known as the *regression coefficient* is the same within each of the treatment groups and is linear in the sense that higher levels of the dependent variable indicate higher levels of the covariate. This assumption is called *homogeneity of regression*. It is based on dividing or partitioning the adjusted within-groups sum of squares for the dependent variable into the *between-regressions* sum of squares and the remaining sum of squares (the remainder). These sums of squares and their associated degrees of freedom are shown in Table 8.17. The between-regressions mean square is its sum of squares divided by its degrees of freedom which is the number of groups

Table 8.17 Between-regressions and remaining sums of squares and degrees of freedom

Source of variation	Degrees of freedom
Between-regressions	No. of groups −1
Remainder	No. of cases − (2 × no. of groups)
Adjusted within groups	No. of cases − no. of groups −1

minus 1. The remainder mean square is its sum of squares divided by its degrees of freedom which is the number of cases minus twice the number of groups. The *F* test for homogeneity of regression is the between-regressions mean square divided by the remainder mean square.

We have already described how to calculate the adjusted within-groups sum of squares for the dependent variable. The between-regressions sum of squares (BR-SS) is the sum of the sum of products for each group (SP1, SP2, ...) squared and then divided by the covariate sum of squares for each group (SS_{1cov}, SS_{2cov}, ...) from which is subtracted the within-groups sum of products (WG-SP) squared and then divided by the within-groups sum of squares ($WG-SS_{cov}$) for the covariate:

$$BR\text{-}SS = \left(\frac{SP_1^2}{SS_{1cov}} + \frac{SP_1^2}{SS_{2cov}} + \ldots\right) - \frac{WG\text{-}SP^2}{WG\text{-}SS_{cov}}$$

The remainder sum of squares is simply obtained by subtracting the between-regressions sum of squares from the adjusted within-groups sum of squares:

$$remainder\ SS = WG\text{-}SS_{adj} - BR\text{-}SS$$

To compute the *F* test for homogeneity of regression we carry out the following steps which will be illustrated with the pre-test and post-test anxiety scores of the men in the cognitive and control groups.

Step 1   Calculate the sum of products for each group by (1) subtracting the covariate group mean from each of its individual scores in the group; (2) subtracting the dependent variable group mean from each of its individual scores in the group; (3) multiplying the deviation for each pair of covariate and dependent individual scores; and (4) summing the products within each group.

The sum of products for the cognitive condition is 1.00:

$$[(3 - 2.3) \times (2 - 1.5)] + [(3 - 2.3) \times (2 - 1.5)] + [(2 - 2.3)$$
$$\times (2 - 1.5)] + [(2 - 2.3) \times (1 - 1.5)] + [(2 - 2.3) \times (1 - 1.5)]$$
$$+ [(2 - 2.3) \times (1 - 1.5)]$$
$$= 1.00$$

The sum of products for the control condition is 1.00:

$$[(3 - 3.7) \times (3 - 3.5)] + [(3 - 3.7) \times (3 - 3.5)] + [(4 - 3.7)$$
$$\times (3 - 3.5)] + [(4 - 3.7) \times (4 - 3.5)] + [(4 - 3.7) \times (4 - 3.5)]$$
$$+ [(4 - 3.7) \times (4 - 3.5)]$$
$$= 1.00$$

Step 2   Calculate the covariate sum of squares for each group by (1) subtracting the covariate group mean from each of its individual scores in the group; (2) squaring them; and (3) summing the products within each group.

The sum of squares for pre-test anxiety in the cognitive condition is 1.333:

$$(3 - 2.33)^2 + (3 - 2.33)^2 + (2 - 2.33)^2 + (2 - 2.33)^2 + (2 - 2.33)^2 + (2 - 2.33)^2 = 1.333$$

The sum of squares for pre-test anxiety in the control condition is 1.333:

$$(3 - 3.67)^2 + (3 - 3.67)^2 + (4 - 3.67)^2 + (4 - 3.67)^2 + (4 - 3.67)^2 + (4 - 3.67)^2 = 1.333$$

Step 3   Calculate the between-regressions sum of squares by substituting the appropriate values into the following formula:

$$\text{BR-SS} = \left(\frac{SP_1{}^2}{SS_{1cov}} + \frac{SP_1{}^2}{SS_{2cov}} + \ldots \right) - \frac{\text{WG-SP}^2}{\text{WG-SS}_{cov}}$$

The between-regressions sum of squares for post-test anxiety is 0:

$$\left(\frac{1.00^2}{1.33} + \frac{1.00^2}{1.33} \right) - \frac{2.0^2}{2.66} = 1.50 - 1.50 = 0$$

Step 4   Calculate the remainder sum of squares by subtracting the between-regressions sum of squares from the adjusted within-groups sum of squares.

The remainder sum of squares for post-test anxiety is 1.5 ($1.50 - 0 = 1.5$).

Step 5   Calculate the between-regressions mean square by dividing the between-regressions sum of squares by its degrees of freedom.

The between-regressions mean square for post-test anxiety is 0 ($0/(2 - 1) = 0$).

Step 6   Calculate the remainder mean square by dividing the remainder sum of squares by its degrees of freedom.

The remainder mean square for post-test anxiety is its sum of squares (1.5) divided by its degrees of freedom ($12 - (2 \times 2) = 8$) which gives 0.19 ($1.5/8$).

Step 7   Calculate the F test for homogeneity of regression by dividing the between-regressions mean square by the remainder mean square.

The F test in this case is 0 ($0/0.19$).

Step 8   Look up the statistical significance of the F ratio in the table in Appendix 5.

With 1 and 8 degrees of freedom in the numerator and denominator respectively, F would have to exceed 5.3177 to be significant at less than the 0.05 level which it is not. Therefore, the regression coefficient is the same in each of the groups.

One-way analysis of covariance may be computed in SPSS with either the **anova** or the **manova** command. The advantage of using the **manova** command is that the output includes the F test for homogeneity of regression. The relevant **anova** command is

anova dependent variable name **by** grouping variable name (value of first group,value of last group) **with** covariate name.

After having selected the men in the sample with the **select if (gen eq 2)** command, we would run the following **anova** command to carry out our one-way analysis of covariance:

anova fol by con(2,3) with pre.

The output for this command is shown in Table 8.18. The F test for the between-groups main effect (called **CON**) is its mean square **(1.000)** divided by the residual mean square **(.167)** which gives a rounded value of **6.000** $(1/0.167 = 5.99)$.

The means and numbers of cases in each group or cell for the dependent variable can be displayed by adding the **/statistics 3.** subcommand to the **anova** command. The output for this command is shown in Table 8.19.

The unadjusted and adjusted group means for the dependent variable can be produced by adding a 1 to the **/statistics** subcommand. The output for this subcommand is displayed in Table 8.20. The adjusted mean for post-test anxiety in the cognitive condition can be calculated by subtracting the deviation adjusted for the covariate **(−.50)** from the grand mean **(2.500)** giving a value of 2. Similarly, the adjusted mean for post-test anxiety in the control condition is worked out by adding the deviation adjusted for the covariate **(.50)** to the grand mean **(2.500)** giving a value of 3.

Eta is the square root of eta squared which in turn is the between-groups variance divided by the total variance. From our manual calculations, the between-groups sum of squares was 12 and the total sum of squares was 15. Dividing 12 by 15 and taking the square root of the result ($\sqrt{0.8}$) yields an eta of 0.89. **Multiple R Squared** is based on the sums of squares shown in Table 8.18. It is the covariate and main effect sums of squares added together **(1.000 + 12.500 = 13.500)** and divided by the total sum of squares **(15.000)** which gives a squared multiple correlation of 0.9 (13.5/15.0 = **.900**). **Multiple R** is the square root of this value ($\sqrt{0.9}$ = **.949**).

Table 8.18 **Anova** output for analysis of covariance

*** ANALYSIS OF VARIANCE ***

POS
BY CON
WITH PRE

Source of Variation	Sum of Squares	DF	Mean Square	F	Signif of F
Covariates	12.500	1	12.500	75.000	.000
PRE	12.500	1	12.500	75.000	.000
Main Effects	1.000	1	1.000	6.000	.037
CON	1.000	1	1.000	6.000	.037
Explained	13.500	2	6.750	40.500	.000
Residual	1.500	9	.167		
Total	15.000	11	1.364		

The general **manova** command for running a one-way analysis of covariance is as follows:

manova dependent variable name **by** grouping variable name (value of first group, value of last group) **with** covariate name
   /**pmeans**
   /**design**
   /**analysis**=dependent variable name
   /**design**=covariate name, grouping variable name, grouping variable name **by** covariate name.

The **pmeans** subcommand provides adjusted means while the **analysis** and the second **design** subcommands produce the *F* test for homogeneity of regression.

Therefore, the following **manova** command would carry out a one-way analysis of covariance on post-test anxiety once the men in the sample had been selected:

manova pos by con(2,3) with pre
   /**pmeans**
   /**design**
   /**analysis=pos**
   /**design=pre, con, con by pre.**

The output for the adjusted and the original or observed (**Obs.**) means for the two conditions are shown in Table 8.21.

The relevant output for the adjusted between-groups effect for post-test anxiety is presented in Table 8.22. The *F* ratio for the adjusted between-groups effect (called **CON**) is its mean square (1.00) divided by the adjusted within-groups (called **WITHIN CELLS**) mean square (**.17**) which gives a rounded value of 6.00 (1.00/0.17 = 5.88).

The output for the *F* test for homogeneity of regression is displayed in

Table 8.19 **Anova** output of cell means and numbers of cases

---

* * * CELL MEANS * * *

                    POS
                  BY CON

TOTAL POPULATION
            2.50
     (12)
CON
            2   3
          1.50   3.50
     (6)   (6)

Table 8.20 Anova output for unadjusted and adjusted means

*** MULTIPLE CLASSIFICATION ANALYSIS ***

POS
BY CON
WITH PRE

Grand Mean = 2.500

Variable + Category	N	Unadjusted Dev'n	Eta	Adjusted for Independents Dev'n	Beta	Adjusted for Independents + Covariates Dev'n	Beta
CON							
2	6	−1.00				−.50	
3	6	1.00				.50	
			.89				.45

Multiple R Squared	.900
Multiple R	.949

Table 8.21 **Manova** output of unadjusted and adjusted means

* * ANALYSIS OF VARIANCE – DESIGN 1 * *

Adjusted and Estimated Means
Variable .. POS

CELL	Obs. Mean	Adj. Mean	Est. Mean	Raw Resid.	Std. Resid.
1	1.500	2.000	1.500	.000	.000
2	3.500	3.000	3.500	.000	.000

Table 8.23. In this test the between-regressions (called **CON BY PRE**) mean square **(.00)** is divided by the residual (called **WITHIN+RESIDUAL**) mean square **(.19)** to produce a figure of **.00** (0/ 0.19 = 0).

SUMMARY

The computation of parametric tests for assessing whether the means of equal interval or ratio data from two or more related samples differ significantly across the samples is described. The related *t* test compares the difference between the means of the two related samples taking into account the extent to which the scores of the two samples are correlated by modifying the way the standard error of the difference in means is computed. Single factor repeated measures analysis of variance determines whether the means of three or more related samples differ. Two-way analysis of variance with repeated measures on one factor compares the means of groups consisting of two factors, one of which is repeated. One-way analysis of covariance compares the means of two or more groups controlling for the effects of a second factor known to be associated with the first factor and called a covariate. Interpretation of the analysis depends on the regression coefficient being the same within each of the groups.

EXERCISES

The data for these exercises are available in Table 6.18.

1 Use the related *t* test to compare educational interest at 12 and 15 for pupils from mixed-sex schools.
   (a) What is the value of the *t* test?
   (b) What are its degrees of freedom?
   (c) What is its two-tailed probability level?
   (d) Is educational interest significantly greater at 15 than at 12 for pupils from mixed-sex schools?

Table 8.22 **Manova** output of adjusted between-groups effects

** ANALYSIS OF VARIANCE – DESIGN 1 **

Tests of Significance for POS using UNIQUE sums of squares

Source of Variation	SS	DF	MS	F	Sig of F
WITHIN CELLS	1.50	9	.17		
REGRESSION	1.50	1	1.50	9.00	.015
CONSTANT	.02	1	.02	.11	.749
CON	1.00	1	1.00	6.00	.037

Table 8.23 **Manova** output of the *F* test for homogeneity of regression

** ANALYSIS OF VARIANCE – DESIGN 2 **

Tests of Significance for POS using UNIQUE sums of squares

Source of Variation	SS	DF	MS	F	Sig of F
WITHIN+RESIDUAL	1.50	8	.19		
CONSTANT	.02	1	.02	.09	.769
PRE	1.50	1	1.50	8.00	.022
CON	.07	1	.07	.37	.561
CON BY PRE	.00	1	.00	.00	1.000

2   Use a single factor repeated measures analysis of variance to compare educational interest at 9, 12 and 15 for pupils from mixed-sex schools.
(a) What is the value of the F test?
(b) What are its degrees of freedom?
(c) What is its probability level?
(d) Does educational interest at 9, 12 and 15 differ significantly for pupils from mixed-sex schools?

3   Use a two-way analysis of variance with repeated measures on one factor to determine whether any change in educational interest between 12 and 15 differs for pupils from single- and mixed-sex schools.
(a) What is the value of the F test?
(b) What are its degrees of freedom?
(c) What is its probability level?
(d) Does any change in educational interest between 12 and 15 differ for pupils from single- and mixed-sex schools?

4   Use a one-way analysis of covariance to determine whether there is a significant difference in educational interest at 12 between single- and mixed-sex schools when socio-economic status is covaried.
(a) What is the value of the F test for the adjusted between-groups effect?
(b) What are its degrees of freedom?
(c) What is its probability level?
(d) What is the value of the F test for homogeneity of regression?
(e) What are its degrees of freedom?
(f) What is its probability level?
(g) Is the regression coefficient the same in the two groups of single- and mixed-sex schools?
(h) What is the adjusted mean of educational interest at 12 for pupils from single-sex schools?
(i) What is the adjusted mean of educational interest at 12 for pupils from mixed-sex schools?
(j) Is educational interest at 12 significantly greater in single- than in mixed-sex schools when socio-economic status is covaried?

Chapter 9

Tests of association for categorical and ordinal data

So far we have looked at statistical tests which determine whether the distribution of two or more variables differs significantly. However, we are often interested in the extent to which two or more variables are associated, the direction of that association and the likelihood of that association occurring by chance. For example, we may wish to know whether married women with children are less likely to be in paid employment than married women without children and what the strength and statistical probability of any such association is. Or, as discussed in the previous chapter, we may want to find out whether higher pre-test anxiety is related to higher post-test anxiety and how strong and statistically significant such a relationship is. In addition, we may wish to discover whether an association between two variables is the result of their association with one or more other variables. For instance, if it was found that children who did best at school were also breastfed as babies, then this association may result from the fact that better educated mothers were more likely both to breastfeed their children and to encourage them to do well at school. To discover the answers to such questions, we would need to carry out the appropriate test of association, the selection of which partly depends on whether the data are categorical, ordinal or interval/ratio. In this chapter we will deal with tests which are suitable for categorical and ordinal data.

CATEGORICAL DATA

Tests of association for categorical data described in this chapter can be divided into those that are derived from chi-square (*phi coefficient, contingency coefficient* and *Cramer's V*) and those that are based on the *proportional reduction in error* (*Goodman and Kruskal's lambda* and *tau*). We will illustrate the computation of these tests with the data in Table 9.1 which show the number of married women either with or without children who are either employed or not.

Table 9.1 Number of married women with and without children in paid
employment

		Children	
		No	*Yes*
Paid employment	No	15	50
	Yes	55	20

Phi coefficient

The phi coefficient is suitable as a measure of association where both
variables are dichotomous. It is computed by dividing Pearson's chi-square
by the total number of cases and taking the square root of the result:

$$\text{phi} = \sqrt{\frac{\text{chi-square}}{\text{no. of cases}}}$$

Its value can vary from zero to +1.0.

To calculate phi, we first have to compute chi-square. As described in
Chapter 5, chi-square is the sum of the squared difference between the
observed and expected frequency for each cell divided by the expected
frequency for that cell. The expected frequency for any cell is its row total
multiplied by its column total divided by the grand total. The expected
frequencies for this example are shown in Table 9.2. In this example, chi-
square is 35.18:

$$\frac{(15-32.5)^2}{32.5} + \frac{(50-32.5)^2}{32.5} + \frac{(55-37.5)^2}{37.5} + \frac{(20-37.5)^2}{37.5}$$

$$= \frac{306.25}{32.5} + \frac{306.25}{32.5} + \frac{306.25}{37.5} + \frac{306.25}{37.5}$$

$$= 9.42 + 9.42 + 8.17 + 8.17 = 35.18$$

Consequently, phi is 0.50 ($\sqrt{(35.18/140)}$). We look up the statistical
significance of this value which has 1 degree of freedom in the table in
Appendix 8. With 1 degree of freedom, chi-square has to be larger than
3.84 to be significant at the two-tailed 0.05 level which it is. Therefore, we
would conclude that there was a statistically significant association between
having children and being in paid employment such that fewer married
women with children were in paid employment than married women
without children.

Table 9.2 Expected frequency of married women with and without children in paid employment

		Children	
		No	Yes
Paid employment	No	32.5	32.5
	Yes	37.5	37.5

The SPSS command for computing phi is **crosstabs** where the keyword **phi** is added to the **statistics** subcommand:

crosstabs table=variable **by** variable
/statistics=phi.

If we wanted Pearson's chi-square as well (which we do to check our own calculations) we would add **chisq** to the **statistics** subcommand.

To calculate chi-square and phi for this example, we would first have to enter the data table with the use of the **weight** command followed by the appropriate **crosstabs** command. The following commands could be used for computing phi:

data list/em 1 ch 3 wt 5-6.
weight by wt.
begin data.
1 1 15
1 2 50
2 1 55
2 2 20
end data.
crosstabs table=em by ch
 /cells=count expected
 /statistics=chisq phi.

The output for **chisq** is shown in Table 9.3. The output for **phi** is presented in Table 9.4; it is about 0.50 ($\sqrt{(35.17949/140)}$ = **.50128**). This output also includes Cramer's V which has the same value as phi when the variables are dichotomous.

Contingency coefficient

When one or both variables have more than two categories, phi may not vary between 0 and +1 because the chi-square value can be greater than the total number of cases in the sample. To obtain a measure that must lie

Table 9.3 Chi-square output

Chi-Square	Value	DF	Significance
Pearson	35.17949	1	.00000
Continuity Correction	33.19795	1	.00000
Likelihood Ratio	36.86740	1	.00000
Mantel–Haenszel test for linear association	34.92821	1	.00000
Minimum Expected Frequency –	32.500		

Table 9.4 Phi output

Statistic	Value	ASE1	T-value	Approximate Significance
Phi	.50128			.00000 *1
Cramer's V	.50128			.00000 *1

*1   Pearson chi-square probability

between 0 and +1, Pearson devised the contingency coefficient in which chi-square has been added to the denominator of the formula for phi:

$$\text{contingency coefficient } C = \sqrt{\frac{\text{chi-square}}{\text{chi-square} + \text{no. of cases}}}$$

The contingency coefficient does not have +1 as its upper limit which depends on the number of categories. For a table made up of an equal number of rows and columns, $n \times n$, the upper limit is calculated by subtracting 1 from n, dividing the result by n and then taking the square root of this division. So, for a 3 × 3 table the upper limit is 0.82 ($\sqrt{[(3 - 1)/3]} = 0.82$), while for a 4 × 4 table it would be 0.87 ($\sqrt{[(4 - 1)/4]} = 0.87$). When the number of rows and columns differ, as in a 3 × 4 table, the upper limit is based on the smaller number. In this case the upper limit would be 0.82.

We will demonstrate the calculation of the contingency coefficient with the example from Chapter 5 of number of women and men in three different years of the course. These data are reproduced in Table 9.5. As calculated in Chapter 5, chi-square for these data is 0.218. Consequently, the contingency coefficient is 0.04 ($\sqrt{[0.218/(0.218 + 112)]} = 0.04$). We would look up the statistical significance of this value in the table in

Table 9.5 Numbers of women and men taking the same course in three
consecutive years

	1991	1992	1993
Women	19	27	24
Men	11	18	13

Appendix 8 with the appropriate degrees of freedom which is the number
of rows minus 1 multiplied by the number of columns minus 1. With 2
degrees of freedom $((2 - 1) \times (3 - 1))$ the contingency coefficient would
have to exceed 5.99 to be significant at the two-tailed 0.05 level which it is
not. Consequently, we would conclude that there was no association
between gender and successive years of intake.

The SPSS command for computing the contingency coefficient is
crosstabs where the keyword **cc** is added to the **statistics** subcommand:

crosstabs table=variable **by** variable
 /**statistics**=**cc.**

To compute the contingency coefficient as well as chi-square for this
example, we would first have to enter the data table with the use of the
weight command followed by the appropriate **crosstabs** command. The
following commands could be used for producing this coefficient:

data list/gen 1 year 3 wt 5-7.
weight by wt.
begin data.
1 1 19
1 2 27
1 3 24
2 1 11
2 2 18
2 3 13
end data.
crosstabs table=gen by year
 /**statistics=chisq cc.**

The output for chi-square and the contingency coefficient is shown in
Table 9.6. The contingency coefficient is about 0.04 ($\sqrt{[.21718/(.21718 + 112)]} = .04399$).

Cramer's V

To make the upper limit of the association +1 for tables greater than

Table 9.6 Chi-square and contingency coefficient output

Chi-Square	Value	DF	Significance
Pearson	.21718	2	.89710
Likelihood Ratio	.21699	2	.89718
Mantel–Haenszel test for linear association	.02482	1	.87483
Minimum Expected Frequency –	11.250		

Statistic	Value	ASE1	T-value	Approximate Significance
Contingency Coefficient	.04399			.89710 *1

*1   Pearson chi-square probability

2×2, Cramer produced V which is computed by dividing chi-square by the total number of cases multiplied by 1 subtracted from the smaller number of rows or columns and then taking the square root of the result:

$$\text{Cramer's } V = \sqrt{\frac{\text{chi-square}}{\text{no. of cases} \times (\text{smaller no. of rows/columns} - 1)}}$$

Where the smaller number of rows or columns is 2, the denominator effectively becomes the number of cases ($N \times (2 - 1) = N$) and therefore Cramer's V is the same as phi.

In this case Cramer's V is 0.04 ($\sqrt{[0.217/(112 \times 1)]} = 0.04$). Thus, as before, we would conclude that there was no association between gender and successive years of intake.

The SPSS command for computing Cramer's V is **crosstabs** where the keyword **phi** is added to the **statistics** subcommand:

crosstabs table=variable **by** variable
  /statistics=phi.

The following command will compute Cramer's V for our example:

crosstabs table=gen by year
  /statistics=phi.

The relevant output for this command is presented in Table 9.7. Cramer's V is about 0.04 ($\sqrt{[.21718/(112 \times 1)]} = .04404$).

Table 9.7 Cramer's *V* output

Statistic	Value	ASE1	T-value	Approximate Significance
Phi	.04404			.89710 *1
Cramer's V	.04404			.89710 *1

*1   Pearson chi-square probability

Goodman and Kruskal's lambda

Lambda is the proportional increase in predicting the outcome of one categorical variable when knowing its combined outcome with a second categorical variable. The value of lambda can vary from 0 to +1. Zero means that there is no increase in predictiveness whereas 1 indicates that prediction can be made without error. Suppose, for example, that we wanted to predict from the data in Table 9.1 the larger number of cases with respect to married women in paid employment regardless of whether they had children. The larger category is married women in paid employment (75). Consequently, if we had to predict whether a particular married woman was in paid employment or not, our best guess would be to say she was in paid employment. If we did this for all 140 women we would be wrong on 65 occasions ($140 - 75 = 65$).

How would our ability to predict whether a particular woman was in paid employment be enhanced by our knowledge of whether she had children? Taking the women without children first, if we knew that 55 of these 70 women were in paid employment, our best guess for predicting which category a particular woman in this group was in would be to say she was in paid employment. If we did this for all 70 women we would be wrong 15 times ($70 - 55 = 15$). Turning next to the women with children, if we knew that 50 of these 70 women were not in paid employment, our best guess for predicting which category a particular women in this group was in would be to say she was not in paid employment. If we did this for all 70 women we would be wrong 20 times ($70 - 50 = 20$). Therefore, if we knew whether women had children or not, we would make 35 errors ($15 + 20 = 35$). Knowing this information would reduce our errors by 30 ($65 - 35 = 30$) which as a proportion of the errors we made initially would be 0.46 ($30/65 = 0.46$). In other words, knowledge of the second variable would reduce the proportion of errors by 0.46. Predicting married women in paid employment from having children results in a lambda of 0.46.

We could also work out lambda for predicting whether married women have children based on knowing whether they were in paid employment. Lambda for this prediction is 0.5:

$$\frac{70 - (20 + 15)}{140 - 70} = \frac{35}{70} = 0.5$$

These two lambdas are called *asymmetric* since they are likely to vary depending on which variable is being predicted. The following formula is used for calculating asymmetric lambda:

$$\text{asymmetric lambda} = \frac{\text{sum of the largest cell frequencies in the columns} - \text{largest row total}}{\text{total number of cases} - \text{largest row total}}$$

Applying this formula to our data, we see that lambda for predicting paid employment is 0.46:

$$\frac{(50 + 55) - 75}{140 - 75} = \frac{30}{65} = 0.46$$

Lambda for predicting having children is 0.5:

$$\frac{(55 + 50) - 70}{140 - 70} = \frac{35}{70} = 0.5$$

The formula for computing symmetric lambda is

$$\frac{\begin{array}{c}\text{sum of the largest}\\ \text{cell frequencies}\\ \text{in the columns}\end{array} + \begin{array}{c}\text{sum of the largest}\\ \text{cell frequencies}\\ \text{in the rows}\end{array} - \begin{array}{c}\text{largest}\\ \text{row}\\ \text{total}\end{array} - \begin{array}{c}\text{largest}\\ \text{column}\\ \text{total}\end{array}}{(2 \times \text{total number of cases}) - \text{largest row total} - \text{largest column total}}$$

Applying this formula to our data we find that symmetric lambda is 0.48:

$$\frac{(55 + 50) + (55 + 50) - 75 - 70}{(2 \times 140) - 75 - 70} = \frac{65}{135} = 0.48$$

The SPSS command for computing lambda is **crosstabs** where the keyword **lambda** is added to the **statistics** subcommand:

crosstabs table=variable **by** variable
 /**statistics**=**lambda.**

The following command will compute lambda for our example:

crosstabs table=**em by ch**
 /**statistics**=**lambda.**

The relevant output for this command is presented in Table 9.8 which shows the asymmetric lambda for paid employment (**EM**) as the dependent variable, the asymmetric lambda for children (**CH**) as the dependent

Table 9.8 Goodman and Kruskal's lambda and tau output

Statistic		Value	ASE1	T-value	Approximate Significance
Lambda :					
symmetric		.48148	.08465	4.54178	
with EM	dependent	.46154	.09445	3.76262	
with CH	dependent	.50000	.08144	4.66667	
Goodman & Kruskal Tau :					
with EM	dependent	.25128	.07311		.00000 *2
with CH	dependent	.25128	.07306		.00000 *2

*2   Based on chi-square approximation

variable and the symmetric lambda. Discussion of asymptotic standard error (**ASE1**) and the *t* statistic is beyond the scope of this book. The **lambda** keyword also gives Goodman and Kruskal's tau for the same data.

Goodman and Kruskal's tau

Lambda assumes that the same prediction is made for all cases in a particular row or column. Goodman and Kruskal's tau, on the other hand, presumes that the predictions are randomly made on the basis of their proportions in row and column totals. For instance, if we predicted whether women were in paid employment ignoring whether they had children, then we would guess this correctly for 0.46 (65/140 = 0.46) of the 65 women who were not in paid employment (i.e. 0.46 × 65 = about 30 women) and for 0.54 (75/140 = 0.54) of the 75 women who were in paid employment (i.e. 0.54 × 75 = about 40 women). In other words, we would guess correctly that about 70 of the women were in paid employment (140 − 30 − 40 = 70 women) and the probability of error would be 0.5 (70/140 = 0.5).

If we now took into account whether these women had children or not, then we would predict correctly whether women were in paid employment for 0.23 (15/65 = 0.23) of the 15 women without children and not in paid employment (i.e. 0.23 × 15 = 3.5 women), 0.77 (50/65 = 0.77) of the 50 women with children and not in paid employment (i.e. 0.77 × 50 = 38.5 women), 0.73 (55/75 = 0.73) of the 55 women without children and in paid employment (i.e. 0.73 × 55 = 40.3 women) and 0.27 (20/75 = 0.27) of the 20 women with children and in paid employment (i.e. 0.27 × 20 = 5.4 women). In other words, the probability of error for guessing whether women were in paid employment knowing whether they had children would be 0.37 ((140 − 3.5 − 38.5 − 40.3 − 5.4)/140 = 0.37). Consequently, the proportional reduction of error in predicting women in paid employment knowing whether they have children is 0.26 ((0.5 − 0.37)/0.5 = 0.26). In the same way, we could also work out Goodman and Kruskal's tau for predicting whether women have children knowing whether they were in paid employment.

The SPSS command for computing Goodman and Kruskal's tau, as we have already seen, is **crosstabs** where the keyword **lambda** is added to the **statistics** subcommand:

crosstabs table=variable **by** variable
/**statistics**=**lambda.**

The SPSS computation of Goodman and Kruskal's tau for our example is shown in Table 9.8 first for women in paid employment as the dependent variable and second for women with children as the dependent variable.

ORDINAL DATA

There are several tests of association for two ordinal variables. Apart from *Spearman's rank order correlation* and *Mantel–Haenszel's chi-square* measure of linear association, the tests discussed in this section (*Kendall's tau a, tau b* and *tau c*; *Goodman and Kruskal's gamma*; and *Somer's d*) are based on comparing all possible pairs of cases. To illustrate the general rationale behind these tests, imagine that two people or judges were asked to rank five women in terms of their leadership potential where a rank of 1 indicated the greatest potential. To indicate the rankings given by these two judges, we have arranged them in Table 9.9 where the rankings for one judge (Judge A) have been listed in order and compared against the rankings of the other judge (Judge B). We can now compare the extent to which the rankings by Judge B are similar to those of Judge A by counting the number of pairs of cases for Judge B in which the first case is ranked higher than the second (called a *concordant* pair), lower (a *discordant* pair) or the same (a *tied* pair). For example, Judge B ranks Ann 2 and Mary 1, so this pair is discordant. On the other hand, both Ann and Jo are ranked

Table 9.9 Example of rankings by two judges

Women	Judge A	Judge B
Ann	1	2
Mary	2	1
Jo	3	2
Sue	4	4
Jane	5	5

2, so this pair is tied, while both Sue and Jane are ranked higher than Ann, so that these two pairs are concordant.

If all pairs of cases for Judge B were concordant, then the rankings of Judge B would be the same as those of Judge A and there would be a perfect direct or *positive* association between the rankings of Judge A and Judge B so that a higher ranking by Judge A would always correspond to a higher ranking by Judge B. Conversely, if all pairs of cases for Judge B were discordant, then there would be a perfect inverse or *negative* association between the rankings of Judge A and Judge B so that a higher ranking by Judge A would always correspond to a lower ranking by Judge B. If there were an equal number of concordant and discordant pairs for Judge B, then there would be no association between the rankings of the two judges. If there are more concordant pairs than discordant pairs, then the association will be positive, while if there are more discordant pairs than concordant pairs, then the association will be negative.

Kendall's rank correlation coefficient or tau *a*

Kendall's tau *a* is used when there are no tied pairs and can vary from −1 to +1. It is the number of concordant pairs minus the number of discordant pairs over the total number of pairs:

$$\text{tau } a = \frac{\text{no. of concordant pairs} - \text{no. of discordant pairs}}{\text{total no. of pairs}}$$

Take the data in Table 9.10 (which are the same as those in Table 9.9 except that the ranking by Judge B of Jo has been changed from 2 to 3) where the numbers of concordant and discordant pairs have been counted. The number of concordant (or discordant) pairs is worked out by taking each case of Judge B in turn, starting with the first case, and counting the number of times that that case is higher (or lower) than the cases below and adding the numbers for all cases. So the ranking by Judge B of Ann is

Table 9.10 Another example of rankings by two judges

Women	Judge A	Judge B	No. of concordant pairs	No. of discordant pairs
Ann	1	2	3	1
Mary	2	1	3	0
Jo	3	3	2	0
Sue	4	4	1	0
Jane	5	5	0	0
			9	1

higher than three of the other rankings (Jo, Sue and Jane), the ranking of Mary is also higher than three of the other rankings (Jo, Sue and Jane) and so on, giving a total of 9 concordant pairs. Tau *a* for this example is 0.8 ($(9 - 1)/10 = 0.8$). Note that the total number of pairs can be calculated by subtracting 1 from the number of cases, multiplying the result by the number of cases and then dividing by 2. If we do this, the total number of pairs is 10 ($(5 - 1) \times 5/2 = 10$).

The SPSS command for computing Kendall's tau *a* is **crosstabs** where the keyword **btau** is added to the **statistics** subcommand:

crosstabs table=variable **by** variable
 /statistics=btau.

The following SPSS commands can be used for running this example:

data list/a 1 b 3.
begin data.
1 2
2 1
3 3
4 4
5 5
end data.
crosstabs tables=a by b
 /statistics=btau.

The output giving tau *a* is shown in Table 9.11. It is called tau *b* since SPSS uses the same computational formula for calculating both tau *b* and tau *a*. This formula, which is described below as an alternative way of computing tau *b*, can be used to calculate tau *a* since it does not involve counting the number of ties.

Kendall's tau *b*

Kendall's tau *b* is used as a test of association for ordinal data when there are tied pairs. It is the number of concordant pairs (*C*) minus the number of discordant pairs (*D*) divided by the square root of the product of the total number of pairs (*T*) minus the number of tied pairs for one variable

Table 9.11 Kendall's tau *a* output

Statistic	Value	ASE1	T-value	Approximate Significance
Kendall's Tau-b	.80000	.21909	3.65148	

(T_1) and the total number of pairs (T) minus the tied pairs for the other variable (T_2):

$$\text{tau } b = \frac{C - D}{\sqrt{(T - T_1) \times (T - T_2)}}$$

Tau b can vary from -1 to $+1$ if the table is square and if none of the row and column totals is zero.

Take the data in Table 9.12 (which are the same as those in Table 9.9). The number of ties for Judge B (the second variable) is 1, the number of concordant pairs is 8 and the number of discordant pairs is 1. There are no tied pairs for Judge A. Consequently, tau b is 0.74:

$$\frac{8 - 1}{\sqrt{(10 - 0) \times (10 - 1)}} = \frac{7}{9.49} = 0.74$$

If we arranged these data into the matrix displayed in Table 9.13 with the ranks of Judge A along the side and the ranks of Judge B along the bottom with the number of ranks in each cell, then we see that this table is

Table 9.12 Number of concordant, discordant and tied pairs of rankings

Women	Judge A	Judge B	C	D	T_1	T_2
Ann	1	2	2	1	0	1
Mary	2	1	3	0	0	0
Jo	3	2	2	0	0	0
Sue	4	4	1	0	0	0
Jane	5	5	0	0	0	0
			8	1	0	1

Table 9.13 Matrix of ranks

Judge A	1	1			
	2	1			
	3	1			
	4		1		
	5			1	
		1 2 4 5			
		Judge B			

not square since it consists of five rows and four columns.

An alternative and easier method of counting the number of concordant, discordant and tied pairs is to use such a matrix. Concordant pairs for a joint ranking are represented by the sum of values which lie below and to the right of that position while discordant pairs are the sum of values which lie below and to the left of that point. So, for the joint ranking located at rank 1 for Judge A and rank 2 for Judge B there are two values below and to the right of it (located at rank 4 of both judges and at rank 5 of both judges) and one value below and to the left of it (at rank 2 for Judge A and at rank 1 for Judge B). Proceeding in this way through the matrix, we can count 8 concordant pairs and 1 discordant pair. Ties are represented by values that lie along either the same rows (for Judge A) or the same columns (for Judge B). So, there is one tie for Judge B.

To illustrate that this second method of counting the number of concordant, discordant and paired ranks is easier to use than the first method, take the data in Table 9.14 (which are the same as that in Table 9.12 except that the ranking of Mary by Judge A has been changed from 2 to 1). If we rearrange the data in matrix form as shown in Table 9.15, we can work out more readily that there are now no discordant pairs since Judge A has given the same ranking to Ann and Mary.

Table 9.14 Number of concordant, discordant and tied pairs of rankings for another example

Women	Judge A	Judge B	C	D	T_1	T_2
Ann	1	2	2	0	1	1
Mary	1	1	3	0	0	0
Jo	3	2	2	0	0	0
Sue	4	4	1	0	0	0
Jane	5	5	0	0	0	0
			8	0	1	1

Table 9.15 Another matrix of rankings

```
          1    1 1
          3      1
Judge A   4        1
          5          1

               1 2 4 5
                Judge B
```

An alternative formula for computing tau b is the difference between the number of concordant (C) and discordant (D) pairs multiplied by 2 and divided by the square root of the squared number of cases (N^2) minus the sum of squared row totals (RT^2) multiplied by the squared number of cases (N^2) minus the sum of squared column totals (CT^2):

$$\text{tau } b = \frac{2 \times (C - D)}{\sqrt{(N^2 - \text{sum of } RT^2) \times (N^2 - \text{sum of } CT^2)}}$$

If we substitute the appropriate values into this formula, then we see that tau b is 0.74:

$$\frac{2 \times (8 - 1)}{\sqrt{[5^2 - (1^2 + 1^2 + 1^2 + 1^2 + 1^2)] \times [5^2 - (1^2 + 2^2 + 1^2 + 1^2)]}}$$

$$= \frac{14}{\sqrt{(25 - 5) \times (25 - 7)}} = \frac{14}{\sqrt{360}} = \frac{14}{19} = 0.74$$

The SPSS command for computing tau b is, as we have already seen, **crosstabs** where the keyword **btau** is added to the **statistics** subcommand:

crosstabs table=variable **by** variable
  /**statistics**=**btau**.

The tau b value for this command and example is shown in Table 9.16.
    The table of rankings produced by this command is presented in Table 9.17.

Kendall's tau c

For a rectangular table Kendall's tau c can come closer to -1 or $+1$. It is the number of concordant pairs (C) minus the number of discordant pairs (D) multiplied by twice the number of columns or rows whichever is the smaller (S), divided by the total number of cases (N) squared times the smaller number of columns or rows minus 1:

Table 9.16 Kendall's tau b output

Statistic	Value	ASE1	T-value	Approximate Significance
Kendall's Tau-b	.73786	.25248	2.68438	

Table 9.17 Contingency table output

A by B

		B				Page 1 of 2
A	**Count**	**1**	**2**	**4**	**5**	**Row Total**
	1		1			1 / 20.0
	2	1				1 / 20.0
	3		1			1 / 20.0
	4			1		1 / 20.0
	5				1	1 / 20.0
	Column Total	1 / 20.0	2 / 40.0	1 / 20.0	1 / 20.0	5 / 100.0

$$\text{tau } c = \frac{(C - D) \times 2 \times S}{N^2 \times (S - 1)}$$

Consequently, for the data in Table 9.12 where the number of columns (4) is smaller than the number of rows (5) tau c is 0.75:

$$\frac{(8 - 1) \times 2 \times 4}{5^2 \times (4 - 1)} = \frac{56}{75} = 0.75$$

The SPSS command for computing tau c is **crosstabs** where the keyword **ctau** is added to the **statistics** subcommand:

crosstabs table=variable **by** variable
  /statistics=ctau.

The tau c value for this command and example is shown in Table 9.18.

Goodman and Kruskal's gamma

Goodman and Kruskal's gamma can range from −1 to +1 and takes no account of ties or the size of the table. It is simply the number of concordant pairs (C) minus the number of discordant pairs (D) divided by the number of concordant and discordant pairs:

Table 9.18 Kendall's tau *c* output

Statistic	Value	ASE1	T-value	Approximate Significance
Kendall's Tau-c	.74667	.27815	2.68438	

$$\text{gamma} = \frac{C - D}{C + D}$$

So, for the data in Table 9.12 gamma is 0.78:

$$\frac{8 - 1}{8 + 1} = \frac{7}{9} = 0.78$$

The SPSS command for computing gamma is **crosstabs** where the keyword **gamma** is added to the **statistics** subcommand:

crosstabs table=variable **by** variable
  /**statistics**=**gamma.**

The output for this command for our example is presented in Table 9.19.

Somer's *d*

Somer's *d* provides an asymmetric as well as a symmetric measure of association and takes account of tied pairs. The formula for computing asymmetric *d* for the first variable as the dependent variable is the difference between the number of concordant (C) and discordant (D) pairs divided by the number of concordant (C), discordant (D) and tied pairs for the first variable (T_1):

$$\text{asymmetric } d = \frac{C - D}{C + D + T_1}$$

For the data in Table 9.12, asymmetric *d* for Judge A as the dependent variable is 0.78:

$$\frac{8 - 1}{8 + 1 + 0} = \frac{7}{9} = 0.78$$

The formula for computing asymmetric *d* for the second variable as the dependent variable is the difference between the number of concordant (C) and discordant (D) pairs divided by the number of concordant (C), discordant (D) and tied pairs for the second variable (T_2):

Table 9.19 Goodman and Kruskall's gamma output

Statistic	Value	ASE1	T-value	Approximate Significance
Gamma	.77778	.24937	2.68438	

$$\text{asymmetric } d = \frac{C - D}{C + D + T_2}$$

Asymmetric d for Judge B as the dependent variable is 0.7:

$$\frac{8 - 1}{8 + 1 + 1} = \frac{7}{10} = 0.7$$

The formula for computing symmetric d is the difference between the number of concordant (C) and discordant (D) pairs divided by the number of concordant (C), discordant (D) and tied pairs for the first variable (T_1) added to the number of concordant (C), discordant (D) and tied pairs for the second variable (T_2) divided by 2:

$$\text{symmetric } d = \frac{C - D}{(C + D + T_1 + C + D + T_2)/2}$$

Symmetric d for this example is 0.74:

$$\frac{8 - 1}{(8 + 1 + 1 + 8 + 1 + 0)/2} = \frac{7}{9.5} = 0.74$$

An alternative formula for computing asymmetric d, where the dependent variable is represented by the row totals of the matrix of ranks, is the difference between the number of concordant (C) and discordant (D) pairs multiplied by 2 and divided by the squared number of cases (N^2) minus the sum of squared column totals (CT^2):

$$\text{asymmetric } d = \frac{2 \times (C - D)}{N^2 - \text{sum of } CT^2}$$

For the data in Table 9.12, asymmetric d for Judge A as the dependent variable is 0.78:

$$\frac{2 \times (8 - 1)}{5^2 - (1^2 + 2^2 + 1^2 + 1^2)} = \frac{14}{25 - 7} = \frac{14}{18} = 0.78$$

The corresponding formula for computing asymmetric d, where the dependent variable is represented by the column totals of the matrix of ranks, is the difference between the number of concordant (C) and discordant (D) pairs multiplied by 2 and divided by the squared number of cases (N^2) minus the sum of squared row totals (RT^2):

$$\text{asymmetric } d = \frac{2 \times (C - D)}{N^2 - \text{sum of } RT^2}$$

Asymmetric d for Judge B as the dependent variable is 0.7:

$$\frac{2 \times (8 - 1)}{5^2 - (1^2 + 1^2 + 1^2 + 1^2 + 1^2)} = \frac{14}{25 - 5} = \frac{14}{20} = 0.7$$

The formula for computing symmetric d is the difference between the number of concordant (C) and discordant (D) pairs multiplied by 4 and divided by the squared number of cases (N^2) minus the sum of squared row totals (RT^2) added to the squared number of cases (N^2) minus the sum of squared column totals (CT^2):

$$\text{symmetric } d = \frac{4 \times (C - D)}{(N^2 - \text{sum of } RT^2) + (N^2 - \text{sum of } CT^2)}$$

Symmetric d is 0.74:

$$\frac{4 \times (8 - 1)}{[5^2 - (1^2 + 1^2 + 1^2 + 1^2 + 1^2)] + [5^2 - (1^2 + 2^2 + 1^2 + 1^2)]}$$

$$= \frac{28}{(25 - 5) + (25 - 7)} = \frac{28}{38} = 0.74$$

The SPSS command for computing Somer's d is **crosstabs** where the keyword **d** is added to the **statistics** subcommand:

crosstabs table=variable **by** variable
    /statistics=d.

The output for this command for our example is presented in Table 9.20.

Spearman's rank order correlation or rho

Spearman's rho ranges from -1 to $+1$ and is based on the amount of disagreement between the ranks for the two variables. More specifically, it involves squaring and then adding together the differences between paired ranks for the two variables for all cases. Rho can be described in terms of the following formula:

Table 9.20 Somer's d output

Statistic		Value	ASE1	T-value	Approximate Significance
Somer's D:					
symmetric		.73684	.25213	2.68438	
with A	dependent	.77778	.24937	2.68438	
with B	dependent	.70000	.26077	2.68438	

$$\text{rho} = 1 - \frac{2 \times \text{sum of differences squared}}{\text{maximum sum of differences squared}}$$

If there are no differences between the ranks, then there will be a perfect positive correlation of +1 ($1 - 0 = 1$) since the differences between the ranks will be zero and zero multiplied by 2 and divided by the maximum sum of differences squared will still be zero. If, on the other hand, the ranks of one variable are the exact reverse of the other, then there will be a perfect negative correlation of -1 ($1 - 2 = -1$) since the sum of differences squared will be the maximum sum which divided by itself will be 1.

When there are no tied ranks, the computational formula for rho is

$$\text{rho} = 1 - \frac{6 \times \text{sum of differences squared}}{N^3 - N}$$

where N is the number of pairs or cases.

When there are tied ranks the computational formula for rho is

$$\text{rho} = \frac{T_1 + T_2 - \text{sum of differences squared}}{2 \times \sqrt{T_1 \times T_2}}$$

where T_1 or T_2 is

$$\frac{[N \times (N^2 - 1)] - [\text{sum of } t \times (t^2 - 1)]}{12}$$

and t is the number of ties at a given rank for either the first or the second variable.

We will illustrate the computation of rho with no tied ranks with the data in Table 9.21 (which are the same as the data in Table 9.9 except that the ranking of Jo by Judge B has been changed from 2 to 3). Substituting the appropriate values in the formula for computing rho when there are no ties, we see that rho is 0.9:

Table 9.21 Initial computations for rho with no tied ranks

Women	Judge A	Judge B	Difference	Difference squared
Ann	1	2	−1	1
Mary	2	1	+1	1
Jo	3	3	0	0
Sue	4	4	0	0
Jane	5	5	0	0
				2

$$1 - \frac{6 \times 2}{5^3 - 5} = 1 - \frac{12}{120} = 1 - 0.1 = 0.9$$

We look up the statistical significance of rho in the table in Appendix 18 where we see that with five cases rho has to be 0.9000 or bigger to be significant at the 0.05 one-tailed level. So if we had anticipated that the two sets of rankings would be positively correlated, we could conclude that the correlation was significantly positive.

Where some of the ranks are tied (as in Table 9.22) we first have to give these ranks the average rank they would have had if they had not been tied, so that the average ranking of Ann and Jo by Judge B is 2.5 ((2 + 3)/2 = 2.5) instead of 2. For the first variable there are no ties, so T_1 is 10:

$$\frac{[5 \times (5^2 - 1)] - [0 \times (0 - 1)]}{12} = \frac{120 - 0}{12} = 10$$

For the second variable there are only two ties (2.5, 2.5) for one rank (2.5) so T_2 is 9.5:

$$\frac{[5 \times (5^2 - 1)] - [2 \times (2^2 - 1)]}{12} = \frac{120 - 6}{12} = 9.5$$

Substituting the appropriate values in the formula for computing rho when there are ties, we find that rho is 0.82:

$$\frac{10 + 9.5 - 3.5}{2 \times \sqrt{10 \times 9.5}} = \frac{16}{19.5} = 0.82$$

As we have already seen, with only five cases this correlation would have to be 0.9 or larger to be significant at the 0.05 one-tailed level.

The SPSS command for computing Spearman's rho is **crosstabs** where the keyword **corr** is added to the **statistics** subcommand:

Table 9.22 Initial computations for rho with some tied ranks

Women	Judge A	Judge B		Difference	Difference squared
Ann	1	2	2.5	−1.5	2.25
Mary	2	1	1.0	1.0	1.00
Jo	3	2	2.5	0.5	0.25
Sue	4	4	4.0	0.0	0.00
Jane	5	5	5.0	0.0	0.00
					3.50

crosstabs table=variable **by** variable
   /**statistics**=**corr.**

The output for this command for the example with ties is shown in
Table 9.23.

Mantel–Haenszel's chi-square

Mantel–Haenszel's chi-square is another linear measure of association for
ordinal data. It is calculated by multiplying the squared Pearson's correlation coefficient by the number of cases minus 1 and it has 1 degree of
freedom. The procedure for computing Pearson's correlation will be
described in the next chapter. However, we can demonstrate the calculation of Mantel–Haenszel's chi-square with the output shown in Table
9.23 which gives Pearson's correlation (**Pearson's R**) as well as Spearman's
correlation. When we square this correlation ($.86603^2 = 0.75$) and
multiply it by 4 ($5 - 1 = 4$), we have a Mantel–Haenszel's chi-square of 3
($0.75 \times 4 = 3$). If we look up this value in the table in Appendix 8, we see
that with 1 degree of freedom chi-square has to exceed 3.84 to be significant at the 0.05 two-tailed level which it is not. Therefore, we would
conclude that the association between these two sets of rankings is not
significant.

   The SPSS command for generating Mantel–Haenzel's chi-square is
crosstabs where the keyword **chisq** is added to the **statistics** subcommand:

crosstabs table=variable **by** variable
   /**statistics**=**chisq.**

The output from this command for this example is displayed in Table 9.24
where we see that Mantel–Haenszel's chi-square is **3.00000**.

Table 9.23 Rho output

Statistic	Value	ASE1	T-value	Approximate Significance
Pearson's R	.86603	.07768	3.00000	.05767
Spearman Correlation	.82078	.23020	2.48868	.08859

Table 9.24 Mantel–Haenszel's chi-square output

Chi-Square	Value	DF	Significance
Pearson	15.00000	12	.24144
Likelihood Ratio	13.32179	12	.34609
Mantel–Haenszel test for linear association	3.00000	1	.08326
Minimum Expected Frequency –	.200		
Cells with Expected Frequency <5 –	20 OF	20 (100.0%)	

A MEASURE OF PARTIAL ASSOCIATION

A significant association between two measures does not necessarily mean that the two variables are causally related. For instance, if better educated people were found to have higher self-esteem, then this relationship does not necessarily imply that there is a causal link between these two variables such that better education leads to higher self-esteem. It is possible that this association is *spurious* in the sense that it is the result of one or more other factors which are genuinely related to the two variables of education and self-esteem. For example, greater parental education may be related to both better education and higher self-esteem in the children. When the parental education of these individuals is taken into account there may be no association between their own education and their self-esteem.

The data in Table 9.25 have been made up to illustrate this point where a 1 indicates a lower level of these characteristics and a 2 a higher level. Comparing the overlap of scores for the 20 cases, although we see that 12 (i.e. 60 per cent) of the cases (indicated with an asterisk at the end of the row) have the same scores on their own education and self-esteem, 11 of these 12 cases (i.e. 92 per cent) also have the same status on parental education. If we take out these 11 cases, then only one of the remaining 8 cases (i.e. about 12 per cent) has the same score on their education and self-esteem. In other words, if we remove the influence of parental

Table 9.25 Data on parental education, children's education and children's
self-esteem

Case no.	Parental education	Children's education	Children's self-esteem	
01	1	1	2	
02	1	1	2	
03	1	1	1	*
04	1	1	1	*
05	1	1	1	*
06	1	1	1	*
07	1	1	1	*
08	1	1	1	*
09	1	2	1	
10	1	2	2	*
11	2	1	2	
12	2	1	2	
13	2	2	2	*
14	2	2	2	*
15	2	2	2	*
16	2	2	2	*
17	2	2	2	*
18	2	2	1	
19	2	2	1	
20	2	2	1	

education, then there does not appear to be any association between a person's own education and self-esteem.

A less extreme version of this situation is one in which part but not all of the association between two measures may be due to one or more other factors. For example, better educated people may have higher self-esteem and may also have better educated parents. Part of their self-esteem may be due to their own education while another part may be due to their parent's education. If we remove the influence of their parent's education on the association between their own education and their self-esteem, then we can assume that the remaining association between these two variables is not the direct result of their parent's education. Similarly, we could remove the influence of their own education from the relationship between their parent's education and self-esteem to determine how much of the association between these two variables was not due to their own education.

Conversely, the absence of a significant association between two measures does not necessarily signify no causal connection between those two variables. It is possible that the relationship is suppressed or hidden by the influence of one or more other variables. For example, education may appear not to be associated with self-esteem because higher aspirations may result in better education, on the one hand, and lower self-esteem, on the other (due to failing to meet those high standards). If we remove the effect of aspirational level, we may find that education is related to self-esteem.

This kind of situation is exemplified by the data in Table 9.26 where 1 indicates a lower level and 2 a higher level of these factors. Comparing the extent to which the two scores are the same for all the cases, we see that only 4 (i.e. 20 per cent) of the 20 cases (denoted with one asterisk at the end of their row) have the same values on education and self-esteem. However, for 10 of the 20 cases (indicated by two asterisks at the end of their row) the aspiration score is the same as the education score but different from the self-esteem score. If in these cases the real relationship between education and self-esteem was positive, then 14 (i.e. 70 per cent) of the 20 cases would have shown such a relationship.

An index of association between two variables where no other variables have been controlled or partialled out is known as a *zero-order* association. A *first-order* association is one where one other variable has been controlled, a *second-order* association is one in which two other variables have been controlled and so on. The two tests of partial association that we shall discuss are *Kendall's partial rank correlation coefficient* and *partial gamma*.

Table 9.26 Data on aspirations, education and self-esteem

Case	Aspirations	Education	Self-esteem	
01	2	1	2	
02	2	1	2	
03	2	1	2	
04	1	1	2	**
05	1	1	2	**
06	1	1	2	**
07	1	1	2	**
08	1	1	2	**
09	1	1	1	*
10	1	1	1	*
11	1	2	1	
12	1	2	1	
13	1	2	1	
14	2	2	1	**
15	2	2	1	**
16	2	2	1	**
17	2	2	1	**
18	2	2	1	**
19	2	2	2	*
20	2	2	2	*

Kendall's partial rank correlation coefficient

The formula for computing the partial rank correlation ($tau_{12.3}$) between two variables (1 and 2) partialling out a third (3) variable is the rank correlation between the first two variables (tau_{12}) minus the product of the rank correlation between one of the two variables (1) and the third variable (tau_{13}) and the rank correlation between the other variable (2) and the third variable (tau_{23}), divided by the square root of the product of 1 minus the squared rank correlation between one of the two variables (1) and the third variable (tau_{13}^2) times 1 minus the squared rank correlation between the other variable (2) and the third variable (tau_{23}^2):

$$tau_{12.3} = \frac{tau_{12} - (tau_{13} \times tau_{23})}{\sqrt{(1 - tau_{13}^2) \times (1 - tau_{23}^2)}}$$

There is no significance level for this statistic.

To compute the rank correlation between own education and self-esteem controlling for parental education using the data in Table 9.25 we would first calculate the Kendall's rank correlation for the three variables. The rank correlation between own education and self-esteem is 0.2, between own education and parental education is 0.6 and between self-esteem and parental education is 0.4. Substituting these values into the formula above, we see that the partial rank correlation is −0.05:

$$\frac{0.2 - (0.6 \times 0.4)}{\sqrt{(1 - 0.6^2) \times (1 - 0.4^2)}} = \frac{0.2 - 0.24}{\sqrt{0.64 \times 0.84}} = \frac{-0.04}{0.73} = -0.05$$

In other words, the rank correlation of 0.2 between own education and self-esteem is reduced to −0.05 when parental education is controlled.

We shall repeat this procedure for computing the rank correlation between own education and self-esteem controlling for aspirations using the data in Table 9.26. The rank correlation between own education and self-esteem is 0.0, between own education and aspirations is 0.4 and between self-esteem and aspirations is −0.6. Placing these values into the above formula, we find that the partial rank correlation is 0.33:

$$\frac{0.0 - (0.4 \times -0.6)}{\sqrt{(1 - 0.4^2) \times (1 - -0.6^2)}} = \frac{0.0 - -0.24}{\sqrt{0.84 \times 0.64}} = \frac{0.24}{0.73} = 0.33$$

The rank correlation of 0.0 between own education and self-esteem is increased to 0.33 when the variable of aspirations is held constant.

SPSS does not compute the partial rank correlation but as we have just seen this is fairly easy to do.

Partial gamma

The formula for partial gamma is the number of concordant pairs (C) minus the number of discordant pairs (D) for the two variables summed across the different levels of the third variable divided by the number of concordant and discordant pairs summed across the different levels of the third variable:

$$\text{partial gamma} = \frac{\text{sum of } C - D}{\text{sum of } C + D}$$

We will demonstrate the calculation of partial gamma with the data in Table 9.25. First we draw up a contingency table as shown in Table 9.27 which contains two subtables, one for cases with less well educated parents (1) and one for those with better educated parents (2). Taking each subtable in turn, we will use the matrix method of counting the number of concordant and discordant pairs for any cell in that subtable where the number of concordant pairs is the sum of cases which lie below and to the right of that cell multiplied by the number in that cell, whereas the number of discordant pairs is the sum of cases which lie below and to the left of that cell multiplied by the number of cases in that cell. Since each subtable only consists of a 2×2 table, there is only one cell below and to the right of the upper left-hand cell which can contain concordant pairs and there is only one cell below and to the left of the upper right-hand cell which can hold discordant pairs. Therefore, for cases with less well educated parents, there are 6 concordant pairs (6×1) and 2 discordant pairs (1×2) whereas for those with better educated parents there are no concordant pairs (0×5) and 6 discordant pairs (3×2). Substituting these values into the formula for computing partial gamma, we see that partial gamma is -0.14:

$$\frac{(6-2)+(0-6)}{(6+2)+(0+6)} = \frac{-2}{14} = -0.14$$

Table 9.27 Contingency table of parental education, own education and self-esteem

				Own education	
				1	2
Parental education	1	Self-esteem	1	6	1
			2	2	1
	2	Self-esteem	1	0	3
			2	2	5

We can work out what zero-order gamma is for the association between own education and self-esteem by drawing up the contingency table as shown in Table 9.28. The number of concordant pairs is 36 (6 × 6) while the number of discordant pairs is 16 (4 × 4). Consequently, gamma is 0.38:

$$\frac{36 - 16}{36 + 16} = \frac{20}{52} = 0.38$$

In other words, the zero-order gamma of 0.38 between own education and self-esteem is reduced to −0.14 when parental education is taken into account.

The SPSS command for computing partial gamma is the **crosstabs** command which takes a slightly different form from that previously shown in that the variables are initially listed together with their minimum and maximum values:

crosstabs variables=first variable (minimum value,maximum value) second variable (minimum value,maximum value) third variable (minimum value,maximum value)
   /tables=first variable **by** second variable **by** third variable
   /statistics gamma.

So, we could use the following **crosstabs** command to compute partial gamma for the data in Table 9.25:

crosstabs variables=se(1,2) ce(1,2) pe(1,2)
   /tables=se by ce by pe
   /statistics gamma.

This command will produce two subtables of the kind shown in Table 9.27, gammas for those two subtables as well as the zero-order gamma and first-order partial gamma.

SUMMARY

The computation of tests of association for categorical and ordinal data is described in this chapter. Tests of association for categorical data can be

Table 9.28 Contingency table of own education and self-esteem

| | | Own education | |
		1	2
Self-esteem	1	6	4
	2	4	6

divided into those derived from chi-square (phi coefficient, contingency coefficient and Cramer's V) and those based on the proportional reduction in error (Goodman and Kruskal's lambda and tau). The phi coefficient is appropriate for two dichotomous variables where it can vary from 0 to +1. When one or both variables have more than two categories, the contingency coefficient may be preferable since it varies between 0 and less than +1 whereas phi may be greater than +1. To make the upper limit +1 for tables greater than 2 × 2, Cramer's V should be used. Goodman and Kruskal's lambda, which varies from 0 to +1, is the proportional increase in predicting one outcome of a categorical variable when knowing its combined outcome with a second categorical variable. Whereas lambda assumes that the same prediction is made for all cases in a particular row or column, Goodman and Kruskal's tau presumes that the predictions are randomly made on the basis of their proportions in row and column totals.

Tests of association for two ordinal variables, which count the number of cases higher (concordant) and lower (discordant) than the others, include Somer's d, Goodman and Kruskal's gamma, and Kendall's tau a, tau b and tau c. Kendall's tau a, which is the number of concordant pairs minus the number of discordant pairs over the total number of pairs, is used when there are no tied pairs and it can vary from −1 to +1. Tau b is employed when there are tied pairs and can vary from −1 to +1 if the table is square and if none of the row and column totals is zero. For a rectangular table tau c can come closer to ±1. Goodman and Kruskal's gamma, which is the number of concordant pairs minus the number of discordant pairs divided by the number of concordant and discordant pairs, can range from −1 to +1 and takes no account of ties or the size of the table. Somer's d provides an asymmetric as well as a symmetric measure of association and includes tied pairs. Spearman's rho ranges from −1 to +1 and is based on the squared difference between the ranks for the two variables. Mantel–Haenszel's chi-square is the squared Pearson's correlation coefficient multiplied by the number of cases minus 1. Partial gamma and Kendall's partial rank correlation coefficent are tests of partial association for ordinal data which partial out a third variable.

EXERCISES

1   Students reading an arts, social science or natural science subject were asked whether they supported an increase in direct taxation. The numbers in favour, against and undecided are shown in Table 9.29. Calculate the association between the students' area of study and their opinion on this issue using the following tests:
    (a) Phi coefficient
    (b) Contingency coefficient
    (c) Cramer's V

Table 9.29 Opinion on increase in direct taxation of arts, social science and
natural science students

	Yes	No	Undecided
Arts	45	15	9
Social science	77	13	11
Natural science	69	27	3

    (d) Goodman and Kruskal's asymmetric lambda with opinion as the
dependent variable

    (e) Goodman and Kruskal's asymmetric tau with opinion as the
dependent variable

2   Calculate the association between educational interest at 12 and at 15
for the data in Table 6.18 using the following tests:

    (a) Kendall's tau b

    (b) Kendall's tau c

    (c) Goodman and Kruskal's gamma

    (d) Somer's asymmetric d with educational interest at 15 as the
dependent variable

    (e) Spearman's rho

    (f) Kendall's partial rank correlation coefficient controlling for edu-
cational interest at 9

    (g) Partial gamma controlling for educational interest at 9

Chapter 10

Tests of association for interval/ratio data

This chapter describes the Pearson's product moment correlation which assesses the strength, direction and probability of the linear association between two interval or ratio variables. Tests for determining whether Pearson's correlations differ for variables which come from the same or different samples are also discussed. We would use these tests to find out, for example, whether the correlation between educational attainment at ages 9 and 12 is similar to that between educational attainment at 12 and 15 for the same group of pupils, or whether the correlation between self-esteem and educational attainment is similar for girls and boys. In addition, Pearson's partial correlation which covaries out the effects of one or more variables which may be related to the two variables of interest is covered, as is eta which provides an index of the non-linear association between an interval/ratio variable and a categorical/ordinal one.

PEARSON'S PRODUCT MOMENT CORRELATION OR r

Pearson's product moment correlation or r is a measure of the linear association between two interval or ratio variables and varies between -1 and $+1$. One way of conceptualising Pearson's correlation is to think of it as the ratio of the variance shared by two variables compared with the overall variance of the two variables. If the shared variance is high, then this variance will be similar to the overall variance and so the correlation will come close to -1 or $+1$. If there is no shared variance (i.e. zero shared variance), then the correlation will be zero. Variance is based on the extent to which scores differ from the mean. If high scores on one variable are associated with high scores on the other variable, then the differences will be in the same direction. A positive difference on one variable will tend to go together with a positive difference on the other variable. Similarly, a negative difference on one variable will tend to be associated with a negative difference on the other. If we multiply these differences, then the product of the differences will largely be positive in direction since a negative value multiplied by another negative value gives a positive value (e.g. $-2 \times -3 = 6$). On the other hand, if high scores on one variable are associated with low scores on the other variable, then a positive difference is likely to go together with a negative difference. If we multiply these differences, then the product of the differences will predominantly be negative since a positive value multiplied by a negative value forms a negative value (e.g. $2 \times -3 = -6$).

One formula for computing Pearson's r is the covariance of the two variables divided by the square root of the product of the separate variances of those variables:

$$r = \frac{\text{covariance of variables } A \text{ and } B}{\sqrt{(\text{variance of variable } A) \times (\text{variance of variable } B)}}$$

Covariance is the sum of products of the deviation of the score of one variable (A) from its mean multiplied by the deviation of the corresponding score of the other variable (B) for all pairs of scores, which is then divided by the number of cases or pairs minus 1:

$$\text{covariance} = \frac{\text{sum } [(\text{mean } A - \text{each } A \text{ score}) \times (\text{mean } B - \text{each } B \text{ score})]}{\text{no. of cases} - 1}$$

Variance is the sum of squares of the deviation of each score from its mean, which is then divided by the total number of cases minus 1:

$$\text{variance} = \frac{\text{sum } (\text{mean} - \text{each score})^2}{\text{no. of cases} - 1}$$

We will demonstrate the computation of Pearson's r with the data in Table 9.9 which have been reproduced in Table 10.1. Table 10.1 shows the sum (15 and 15) and mean score (3 and 3) for the two variables (A and B), the difference of each score from their respective means (D_A and D_B), the squares (D_A^2 and D_B^2) and sum of squares of these differences (10 and

Table 10.1 Data and initial computations for Pearson's correlation showing a strong positive relationship

	A	B	D_A	D_A^2	D_B	D_B^2	D_{AB}
	1	2	2	4	1	1	2
	2	1	1	1	2	4	2
	3	3	0	0	0	0	0
	4	4	−1	1	−1	1	1
	5	5	−2	4	−2	4	4
Sum	15	15		10		10	9
Mean	3	3					

10), and the cross-product of these differences for the two variables (D_{AB}) and its sum (9). The variances of A and B are the same, 2.5 $(10/(5 - 1) = 2.5)$, while the covariance is 2.25 $(9/(5 - 1) = 2.25)$. Consequently, Pearson's r is 0.9 $(2.25/\sqrt{(2.5 \times 2.5)} = 0.9)$. We look up the statistical significance of this correlation in the table in Appendix 19 where the degrees of freedom is the number of cases minus 2. With 3 degrees of freedom the correlation would have to be 0.8783 or bigger to be significant at the 0.05 two-tailed level, which it is. Consequently, we could conclude that there is a statistically significant positive correlation between the two variables.

The percentage of variation that is shared between two variables can be calculated by squaring Pearson's r to give what is known as the *coefficient of determination*. So, the percentage of shared variation represented by a correlation of 0.9 is 81. It should be noted that the amount of shared variation is not a direct function of the size of a correlation since, for example, although a correlation of 0.4 is twice the size of a correlation of 0.2, the amount of shared variation denoted by a correlation of 0.4 (16 per cent) is four times that of a correlation of 0.2 (4 per cent). The size of a correlation is usually described verbally in terms of its amount of shared variation so that correlations in the range 0.1–0.3 (reflecting 1–9 per cent of shared variation) are often described as small, weak or low; correlations in the range 0.4–0.6 (16–36 per cent) as moderate or modest; and correlations in the range 0.7–0.9 (49–81 per cent) as large, strong or high.

One SPSS command for computing Pearson's r is **crosstabs** where the keyword **corr** is added to the **statistics** subcommand:

crosstabs table=variable **by** variable
   /**statistics**=**corr.**

The output for this command for our example is shown in Table 10.2. The value of Pearson's r is the same as that of Spearman's rho since Spearman's rho is a Pearson's r for ranked data with no ties.

Another SPSS command for computing Pearson's r is the **correlation** command:

correlation variable names.

Table 10.2 **Crosstabs** output of Pearson's correlation

Statistic	Value	ASE1	T-value	Approximate Significance
Pearson's R	.90000	.05431	3.57624	.03739
Spearman Correlation	.90000	.16432	3.57624	.03739

When the **statistics** subcommand is added with a **1** on it the means, standard deviations and number of cases for these variables will be displayed. When a **2** is included on it the sum of the cross-product differences and covariance are presented. When the **options** subcommand is included with a **5** on it the number of cases for each correlation will be shown together with its one-tailed probability level.

So, to produce these statistics for our example the **correlation** command is

correlation a b
/options 5
/statistics 1 2.

The output for this command is presented in Table 10.3. The sum of the cross-product differences (**Cross-Prod Dev**) is **9.000** and the covariance (**Variance-Covar**) is **2.2500**, as we have calculated previously. We can work out the correlation by dividing the covariance by the product of the standard deviation of the two variables:

$$r = \frac{\text{covariance}}{\text{std dev of } A \times \text{std dev of } B}$$

If we do this, r is **.90000** $(2.2500/[\sqrt{(1.5811)} \times \sqrt{(1.5811)}] = 0.895)$. The correlations are printed in the form of a square matrix where the leading diagonal consists of the correlation of the variable with itself and the information in the left triangle (which in this case is a single correlation) is the same as that in the right triangle.

Table 10.3 **Correlations** output of Pearson's correlation

Variable	Cases	Mean	Std Dev
A	5	3.0000	1.5811
B	5	3.0000	1.5811

Variables	Cases	Cross-Prod Dev	Variance-Covar
A B	5	9.0000	2.2500

Correlations:	A	B
A	1.0000	.9000
	(5)	(5)
	P= .	P= .019
B	.9000	1.0000
	(5)	(5)
	P= .019	P= .

(Coefficient / (Cases) / 1-tailed Significance)
" . " is printed if a coefficient cannot be computed

Pearson's *r* is a measure of linear association in that it assesses the extent to which higher scores on one variable are related to higher scores on another variable. However, if there is a *curvilinear* relationship between the two variables such that up to a certain point the higher scores on one variable are associated with higher scores on the other variable but after that point the higher scores are associated with lower scores, then *r* may be zero. A possible example of such a curvilinear relationship may be the relationship between being popular and being talkative. People who talk too little or too much may be more unpopular than those who are reasonably talkative.

The most convenient way of determining whether there is a curvilinear relationship between two variables is to plot the position of the two variables on a graph as shown in Figure 10.1. Such a diagram is known as a *scatterplot* or *scattergram*. The scatter of the points in this plot or diagram takes the shape of an inverted-U curve. The data for this graph are taken from Table 10.4 which presents the talkativeness and popularity scores for seven cases. The popularity scores are plotted along the vertical axis or *ordinate* while the talkativeness scores are arranged along the horizontal axis or *abscissa*. The point on the graph of the talkativeness and popularity scores for the first case is where the horizontal line drawn from 1 on the vertical axis intersects with the vertical line drawn from 1 on the horizontal axis. The two scores for each of the seven cases are plotted in this way.

The simplest SPSS command for producing a scatterplot is the **plot** command with the **plot** subcommand specifying which variable is to be placed on the vertical axis and which variable on the horizontal axis:

plot
/**plot** vertical axis variable **with** horizontal axis variable.

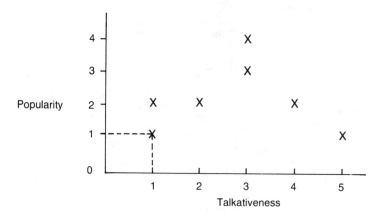

Figure 10.1 A scatterplot of talkativeness and popularity

Table 10.4 Talkativeness and popularity scores

Cases	Talkativeness	Popularity
1	1	1
2	1	2
3	2	2
4	3	3
5	3	4
6	4	2
7	5	1

The scatterplot shown in Figure 10.2 could be produced by the following SPSS commands:

```
data list/ p 1 t 3.
begin data.
1 1
1 2
2 2
3 3
3 4
4 2
5 1
end data.
plot
  /plot p with t.
```

The number of cases for the intersection of a particular pair of scores is displayed in the scatterplot. In this example there is only one case for each unique pair of scores.

The form of the scatterplot can be modified by adding various sub-commands. For example, the points on the scatterplot representing cases can be changed from frequencies to an asterisk by incorporating a **symbols** **'*'** subcommand. The variable name **p** on the vertical axis can be written as **popularity** by having a **vertical 'popularity'** subcommand. Similarly, the variable label **t** on the horizontal axis can be expanded to **talkativeness** by including a **horizontal 'talkativeness'** subcommand. If the minimum value of zero is specified on this subcommand with **min(0)** then the observed minimum of 1 is replaced with 0. If a maximum value of 6 is included with **max(6)**, then whole number values will be indicated on the horizontal axis. A full title for the scatterplot can be given with the subcommand **title 'Plot of popularity with talkativeness'**. With these additions, the **plot** command is as follows:

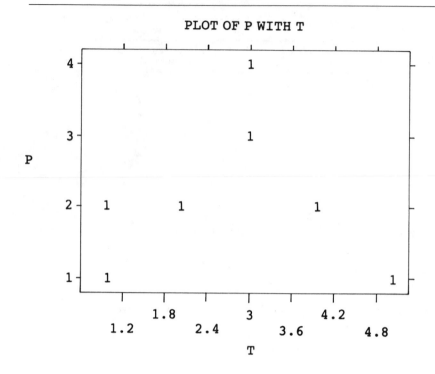

Figure 10.2 Basic **plot** output of a scatterplot

plot
 /**symbols '*'**
 /**vertical 'popularity'**
 /**horizontal 'talkativeness' min(0) max(6)**
 /**title 'Plot of popularity with talkativeness'**
 /**plot p with t.**

The output for this command is shown in Figure 10.3.

As can be seen from the calculations shown in Table 10.5, Pearson's *r* for these data on talkativeness and popularity is about 0.06. When the relationship between two variables is curvilinear, a more appropriate measure of the relationship is *eta* which is described at the end of this chapter.

The size of Pearson's *r* is affected by the variance of one or both variables as well as the presence of extreme scores or *outliers* which will affect the variance. Take, for example, the data in Table 10.6 which could represent the respective listening and popularity scores of seven cases. Pearson's *r* between these two variables is about 0.9 as shown in the calculations in Table 10.7. In other words, there is a strong positive

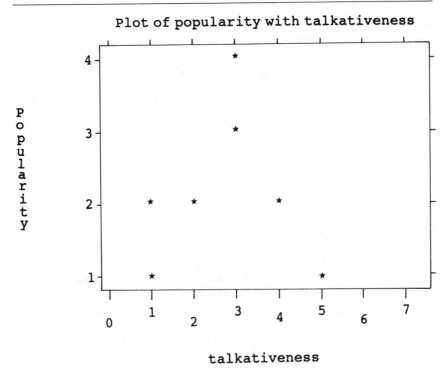

Figure 10.3 Scatterplot produced with additional **plot** subcommands

Table 10.5 Data and initial computations for Pearson's correlation showing a
curvilinear relationship

	T	P	D_T	D_T^2	D_P	D_P^2	D_{TP}
	1	1	1.7	2.9	1.1	1.2	1.9
	1	2	1.7	2.9	0.1	0.0	0.2
	2	2	0.7	0.5	0.1	0.0	0.1
	3	3	−0.3	0.1	−0.9	0.8	0.3
	3	4	−0.3	0.1	−1.9	3.6	0.6
	4	2	−1.3	1.7	0.1	0.0	−0.1
	5	1	−2.3	5.3	1.1	1.2	−2.5
Sum	19	15		13.5		6.8	0.5
Mean	2.7	2.1					
Variance				2.3		1.1	
Covariance							0.1

Note $r = \dfrac{0.1}{2.3 \times 1.1} = \dfrac{0.1}{1.6} = 0.06$

Table 10.6 Listening and popularity scores of seven cases

Cases	Listening	Popularity
1	1	1
2	2	2
3	2	3
4	3	2
5	3	4
6	4	4
7	5	4

correlation between these two variables such that people who listen more are more popular.

Now, we will introduce an extreme score in these data by replacing the 2 of the fourth case by a 9. When we do this, the Pearson's *r* is reduced from 0.9 to 0.4 as can be seen from the calculations in Table 10.8. Note that outliers may increase as well as decrease the size of a correlation.

If we reduced the variance in the original data by excluding the first three cases who have low scores on both listening and popularity, Pearson's *r* between these two variables decreases from 0.9 to about 0.5 as shown in the calculations in Table 10.9.

TESTS OF DIFFERENCE FOR UNRELATED PEARSON'S CORRELATIONS

If we wanted to determine whether the size of a correlation differed between two unrelated samples we could carry out a z test where the difference between the two correlations converted into z correlations (z_1 and z_2) is divided by the the standard error of the difference between the transformed correlations of the two samples (N_1 and N_2):

$$z = \frac{z_1 - z_2}{\sqrt{[1/(N_1 - 3)] + [1/(N_2 - 3)]}}$$

Suppose, for example, we wished to find out whether the correlation of 0.45 between listening and popularity for a sample of 30 women was different from that of 0.30 for a sample of 40 men. Using the table in Appendix 20 we first convert these two correlations into their respective z correlations which are 0.485 and 0.310. Inserting the appropriate values into the above formula, z is 0.69:

$$\frac{0.485 - 0.310}{\sqrt{[1/(30 - 3)] + [1/(40 - 3)]}} = \frac{0.175}{0.253} = 0.69$$

Table 10.7 Computations for Pearson's correlation between listening and popularity

L	P	D_L	$D_L{}^2$	D_P	$D_P{}^2$	D_{LP}
1	1	1.9	3.6	1.9	3.6	3.6
2	2	0.9	0.8	0.9	0.8	0.8
2	3	0.9	0.8	−0.1	0.0	0.7
3	2	−0.1	0.0	0.9	0.8	−0.1
3	4	−0.1	0.0	−1.1	1.2	0.1
4	4	−1.1	1.2	−1.1	1.2	1.2
5	4	−2.1	4.4	−1.1	1.2	2.3
Sum 20	20		10.8		8.8	8.6
Mean 2.9	2.9					
Variance			1.8		1.5	
Covariance						1.4

Note: $r = \dfrac{1.4}{\sqrt{1.8 \times 1.5}} = \dfrac{1.4}{1.6} = 0.9$

Table 10.8 Computations for Pearson's correlation between listening and popularity with one extreme score

L	P	D_L	$D_L{}^2$	D_P	$D_P{}^2$	D_{LP}
1	1	1.9	3.6	2.9	8.4	5.5
2	2	0.9	0.8	1.9	3.6	1.7
2	3	0.9	0.8	0.9	0.8	0.8
3	9	−0.1	0.0	−5.1	26.0	0.5
3	4	−0.1	0.0	−0.1	0.0	0.0
4	4	−1.1	1.2	−0.1	0.0	0.0
5	4	−2.1	4.4	−0.1	0.0	0.2
Sum 20	27		10.8		38.8	8.7
Mean 2.9	3.9					
Variance			1.8		6.5	
Covariance						1.5

Note: $r = \dfrac{1.5}{\sqrt{1.8 \times 6.5}} = \dfrac{1.5}{3.4} = 0.4$

Table 10.9 Computations for Pearson's correlation between listening and
popularity with reduced variance

	L	P	D_L	D_L^2	D_P	D_P^2	D_{LP}
	3	2	0.8	0.6	1.5	2.3	1.2
	3	4	0.8	0.6	−0.5	0.3	−0.4
	4	4	−0.2	0.0	−0.5	0.3	0.1
	5	4	−1.2	1.4	−0.5	0.3	0.6
Sum	15	14		2.6		3.2	1.5
Mean	3.8	3.5					
Variance				0.9		1.1	
Covariance							0.5

Note: $r = \dfrac{0.5}{\sqrt{0.9 \times 1.1}} = \dfrac{0.5}{1.0} = 0.5$

Looking up the significance of this value in the table in Appendix 6, we see
that for z to be significant it would have to be 1.96 or more at the 0.05 two-
tailed level and 1.65 or more at the 0.05 one-tailed level which it is not.
Consequently, we would conclude that there was no significant difference
in the size of these two correlations. Note that it does not matter which way
round in the formula we put the two z correlations or the two sample sizes.

If we had a large number of such correlations to compare it might be
more convenient to write a few SPSS commands to do this for us. To save
us looking up the appropriate z correlations, we could compute these
ourselves using the following formula:

$$z_r = 0.5 \times \log_e(1 + r) - 0.5 \times \log_e(1 - r)$$

Our command file for carrying out this z test on these data could be as
follows:

```
data list /no 1-2 r1 4-7 n1 9-11 r2 13-16 n2 18-20.
begin data.
 1 .45 30 .30 40
end data.
compute zr1=0.5 * ln(1+r1) - 0.5 * ln(1-r1).
compute zr2=0.5 * ln(1+r2) - 0.5 * ln(1-r2).
compute dif=zr1-zr2.
compute se=sqrt(1/(n1-3)+1/(n2-3)).
compute z=dif/se.
format r1 zr1 n1 r2 zr2 n2 dif se z (f5.3).
list.
```

We first list the variable names and column locations (**data list**). We then include the data (**begin ... end data**). We compute the two z correlations (**zr1** and **zr2**), the difference (**dif**) between them, the standard error of the difference (**se**) and the z value (**z**). If we want the numbers to be displayed to three decimal places we need to add the **format** command; otherwise only two decimal places will be shown. The output of the listing of these variables is presented below:

NO	R1	N1	R2	N2	ZR1	ZR2	DIF	SE	Z
1	.450	30.00	.300	40.00	.485	.310	.175	.253	.692

If we are not interested in the values of the difference between the two z correlations and the standard error of the difference, we could compute the z value with this single command:

compute z=(zr1-zr2)/sqrt(1/(n1-3)+1/(n2-3)).

A TEST OF DIFFERENCE FOR RELATED PEARSON'S CORRELATIONS WITH A SHARED VARIABLE

The tests for comparing the size of two correlations from related data are more complicated and depend on whether the two correlations include the same variable (Steiger 1980). One test for comparing two related correlations (r_{12} and r_{13}) which have a variable in common is Williams' modification of Hotelling's T_1 which is called T_2. The formula for T_2 is

$$(r_{12} - r_{13}) \times \sqrt{\frac{(N-1) \times (1 + r_{23})}{[2 \times (N-1)/(N-3) \times A] + [B^2 \times (1 - r_{23})^3]}}$$

where

$$A = (1 - r_{12}^2 - r_{13}^2 - r_{23}^2) + (2 \times r_{12} \times r_{13} \times r_{23})$$

and

$$B = 0.5 \times (r_{12} + r_{13})$$

Suppose that for a very small sample of seven cases we found that the correlation between parental education and children's self-esteem was 0.78 while that between children's education and children's self-esteem was 0.49. We wished to find out whether the correlation between parental education and children's self-esteem was significantly bigger than that between children's education and children's self-esteem. Since these two correlations were from the same sample of cases and had the variable of children's self-esteem in common we could use T_2 to determine whether the two correlations differed. To do this we would also need to know the correlation between parental education and children's education which was 0.85. Substituting the appropriate values in the above formula, we see that T_2 is 1.97:

$$A = (1 - 0.78^2 - 0.49^2 - 0.85^2) + (2 \times 0.78 \times 0.49 \times 0.85)$$
$$= (1 - 0.61 - 0.24 - 0.72) + 0.65 = 0.08$$

and

$$B = 0.5 \times (0.78 + 0.49) = 0.635$$

$$T_2 = (0.78 - 0.49) \times \sqrt{\frac{(7 - 1) \times (1 + 0.85)}{[2 \times (7 - 1)/(7 - 3) \times A] + [B^2 \times (1 - 0.85)^3]}}$$

$$= 0.29 \times \sqrt{\frac{11.10}{(3 \times 0.08) + (0.40 \times 0.003)}} = 0.29 \times \sqrt{\frac{11.10}{0.24 + 0.001}}$$

$$= 0.29 \times \sqrt{\frac{11.10}{0.24}} = 0.29 \times 6.80 = 1.97$$

We look up the value of T_2, whose degrees of freedom is the number of cases minus 3, in the table in Appendix 15. With 4 degrees of freedom, t would have to be 2.132 or larger to be significant at the 0.05 one-tailed level which it is not. Thus, we would conclude that the correlation between parental education and children's self-esteem was not significantly more positive than that between children's education and children's self-esteem.

The following SPSS commands could be employed to compute T_2:

```
data list/ no 1-2 n 4-6 r12 8-11 r13 13-16 r23 18-21.
begin data.
 1 7 .78 .49 .85
end data.
compute a=(1-r12**2-r13**2-r23**2)+(2*r12*r13*r23).
compute b=0.5*(r12+r13).
compute num=(n-1)*(1+r23).
compute den=2*(n-1)/(n-3)*a+b**2*((1-r23)**3).
compute t2=(r12-r13)*sqrt(num/den).
format r12 r13 r23 (f3.2).
list.
```

The relevant output for these commands is shown below:

NO	N	R12	R13	R23	A	B	NUM	DEN	T2
1	7	.78	.49	.85	.08	.64	11.10	.24	1.98

A TEST OF DIFFERENCE FOR RELATED PEARSON'S CORRELATIONS WITH NO SHARED VARIABLE

A test for comparing two correlations from the same sample which have no variable in common is Z_2^*, which has the following formula:

$$\sqrt{N-3} \times (z_{r12} - z_{r34}) \times 1/\sqrt{2 - (2 \times A/B)}$$

where

$$A = 0.5 \times (\{[r_{13} - (r_{12} \times r_{23})] \times [r_{24} - (r_{23} \times r_{34})]\} + \\ \{[r_{14} - (r_{13} \times r_{34})] \times [r_{23} - (r_{12} \times r_{13})]\} + \\ \{[r_{13} - (r_{14} \times r_{34})] \times [r_{24} - (r_{12} \times r_{14})]\} + \\ \{[r_{14} - (r_{12} \times r_{24})] \times [r_{23} - (r_{24} \times r_{34})]\})$$

and

$$B = (1 - r_{12}^2) \times (1 - r_{34}^2)$$

Imagine that we wanted to find out whether the correlation between self-esteem and educational attainment at 9 years of age differed from that at 15 for the same group of 10 individuals where the correlation at 9 and 15 was 0.3 (r_{12}) and 0.4 (r_{34}) respectively. In order to conduct a Z_2^* test we would also need to know the four other correlations between the four variables. We shall say that the (test–retest) correlation between 9 and 15 for both these measures is 0.6 for self-esteem (r_{13}) and 0.8 for educational attainment (r_{24}). The (cross-lagged) correlation between self-esteem at 9 and educational attainment at 15 is 0.1 (r_{14}) and that between educational attainment at 9 and self-esteem at 15 is 0.2 (r_{23}). All six correlations for this example are shown in Figure 10.4. Placing the appropriate values in the formula we find that Z_2^* is −0.32:

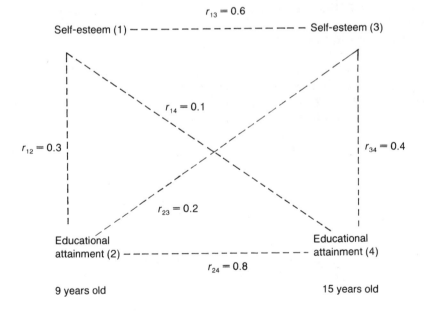

Figure 10.4 Correlations between four variables

$$A = 0.5 \times \left(\{[0.6 - (0.3 \times 0.2)] \times [0.8 - (0.2 \times 0.4)]\} \right.$$
$$+ \{[0.1 - (0.6 \times 0.4)] \times [0.2 - (0.3 \times 0.6)]\}$$
$$+ \{[0.6 - (0.1 \times 0.4)] \times [0.8 - (0.3 \times 0.1)]\}$$
$$\left. + \{[0.1 - (0.3 \times 0.8)] \times [0.2 - (0.8 \times 0.4)]\} \right)$$
$$= 0.5 \times [(0.54 \times 0.72) + (-0.14 \times 0.02)$$
$$+ (0.56 \times 0.77) + (-0.14 \times -0.12)]$$
$$= 0.5 \times [0.39 + -0.003 + 0.43 + 0.02]$$
$$= 0.5 \times 0.84$$
$$= 0.42$$

and

$$B = (1 - 0.30^2) \times (1 - 0.40^2) = 0.91 \times 0.84 = 0.76$$

$$Z_2{}^* = \sqrt{10 - 3} \times (0.310 - 0.424) \times 1/\sqrt{2 - (2 \times 0.42/0.76)}$$
$$= 2.65 \times -0.114 \times 1/\sqrt{2 - 1.11} = -0.30 \times 1.06 = -0.318$$

We look up this value in the table in Appendix 6 where we see that to be significant a z value would have to be ($\pm$) 1.96 or more at the 0.05 two-tailed level and ($\pm$) 1.65 or more at the 0.05 one-tailed level which it is not. Consequently, we would conclude that there was no significant difference in the size of these two correlations. Note that it does not matter which way round we put the two z correlations.

The following SPSS commands could be employed to compute $Z_2{}^*$:

data list /no 1-2 n 4-6 r12 8-11 r34 13-16 r13 18-21
r24 23-26 r14 28-31 r23 33-36.
begin data.
 1 10 .30 .40 .60 .80 .10 .20
end data.
compute zr12=0.5*ln(1+r12)-0.5*ln(1-r12).
compute zr34=0.5*ln(1+r34)-0.5*ln(1-r34).
compute a=0.5*((r13-r12*r23)*(r24-r23*r34)+
          (r14-r13*r34)*(r23-r12*r13)+
          (r13-r14*r34)*(r24-r12*r14)+
          (r14-r12*r24)*(r23-r24*r34)).
compute b=(1-r12**2)*(1-r34**2).
compute z2=sqrt(n-3)*(zr12-zr34)*(1/(sqrt(2-2*a/b))).
format r12 r34 r13 r24 r14 r23 (f3.2) zr12 zr34 a b (f5.3) z2 (f7.3).
list.

The relevant output for these commands is shown below:

NO	N	R12	R34	R13	R24	R14	R23	ZR12	ZR34	A	B	Z2
1	10	.30	.40	.60	.80	.10	.20	.310	.424	.417	.764	−.317

AVERAGING PEARSON'S CORRELATIONS

To find the average of a number of Pearson's correlations, we need (1) to convert them into z correlations; (2) to weight each one of them by multiplying the z correlation by the number of cases in that sample minus 3; (3) to sum the results and divide by the sum of, for each sample, the number of cases minus 3; and (4) to convert this average z into an average r. We would use this procedure if we wanted to report, for instance, the average correlation between self-esteem and educational attainment for a number of samples. An example of this procedure is shown in Table 10.10 where the average r for the three samples is 0.27. As you can see from the table in Appendix 20, r correlations are very similar in size to z_r correlations when they are small. For example, an r of 0.300 is equal to a z_r of 0.310. Consequently, when r correlations are small and when the number of cases is similar in the different samples, simply summing the r correlations and dividing by the number of samples will provide a very close approximation to the more involved procedure. For instance, the simple procedure for our example will give an average r of 0.263 compared with an average r of 0.270 using the more complicated method.

PEARSON'S PARTIAL CORRELATION

To remove the influence of one or more variables from a Pearson's correlation (r_{12}) between the two main variables of interest, we calculate the Pearson's partial correlation. For a first-order partial correlation ($r_{12.3}$) the following formula is used:

$$r_{12.3} = \frac{r_{12} - (r_{13} \times r_{23})}{\sqrt{(1 - r_{13}^2) \times (1 - r_{23}^2)}}$$

To calculate a second-order partial correlation ($r_{12.34}$), which involves controlling two variables, the same general formula holds except that the zero-order correlations are replaced with first-order correlations:

Table 10.10 Computations for averaging Pearson's correlations

Sample	N	N − 3	r	z_r	$z_r \times (N-3)$
1	41	38	0.25	0.255	9.690
2	53	50	0.31	0.321	16.050
3	37	34	0.23	0.234	7.956
Sum		122			33.696

Notes: Average z_r = 33.696/122 = 0.276; average r = 0.270

$$r_{12.34} = \frac{r_{12.3} - (r_{14.3} \times r_{24.3})}{\sqrt{(1 - r^2_{14.3}) \times (1 - r^2_{24.3})}}$$

Similarly, third-order partial correlations are based on second-order partial correlations and so on.

Suppose we wished to calculate the second-order partial correlation between self-esteem and educational attainment controlling for the two variables of parental education and parental acceptance which we knew to be positively related to these two variables. The correlations between these four variables are presented in Table 10.11 while the raw data on which they are based are shown in Table 10.12. We would initially have to calculate the first-order partial correlations between self-esteem and educational attainment partialling out each of these control variables. We will demonstrate the calculation of this first-order partial correlation controlling for parental acceptance. Inserting the appropriate correlations into the formula, we see that this partial correlation is 0.35:

$$r_{12.3} = \frac{0.48 - (0.65 \times 0.36)}{\sqrt{(1 - 0.65^2) \times (1 - 0.36^2)}}$$

Table 10.11 Correlations between parental acceptance, parental education, educational attainment and self-esteem

	Parental acceptance	Parental education	Educational attainment
Parental education	0.15		
Educational attainment	0.36	0.87	
Self-esteem	0.65	0.11	0.48

Table 10.12 Scores for parental acceptance, parental education, educational attainment and self-esteem

Case no.	Parental acceptance	Parental education	Educational attainment	Self-esteem
1	3	1	1	3
2	1	3	2	1
3	3	1	1	3
4	4	3	2	2
5	2	5	4	3
6	5	4	3	3
7	5	4	5	4

$$= \frac{0.48 - 0.23}{\sqrt{0.58 \times 0.87}}$$

$$= \frac{0.25}{0.71} = 0.35$$

The correlation between self-esteem and educational attainment is reduced from 0.48 to 0.35 when we control for parental acceptance.

In order to calculate this second-order partial correlation we also need to compute the first-order partial correlation of self-esteem and parental education controlling for parental acceptance and that of educational attainment and parental education controlling for parental acceptance. The partial correlation of self-esteem and parental education controlling for parental acceptance is 0.01:

$$r_{14.3} = \frac{0.11 - (0.65 \times 0.15)}{\sqrt{(1 - 0.65^2) \times (1 - 0.15^2)}}$$

$$= \frac{0.11 - 0.10}{\sqrt{0.58 \times 0.98}}$$

$$= \frac{0.01}{0.75} = 0.01$$

The partial correlation of educational attainment and parental education controlling for parental acceptance is 0.89:

$$r_{24.3} = \frac{0.87 - (0.36 \times 0.15)}{\sqrt{(1 - 0.36^2) \times (1 - 0.15^2)}}$$

$$= \frac{0.87 - 0.05}{\sqrt{0.87 \times 0.98}}$$

$$= \frac{0.82}{0.92} = 0.89$$

The second-order partial correlation between self-esteem and educational attainment covarying out parental education and parental acceptance is 0.74:

$$r_{12.34} = \frac{0.35 - (0.01 \times 0.89)}{\sqrt{(1 - 0.01^2) \times (1 - 0.89^2)}}$$

$$= \frac{0.35 - 0.01}{\sqrt{1.00 \times 0.21}}$$

$$= \frac{0.34}{0.46} = 0.74$$

In other words, the correlation between self-esteem and educational attainment increases from 0.48 to 0.74 when both parental education and parental acceptance are controlled.

The PC version of SPSS does not have a direct command for carrying out Pearson's partial correlation. However, partial correlations can be produced with the **regression** command. The way this can be done will be outlined here although regression itself will not be described until the next chapter. Where the original data are unavailable it is necessary to provide with the **data list** command a data matrix containing the means, standard deviations, correlations and number of cases. The appropriate command and information for our example are shown below:

data list matrix /pa 1-4 pe 7-10 ea 13-16 se 19-2.
begin data.
3.29 3.00 2.57 2.71
1.50 1.53 1.51 0.95
1.00 0.15 0.36 0.65
0.15 1.00 0.87 0.11
0.36 0.87 1.00 0.48
0.65 0.11 0.48 1.00
7
end data.

The first line of the data matrix contains the means of the four variables **pa** (parental acceptance), **pe** (parental education), **ea** (educational attainment) and **se** (self-esteem) respectively, while the second line lists their standard deviations. The next four lines include the correlation matrix while the seventh line of the matrix states the number of cases in the sample.

The appropriate **regression** command for reading this matrix and providing the first-order partial correlation between self-esteem and educational attainment controlling for parental acceptance is presented below:

regression variables=pa pe ea se
 /read mean stddev corr n
 /statistics zpp
 /dep se
 /enter pa ea.

All the variable names of the data matrix need to be listed initially for the matrix to be processed by the **read** subcommand. The **statistics** subcommand requests only that the zero-order, part and partial correlations (**zpp**) are displayed. The dependent variable (**dep**) can be either self-esteem or educational attainment. The last subcommand specifies the order in which the other two variables are to be entered (**enter**). The variables that are to be partialled out have to be listed before the other main variable. Since we want to partial out parental acceptance we need to add this variable before that of educational attainment. If we wished to partial out both parental acceptance and parental education we would include both these variables before educational attainment (i.e. **enter pa pe ea**).

The relevant output for this command is presented in Table 10.13 where the first-order partial correlation between self-esteem (**SE**) and educational attainment (**EA**) controlling for parental acceptance (**PA**) is shown as **.346976** (i.e. about 0.35).

The relevant output for the second-order partial correlation between self-esteem and educational attainment controlling for both parental acceptance and parental education is presented in Table 10.14 where it is calculated to be **.712713** (i.e. about 0.71) which is close to our value of 0.74.

Since the PC version of SPSS does not have a specific command for producing partial correlations, the mainframe version of doing this will be illustrated together with examples of the relevant output. Where the raw data are unavailable, a **matrix data** command is required. The appropriate command and information for our example are as follows:

matrix data variables=rowtype_ pa pe ea se
begin data
n 7 7 7 7

Table 10.13 **Regression** output of a first-order partial correlation

* * * * MULTIPLE REGRESSION * * * *			
Equation Number 1		**Dependent Variable ..**	**SE**
Variable(s) Entered on Step Number			
1 ..	EA		
2 ..	PA		
– – – – – Variables in the Equation – – – – –			
Variable	**Correl**	**Part Cor**	**Partial**
EA	.480000	.263679	.346976
PA	.650000	.511495	.583054

Table 10.14 **Regression** output of a second-order partial correlation

******MULTIPLE REGRESSION******

Equation Number 1   **Dependent Variable ..   SE**

Variable(s) Entered on Step Number
  1..   EA
  2..   PA
  3..   PE

       – – – – – Variables in the Equation – – – – –

Variable	Correl	Part Cor	Partial
EA	.480000	.541540	.712713
PA	.650000	.310342	.503185
PE	.110000	–.473180	–.663904

corr 1
corr   .15 1
corr   .36   .87 1
corr   .65   .11   .48 1
end data

The mainframe SPSS command for computing partial correlations is called **partial corr** and takes the following general form:

partial corr variables=variables **by** control variables (order of partial correlation)

The following **matrix** subcommand is added if the data are to be read from a matrix:

  /matrix=in(*)

So to compute the first-order partial correlation between self-esteem and educational attainment controlling for parental acceptance we could use the following **partial corr** command:

partial corr variables=se ea by pa(1)
  /matrix=in(*)

A **1** is inserted in parenthesis to indicate that we want a first-order partial correlation although in this situation there is no other alternative.

  To compute the second-order partial correlation between self-esteem and educational attainment controlling for both parental acceptance and parental education we could employ the following command:

partial corr variables=se ea by pa pe(2)
  /matrix=in(*)

Since we have not included a **1** in parenthesis no first-order partial correlations will be displayed.

If we were calculating the partial correlations from raw data and we wished to display the means, standard deviations and zero-order correlations as well we would add the following **statistics** subcommand:

/statistics corr descriptives

The relevant output for the first-order partial correlation is presented in Table 10.15 and for the second-order partial correlation in Table 10.16.

Table 10.15 **Partial corr** output of a first-order partial correlation

	– – – – PARTIAL CORRELATION COEFFICIENTS – – – –	
CONTROLLING FOR ..	**PA**	
	SE	**EA**
SE	1.0000	.3470
	(0)	(4)
	P = .	P = .250
EA	.3470	1.0000
	(4)	(0)
	P = .250	P = .

(COEFFICIENT / (D.F.) / SIGNIFICANCE)
(" . " IS PRINTED IF A COEFFICIENT CANNOT BE COMPUTED)

Table 10.16 **Partial corr** output of a second-order partial correlation

	– – – – PARTIAL CORRELATION COEFFICIENTS – – – –	
CONTROLLING FOR ..	**PA**	**PE**
	SE	**EA**
SE	1.0000	.7127
	(0)	(3)
	P = .	P = .088
EA	.7127	1.0000
	(3)	(0)
	P = .088	P = .

(COEFFICIENT / (D.F.) / SIGNIFICANCE)
(" . " IS PRINTED IF A COEFFICIENT CANNOT BE COMPUTED)

ETA

The eta coefficient provides a useful measure of the strength of the association between an interval/ratio variable (the dependent variable) and a categorical/ordinal variable (the independent variable) when this association is non-linear. Eta varies from 0 to +1 and eta squared indicates the percentage of the total variation in the dependent variable that can be accounted for by the independent variable. As we have seen in Chapter 7, eta squared is the between-groups sum of squares divided by the total sum of squares. In this section we will demonstrate how eta can be calculated for the data in Table 10.4 which represent a curvilinear relationship between talkativeness and popularity. As eta is an asymmetric measure we could compute eta with talkativeness as the dependent variable and popularity as the independent variable, or vice versa. In drawing a graph it is customary to place the independent variable along the horizontal axis and the dependent variable along the vertical axis. Note that the shape of the relationship between talkativeness and popularity would not be curvilinear if talkativeness was the dependent variable and popularity the independent variable. Consequently, we will compute eta with popularity as the dependent variable.

The data in Table 10.4 have been arranged in Table 10.17 such that the popularity scores have been grouped in terms of the talkativeness scores.

Step 1 Calculate the between-groups sum of squares by subtracting the grand mean from the group means, squaring the differences, multiplying the squared differences by the number of cases in each group and summing the products for all the groups.

The between-groups sum of squares for these data is 5.85:

$$[(1.5 - 2.1)^2 \times 2] + [(2.0 - 2.1)^2 \times 1] + [(3.5 - 2.1)^2 \times 2]$$
$$+ [(2.0 - 2.1)^2 \times 1] + [(1.0 - 2.1)^2 \times 1]$$
$$= 0.72 + 0.0 + 3.92 + 0.0 + 1.21$$
$$= 5.85$$

Step 2 Calculate the total sum of squares by subtracting each score from the grand mean, squaring them and summing them.

Table 10.17 Data and initial computations for eta

	1	2	Talkativeness 3	4	5		
	1	2	3	2	1		
	2		4				
Sum	3	2	7	2	1	Grand sum	15
Mean	1.5	2	3.5	2	1	Grand mean	2.1

The total sum of squares for these data is 6.8:

$$(2.1 - 1)^2 + (2.1 - 2)^2 + (2.1 - 2)^2 + (2.1 - 3)^2 + (2.1 - 4)^2$$
$$+ (2.1 - 2)^2 + (2.1 - 1)^2$$
$$= 1.2 + 0.0 + 0.0 + 0.8 + 3.6 + 0.0 + 1.2$$
$$= 6.8$$

Step 3   Divide the between-groups sum of squares by the total sum of squares and take the square root of the result to give eta. For this example, eta is 0.92 ($\sqrt{(5.85/6.8)} = 0.92$).

One SPSS command for computing eta is the **crosstabs** command with **eta** on the **statistics** subcommand:

crosstabs tables=variable name **by** variable name
  /**statistics eta.**

The output from this command for this example is presented in Table 10.18.

Another SPSS command for computing eta is the **anova** command with **1** on the **statistics** subcommand:

anova dependent variable name **by** independent variable name (value of first group,value of last group)
  /**statistics 1.**

The relevant output from this command for this example is displayed in Table 10.19.

SUMMARY

The computation of Pearson's product moment correlation and first- and second-order partial correlations is described together with the calculation of eta and tests for determining whether correlations from the same or different samples differ. Pearson's correlation assesses the strength, direction and probability of the linear association between two interval or ratio variables and varies from -1 to $+1$. It reflects the ratio of the variance shared by two variables compared with the overall variance of the two

Table 10.18 **Crosstabs** output of eta

Statistic		Value	ASE1	T-value	Approximate Significance
Eta:					
with T	dependent	.23820			
with P	dependent	.92421			

Table 10.19 **Anova** output of eta

*** ANALYSIS OF VARIANCE ***

P
BY T

Source of Variation	Sum of Squares	DF	Mean Square	F	Signif of F
Main Effects	5.857	4	1.464	2.929	.270
T	5.857	4	1.464	2.929	.270
Explained	5.857	4	1.464	2.929	.270
Residual	1.000	2	.500		
Total	6.857	6	1.143		

*** MULTIPLE CLASSIFICATION ANALYSIS ***

P
BY T

Grand Mean = 2.143

Variable + Category	N	Unadjusted Dev'n	Eta	Adjusted for Independents Dev'n	Beta	Adjusted for Independents + Covariates Dev'n	Beta
T							
1	2	−.64		−.64			
2	1	−.14		−.14			
3	2	1.36		1.36			
4	1	−.14		−.14			
5	1	−1.14		−1.14			
			.92		.92		

Multiple R Squared		.854
Multiple R		.924

variables. The percentage of variation shared by the two variables is the square of Pearson's correlation and is called the coefficient of determination. A correlation of close to zero may mean that the relationship between the two variables is curvilinear which can be checked with a scatterplot. The size of Pearson's correlation is affected by the variance of one or both variables as well as the presence of extreme scores which influence the variance. The z test determines whether the size of two correlations from different samples differs significantly. For correlations from the same sample, the T_2 test compares those having a variable in common while the Z_2^* test compares those having no variable in common. Eta measures the strength of a non-linear association between an interval/ratio variable and a categorical/ordinal variable and varies from 0 to +1.

Eta squared indicates the percentage of the total variation in the dependent variable explained by the independent variable.

EXERCISES

Use the data in Table 6.18 for the following exercises.

1 Calculate Pearson's correlation between educational interest at 12 and at 15.
   (a) What is the size of the correlation?
   (b) What are its degrees of freedom?
   (c) What is its two-tailed probability value?
   (d) Are educational interest at 12 and 15 significantly positively correlated?

2 Compare the size of the correlation between educational interest at 12 and 15 for single- and mixed-sex schools.
   (a) Which test would you use?
   (b) What is the correlation for single-sex schools?
   (c) What is the correlation for mixed-sex schools?
   (d) What is the value of this test?
   (e) What is its two-tailed probability value?
   (f) Do the two correlations differ significantly?

3 Compare the size of the correlation of educational interest at 12 and 15 with that at 9 and 12.
   (a) Which test would you use?
   (b) What is the correlation between educational interest at 9 and 12?
   (c) What is the value of this test?
   (d) What are its degrees of freedom?
   (e) What is its two-tailed probability value?
   (f) Do the two correlations differ significantly?

4 Compare the size of the correlation between socio-economic status and educational interest at 9 with that of educational interest at 12 and 15.
   (a) Which test would you use?
   (b) What is the correlation between socio-economic status and educational interest at 9?
   (c) What is the value of this test?
   (d) What is its probability value?
   (e) Do the two correlations differ significantly?

5 What is Pearson's correlation between educational interest at 12 and at 15 controlling for educational interest at 9?

6 What is the value of eta for socio-economic status and educational interest at 15?

Chapter 11

Bivariate and multiple regression

Regression analysis estimates or predicts the scores of one variable (called the *criterion* or the dependent variable) from one or more other variables (called *predictors* or independent variables). In order to predict the criterion, the criterion is related to or regressed onto the predictor(s). *Simple* or *bivariate* regression involves one predictor whereas *multiple* regression uses two or more predictors. One of the main purposes of multiple regression in the social sciences is not so much to predict the score of one variable from others but to determine the minimum number of a set of variables which are most strongly related to the criterion and to estimate the percentage of variation in the criterion explained by those variables. For example, we may be interested in finding out which variables are most strongly related to self-esteem and how much of the variation in self-esteem those variables explain. Generally, the variable which is most highly related to self-esteem is entered first into the regression equation followed by variables which are the next most strongly related to self-esteem once their relationship with the other variables is taken into account. If later variables are strongly associated with the variables already entered, then it is less likely that they will independently account for much more of the variation than those previously entered and so they are unlikely to be included as predictors. Although we will demonstrate the calculation of multiple regression with a few cases, this technique should only be used when a relatively large number of cases are available. Under these circumstances, multiple regression is a very valuable statistical procedure. We will begin by describing bivariate regression which just involves one predictor.

BIVARIATE REGRESSION

If we want to predict a score on a criterion from a score on another variable and we know that there is no association between the two variables, then our best guess is the mean of the criterion since this score is the closest to all other scores. If, on the other hand, the two variables are perfectly correlated, then we could predict the criterion perfectly. Indeed, the higher the correlation the more accurate our prediction could be. However, the correlation only tells us how much of the variation is shared by both variables. It does not by itself enable us to predict the actual score of the criterion from the score of the other variable. In order to do this we also need to know the way in which those scores are scaled. What linear regression does is to find the straight line that lies closest to the joint values of the two variables. Provided that there is variation on both variables, the closer the joint values are to the straight line the more accurately we can predict the scores of the criterion.

Linear regression is best explained in terms of the scatterplot of two variables where it is possible to draw the straight line that comes closest to the points on the graph. Take our earlier example of the leadership rankings of Judges A and B in Table 9.10 which have been re-presented in Table 11.1 and which we shall call scores. Previously we worked out that the Pearson's correlation between the scores of these two judges was 0.9. In other words, there is a near perfect association between these two sets of scores. Consequently, we should be able to predict the scores of one judge (say Judge A) from those of the other (Judge B) provided that we know the scales of the two sets of scores. The scatterplot of these two sets of scores is shown in Figure 11.1 where, as is usual, the vertical axis represents the criterion (Judge A) and the horizontal axis the predictor (Judge B).

The following equation is used to calculate where the line should be run through the points:

criterion predicted score = *intercept constant* (or *a*) + [*regression coefficient* (or *b*) × predictor score]

The formula for the regression coefficient (also known as *b* or the slope) is the sum of products of the deviation of the score of the criterion (*A*) from its mean multiplied by the deviation of the corresponding score of the predictor (*B*) for all pairs of scores, which is then divided by the sum of squares of the predictor:

$$b = \frac{\text{sum of products of the criterion and predictor}}{\text{sum of squares of the predictor}}$$

Table 11.1 Scores of two judges

Women	Judge A	Judge B
Ann	1	2
Mary	2	1
Jo	3	3
Sue	4	4
Jane	5	5

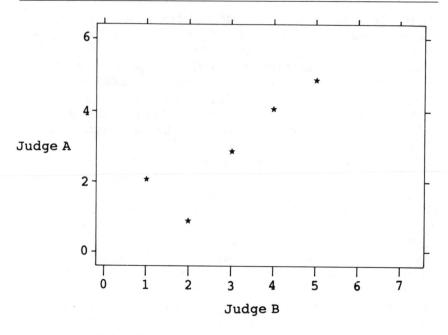

Figure 11.1 Scatterplot of scores of two judges

The intercept constant (or *a*) is the point where the regression line intercepts the vertical axis representing the criterion scores. Its formula is the predictor mean score multiplied by the regression coefficient which is then subtracted from the criterion mean score:

a = criterion mean − (regression coefficient × predictor mean)

The regression line runs from the intercept constant on the vertical axis through the point where the means of the predictor and criterion meet.

So to determine the regression line we first have to compute the regression coefficient. The steps involved in calculating this coefficient for our example are presented in Table 11.2. The means of the criterion (*A*) and the predictor (*B*) are first calculated, followed by the deviation of each score from its mean (D_A and D_B). Squaring (D_B^2) and summing the deviations of the predictor scores gives a sum of squares of 10, while multiplying the deviations of the criterion and predictor (D_{AB}) and summing them produces a sum of products of 9. Dividing the sum of products of the criterion and predictor by the sum of squares of the predictor produces a regression coefficient of 0.9 (9/10 = 0.9).

Once we have calculated the regression coefficient, we can work out the intercept constant which is 0.3 (3 − (0.9 × 3) = 0.3). We can then draw a regression line which stretches from the point on the vertical axis of 0.3

Table 11.2 Computations for a regression coefficient

	A	B	D_A	D_B	$D_B{}^2$	D_{AB}
	1	2	2	1	1	2
	2	1	1	2	4	2
	3	3	0	0	0	0
	4	4	−1	−1	1	1
	5	5	−2	−2	4	4
Sum	15	15			10	9
Mean	3	3				

Note: $b = \dfrac{9}{10} = 0.9$.

through the intersection of the means of the two variables as shown in Figure 11.2.

Knowing the regression coefficient and the intercept constant, we can use the regression equation to predict the value of the criterion from any value of the predictor. For example, using this information we would predict that if Judge B gave a score of 1 Judge A would give a score of 1.2 $(0.3 + (0.9 \times 1) = 1.2)$. Note that in the particular case where Judge B gave a score of 1, Judge A gave one of 2. In other words, there is a difference between the predicted score and the actual score of the criterion which in this case is 0.8 $(2 - 1.2 = 0.8)$. This difference is called a *residual.* Although this residual is positive, others will be negative. For example, a score by Judge B of 2 would lead to a predicted score of 2.1 $(0.3 + (0.9 \times 2) = 2.1)$ by Judge A although the actual score of Judge A is 1. In other words, the difference between the actual and the predicted score is −1.1 $(1 - 2.1 = -1.1)$. The actual criterion value is given by the following equation:

criterion value $= a + (b \times$ predictor value$) +$ residual

Therefore, if Judge B gives a score of 1, the score of Judge A is 2.0:

$0.3 + (0.9 \times 1) + 0.8 = 2.0$

Note that the regression coefficient or slope is the average amount of change in the criterion that is predicted by a change of one unit in the predictor. The slope of the line can be defined as the vertical distance divided by the horizontal distance between any two points on the line:

slope $= \dfrac{\text{vertical distance}}{\text{horizontal distance}}$

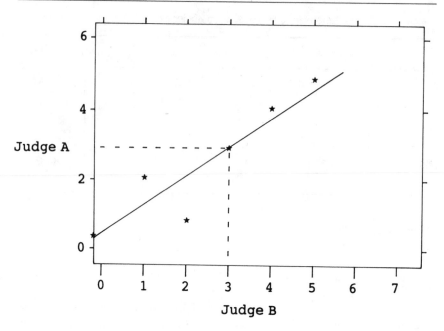

Figure 11.2 Regression line

Take the following two points on the regression line in Figure 11.2: (1) the point defined by 1 on the horizontal axis and 1.2 on the vertical axis; and (2) the point defined by 2 on the horizontal axis and 2.1 on the vertical axis. Dividing the vertical distance (2.1 − 1.2 = 0.9) by the horizontal distance (2 − 1 = 1) between these two points gives a slope or regression coefficient of 0.9 (0.9/1 = 0.9). In other words, the average amount of change in the scores of Judge A that is predicted by a change of one unit in the scores of Judge B is 0.9. Consequently, when the score of Judge B increases from 2 to 3, the predicted score of Judge A should increase from 2.1 to 3 (2.1 + 0.9 = 3).

The regression line is the straight line that is closest to the points on the scatterplot. If we simply added the residuals together, they would sum to zero since the sum of the negative differences equals the sum of the positive differences as shown in Table 11.3. Consequently, they are first squared and then summed to give the sum of squared residuals. Since the sum of squared residuals is the smallest it can be, the regression line is called the *least-squares line* or *line of best fit.*

A measure of the accuracy of prediction is the *standard error of estimate* which is the square root of the sum of squared residuals divided by the number of cases minus 2:

Table 11.3 Sum of residuals and residuals squared

Judge A scores

Actual	Predicted	Residuals	Residuals²
1	0.3 + (0.9 × 2) = 2.1	1 − 2.1 = −1.1	1.21
2	0.3 + (0.9 × 1) = 1.2	2 − 1.2 = 0.8	0.64
3	0.3 + (0.9 × 3) = 3.0	3 − 3.0 = 0.0	0.00
4	0.3 + (0.9 × 4) = 3.9	4 − 3.9 = 0.1	0.01
5	0.3 + (0.9 × 5) = 4.8	5 − 4.8 = 0.2	0.04
Sum		0.0	1.90

$$\text{standard error of estimate} = \sqrt{\frac{\text{sum of squared residuals}}{N-2}}$$

It is the standard deviation of the errors of prediction. It provides an estimate of the probability of a particular criterion score occurring in that 68 per cent of scores will lie within one standard deviation of the predicted score, 95 per cent within two standard deviations and 99 per cent within three standard deviations. The standard error of estimate of the scores of Judge A is about 0.8 ($\sqrt{[1.9/(5-2)]} = 0.79582$). For example, when the score of Judge B is 2, the predicted score for Judge A is calculated to be 2.1 using the regression equation. As the standard error of estimate of the scores of Judge A is about 0.8 there is a 68 per cent probability that the actual score of Judge A will fall within the range 2.1 ± 0.8 (i.e. 1.3 to 2.9), a 95 per cent probability that it will fall within 2.1 ± 1.6 (2 × 0.8 = 1.6) and a 99 per cent probability that it will fall within 2.1 ± 2.4 (3 × 0.8 = 2.4).

The *standard error of the regression coefficient* is the sum of squared residuals divided by the number of cases minus 2, which is then divided by the sum of squares of the predictor variable and the square root is taken of this result:

$$\text{standard error of } b = \sqrt{\frac{\text{sum of squared residuals}/(N-2)}{\text{sum of squares of predictor}}}$$

If the sample size is greater than 200, it gives an estimate of the probability of the regression coefficient occurring within one standard deviation of its value. For our example it is about 0.25:

$$\sqrt{\frac{1.90/(5-2)}{10}} = 0.25166$$

Consequently, the regression coefficient would have a 95 per cent probability of falling within the range $0.9 \pm (0.25 \times 1.96)$ if the sample was greater than 200. With smaller samples, the b estimates follow the t distribution with the degrees of freedom equal to the number of cases minus 2. According to the table in Appendix 15, the t value for 3 degrees of freedom is 3.182 at the 0.05 two-tailed level. Therefore, the regression coefficient has a 95 per cent probability of falling within the interval $0.9 \pm (0.25 \times 3.182)$.

The *standard error of the intercept* is (1) the sum of squared residuals divided by the number of cases minus 2, which is then (2) multiplied by 1 divided by the number of cases plus the square of the predictor mean divided by the predictor sum of squares, and (3) the square root is then taken of this result:

$$\text{standard error of } a = \sqrt{\frac{\text{sum of squared residuals}}{n-2} \times \left(\frac{1}{n} + \frac{\text{predictor mean squared}}{\text{predictor sum of squares}}\right)}$$

For our example it is about 0.83:

$$\sqrt{\frac{1.90}{5-2} \times \left(\frac{1}{5} + \frac{3^2}{10}\right)} = \sqrt{\frac{1.9}{3} \times (0.2 + 0.9)} = \sqrt{0.6966} = 0.8346$$

With samples greater than 200, the intercept would have a 95 per cent probability of falling within the range $0.3 \pm (0.83 \times 1.96)$. With smaller samples, the a estimates follow the t distribution with the degrees of freedom equal to the number of cases minus 2. According to the table in Appendix 15, the t value for 3 degrees of freedom is 3.182 at the 0.05 two-tailed level. Therefore, the intercept has a 95 per cent probability of falling within the interval $0.3 \pm (0.83 \times 3.182)$.

Note that in this example the regression coefficient is the same size as the correlation coefficient since the variance of the two variables is the same. If the variances differ, as is usually the case, the regression coefficient and the correlation coefficient will vary. The formula for the correlation coefficient is essentially the sum of products of the criterion and predictor divided by the square root of the product of the sum of squares of the criterion and the predictor:

$$r = \frac{\text{sum of products of criterion and predictor}}{\sqrt{\text{criterion sum of squares} \times \text{predictor sum of squares}}}$$

Consequently, if the sum of squares for both the criterion and the predictor is the same, then the denominator of this formula is the sum of squares of the predictor.

Notice also that when the variances of the two variables differ, the regression coefficient for predicting the scores of Judge B from those of

Judge A will not be the same as that for predicting the scores of Judge A from those of Judge B since the sum of squares in the denominator will differ. However, when the criterion and the predictor are standardised so that they both have a standard deviation of 1, the regression coefficient is standardised so that the *standardised* regression coefficient or *B* is the same for predicting the scores of Judge A from those of Judge B and for predicting the scores of Judge B from those of Judge A. The standardised regression coefficient is the same as Pearson's correlation and can be calculated by multiplying the unstandardised regression coefficient by the standard deviation of the predictor and dividing by the standard deviation of the criterion:

$$\text{standardised regression coefficient} = \text{unstandardised regression coefficient} \times \frac{\text{predictor std dev}}{\text{criterion std dev}}$$

Since the standard deviations for our two variables are the same, the standardised and unstandardised regression coefficients are the same (i.e. 0.9).

Regression analysis can be thought of in terms of analysis of variance where the total sum of squares for the criterion can be divided or partitioned into a sum of squares due to regression and a residual sum of squares which is left over:

$$\text{criterion total sum of squares} = \text{regression sum of squares} + \text{residual sum of squares}$$

The total sum of squares for the criterion can be calculated by subtracting the criterion mean score from each of its individual scores, squaring and summing them. If we do this for the scores of Judge A, the total sum of squares for Judge A is 10. The regression sum of squares is the sum of squared differences between the predicted criterion score and the mean criterion score:

$$\text{regression sum of squares} = \text{sum of (predicted criterion score} - \text{mean criterion score})^2$$

Alternatively, subtracting the residual sum of squares from the criterion total sum of squares gives the regression sum of squares:

$$\text{regression sum of squares} = \text{criterion total sum of squares} - \text{residual sum of squares}$$

Therefore, the regression sum of squares for our example is 8.1 (10 − 1.9 = 8.1).

The *squared multiple correlation* or R^2 is the proportion of the regression sum of squares over the criterion total sum of squares:

$$R^2 = \frac{\text{regression sum of squares}}{\text{criterion total sum of squares}}$$

It represents the proportion of variation in the criterion accounted for by the linear combination of the independent variables which in this case is only one variable. The squared multiple correlation for our example is 0.81 ($8.1/10 = 0.81$). In other words, 81 per cent of the variation in the scores of Judge A is explained by or shared with the scores of Judge B.

The *multiple correlation* or *R* is the square root of the squared multiple correlation:

$$R = \sqrt{(R^2)}$$

The multiple correlation for our example is 0.9 ($\sqrt{(0.81)} = 0.9$).

The statistical significance of the squared multiple correlation can be tested by computing the *F* ratio of the regression mean square to the residual mean square:

$$F = \frac{\text{regression mean square}}{\text{residual mean square}}$$

The regression mean square is the regression sum of squares divided by its degrees of freedom which is the number of predictors in the regression equation. The residual mean square is the residual sum of squares divided by its degrees of freedom which is the number of cases minus the number of predictors minus 1.

For our example the regression mean square is 8.1 ($8.1/1 = 8.1$) and the residual mean square is 0.6333 ($1.9/(5 - 1 - 1) = 0.63333$). Therefore, the *F* ratio is 12.79 ($8.1/0.6333 = 12.79$). With 1 and 3 degrees of freedom in the numerator and denominator respectively, the *F* ratio has to be 10.128 or larger to be significant at the 0.05 level, which it is. Consequently we would conclude that the squared multiple correlation between the scores of Judge A and Judge B is significantly positive.

An alternative method of computing the *F* ratio for the squared multiple correlation is multiplying the squared multiple correlation by the degrees of freedom for the residual sum of squares and dividing the result by the squared multiple correlation subtracted from 1 and multiplied by the degrees of freedom for the regression sum of squares:

$$F = \frac{R^2 \times (\text{no. of cases} - \text{no. of predictors} - 1)}{(1 - R^2) \times \text{no. of predictors}}$$

This *F* ratio for our example is 12.79:

$$\frac{0.81 \times (5 - 1 - 1)}{(1 - 0.81) \times 1} = \frac{0.81 \times 3}{0.19 \times 1} = \frac{2.43}{0.19} = 12.789$$

The degrees of freedom for this *F* ratio is the same as the previous one.

Bivariate regression can be carried out by SPSS with either the **plot** or the **regression** command. The basic **plot** command for producing a simple regression is as follows:

plot
  /format regression
  /plot criterion **with** predictor.

To analyse the data for our example, the following **plot** command was used:

plot
  /symbols '*'
  /horizontal 'Judge B' min(0) max(6)
  /vertical 'Judge A' min(0) max(6)
  /format regression
  /plot a with b.

The relevant output for this command is presented in Figure 11.3. The intercepts on each axis for the regression line are marked with the letter **R**. The statistics include Pearson's correlation (**.90000**), the correlation

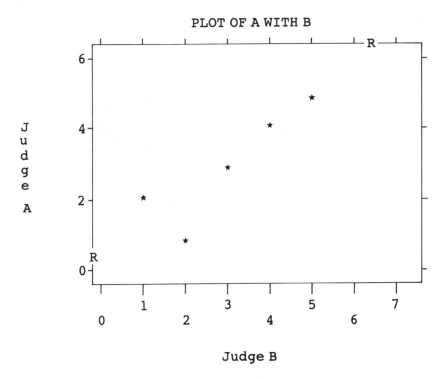

5 cases plotted. Regression statistics of A on B:

Correlation .90000 R Squared .81000 S.E. of Est .79582 Sig. .0374
Intercept (S.E.) .30000 (.83467) Slope (S.E.) .90000 (.25166)

Figure 11.3 **Plot** output of bivariate regression

squared (**R Squared .81000**), the standard error of estimate (**S. E. of Est .79582**), the two-tailed significance level of the correlation (**Sig. .0374**), the intercept (**.30000**), its standard error (**.83467**), the slope or unstandardised regression coefficient (**.90000**) and its standard error (**.25166**).

The basic **regression** command for computing a bivariate regression is

regression variables criterion predictor
 /**dep** criterion
 /**method enter** predictor.

Particular statistics can be requested with a **statistics** subcommand and the appropriate keywords while a standardised scatterplot will be produced with a **scatterplot** subcommand in which the names of the criterion and predictor are placed in parentheses.

The following **regression** command was run to analyse the data for our example:

regression variables a b
 /**statistics r anova coeff ci**
 /**dep a**
 /**method enter b**
 /**scatterplot (a,b).**

The keyword **r** includes the multiple correlation, the squared and adjusted multiple correlation and the standard error of estimate. These statistics are displayed in Table 11.4. Since there is only one predictor, the multiple correlation reflects a single predictor. The adjusted squared multiple correlation is a more conservative estimate of explained variance than the squared multiple correlation since it takes into account the size of the sample and the number of predictors in the equation. Its formula is

Table 11.4 **Regression** output with **r** keyword

---

* * * * MULTIPLE REGRESSION * * * *

Equation Number 1   **Dependent Variable ..**   **A**

Variable(s) Entered on Step Number
   1 ..   B

Multiple R	.90000
R Square	.81000
Adjusted R Square	.74667
Standard Error	.79582

F = 12.78947   **Signif F = .0374**

$$\text{adjusted } R^2 = R^2 - \frac{(1 - R^2) \times \text{no. of predictors}}{\text{no. of cases} - \text{no. of predictors} - 1}$$

Since there is only one predictor in this equation, the adjusted squared multiple correlation is about 0.75:

$$0.81 - \frac{(1 - 0.81) \times 1}{5 - 1 - 1} = 0.81 - \frac{0.19}{3} = 0.81 - 0.06333 = 0.74667$$

The keyword **anova** displays the regression and residual sum of squares and mean square, the F ratio and its probability. This output is presented in Table 11.5.

The keyword **coeff**, as shown in Table 11.6, produces the regression coefficient (**B**), the standard error of the regression coefficient (**SE B**), the standardised regression coefficient (**Beta**), the t value (**T**) and its two-tailed probability level (**Sig T**). Note that SPSS output refers to the unstandard-ised regression coefficient as **B** and the standardised regression coefficient as **Beta**. The t test, which is the unstandardised regression coefficient divided by its standard error, is **3.576 (.900000/.251661 = 3.5762)**. Its degrees of freedom are equal to those associated with the residual sum of squares. Using the table in Appendix 15, we see that with 3 degrees of freedom t has to be 3.182 or bigger to be significant at the 0.05 level, which it is.

The keyword **ci**, as displayed in Table 11.7, gives the 95 per cent confidence interval of the unstandardised regression coefficient.

Table 11.5 **Regression** output with **anova** keyword

Analysis of Variance

	DF	Sum of Squares	Mean Square
Regression	1	8.10000	8.10000
Residual	3	1.90000	.63333

F =	12.78947		Signif F =	.0374

Table 11.6 **Regression** output with **coeff** keyword

------------ Variables in the Equation ------------

Variable	B	SE B	Beta	T	Sig T
B	.900000	.251661	.900000	3.576	.0374
(Constant)	.300000	.834666		.359	.7431

Table 11.7 **Regression** output with **ci** keyword

	---- Variables in the Equation ----	
Variable	95% Confdnce	Intrvl B
B	.099114	1.700886
(Constant)	−2.356240	2.956240

When both **coeff** and **ci** are specified together the output is displayed as in Table 11.8.

The **scatterplot** subcommand produces the residuals statistics shown in Table 11.9 and the scatterplot of standardised variables in Figure 11.4. The residuals statistics include the unstandardised predicted values of the criterion (**PRED**), the unstandardised residuals (**RESID**), the standardised predicted values (**ZPRED**) and the standardised residuals (**ZRESID**). As can be seen from Table 11.3 the minimum unstandardised predicted value is 1.2 for case 2 and the maximum unstandardised predicted value is 4.8 for case 5, while the minimum unstandardised residual is −1.1 for case 1 and the maximum unstandardised residual is 0.8 for case 2. The predicted values are standardised by subtracting the mean value from them and dividing the result by the standard deviation. So the predicted value of 1.2 minus the mean of 3.0 becomes −1.8 which, divided by the standard deviation of 1.423, makes −1.2649 $((1.2 - 3.0)/1.423 = -1.26493)$. The scores of the two variables are standardised in the same way by subtracting the mean from them and dividing by their standard deviation. Since the

Table 11.8 **Regression** output with **coeff** and **ci** keyword

Equation Number 1	Dependent Variable ..		A		
	----------- Variables in the Equation -----------				
			95%		
Variable	B	SE B	Confdnce	Intrvl B	Beta
B	.900000	.251661	.099114	1.700886	.900000
(Constant)	.300000	.834666	−2.356240	2.956240	
	---- in ----				
Variable	T	Sig T			
B	3.576	.0374			
(Constant)	.359	.7431			

Table 11.9 **Regression** output of residuals with **scatterplot** subcommand

Residuals Statistics:

	Min	Max	Mean	Std Dev	N
*PRED	1.2000	4.8000	3.0000	1.4230	5
*RESID	−1.1000	.8000	.0000	.6892	5
*ZPRED	−1.2649	1.2649	.0000	1.0000	5
*ZRESID	−1.3822	1.0052	.0000	.8660	5

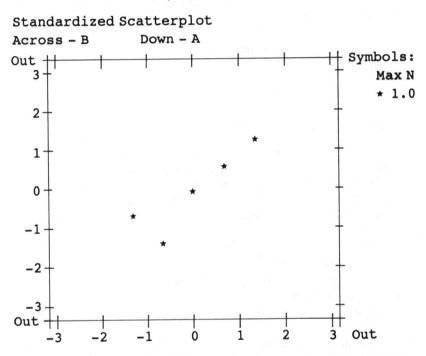

Figure 11.4 **Regression** output of standardised scatterplot with **scatterplot** subcommand

means and standard deviations of the two variables are the same (3.0 and 1.58) a score of 1 becomes a standardised score of −1.27 ((1 − 3)/1.58 = −1.2658) for both variables. Residuals are standardised by dividing them by the standard error of estimate. So the unstandardised residual of −1.1 becomes a standardised residual of 1.38 when divided by the standard error of estimate (−1.1/0.79582 = 1.3822).

Correlation and regression provide a good index of the association between two variables when the assumptions of normality, linearity and *homoscedasticity* are met. Homoscedasticity refers to the variance of one variable being similar for all values of the other variable. A way of checking these three assumptions visually is to produce a scatterplot of the residuals with the predicted values. The assumption of normality is met if the residuals are normally distributed around each predicted score so that most of the residuals for that predicted score are concentrated at the centre of its distribution. The assumption of linearity holds if the overall shape of the distribution of points is rectangular. A curved shape implies that the relationship is not linear. The assumption of homoscedasticity is fulfilled if the spread of residuals does not change with an increase in the predicted values. An example of heteroscedasticity is when the distribution of residuals becomes wider at higher values.

The scatterplot between the residuals and the predicted values can be produced with the following **scatterplot** subcommand as part of the **regression** command:

/**scatterplot** (*****resid,*****pred).

MULTIPLE REGRESSION

Multiple regression is the extension of bivariate regression to two or more predictors. We would use multiple regression if we wanted to find out, for example, how much of the variation in self-esteem was explained by the predictors of parental acceptance, educational attainment and parental education. The regression equation for multiple regression is as follows:

criterion predicted score $= a + (b_1 \times \text{predictor}_1 \text{ score}) + (b_2 \times \text{predictor}_2 \text{ score}) + \ldots$

where b_1 is the unstandardised partial regression coefficient of the criterion with the first predictor controlling for the other predictors in the equation, b_2 is the unstandardised partial regression coefficient of the criterion with the second predictor controlling for the other predictors in the equation and so on.

As the calculation of partial regression coefficients with more than two predictors is complicated and is more appropriately carried out with matrix algebra, we will only demonstrate the calculation of a multiple regression with two predictors. The formula for computing the standardised partial regression coefficient of the criterion (c) with the first predictor (1) controlling for the second predictor (2) is

$$B_1 = \frac{r_{c1} - (r_{c2} \times r_{12})}{1 - r_{12}^2}$$

To convert the standardised partial regression coefficient into the unstandardised coefficient, we multiply the standardised coefficient by the standard deviation of the criterion divided by the standard deviation of the predictor:

$$b_1 = \frac{\text{criterion std dev}}{\text{predictor}_1 \text{ std dev}} \times B_1$$

Similarly, the formula for computing the standardised partial regression coefficient of the criterion (c) with the second predictor (2) controlling for the first predictor (1) is

$$B_2 = \frac{r_{c2} - (r_{c1} \times r_{12})}{1 - r_{12}^2}$$

The formula for the unstandardised partial regression coefficient is

$$b_2 = \frac{\text{criterion std dev}}{\text{predictor}_2 \text{ std dev}} \times B_2$$

As an illustration, we will compute the multiple regression between the criterion of self-esteem and the two predictors of parental acceptance and educational attainment for the data previously shown in Table 10.11. To be able to do this we need to know the means, standard deviations and inter-correlations of the three variables together with the number of cases in the sample which are presented in Table 11.10.

Using the above formulae we find that the standardised partial regression coefficient between self-esteem and parental acceptance is about 0.55 while the unstandardised partial regression coefficient is about 0.35:

$$B_1 = \frac{0.65 - (0.48 \times 0.36)}{1 - 0.36^2} = \frac{0.4772}{0.8704} = 0.548$$

$$b_1 = \frac{0.95}{1.50} \times 0.548 = 0.347$$

Table 11.10 Correlations, means and standard deviations for parental acceptance, parental education, educational attainment and self-esteem

	Parental acceptance	Parental education	Educational attainment	Self-esteem
Parental acceptance	–			
Parental education	0.15	–		
Educational attainment	0.36	0.87	–	
Self-esteem	0.65	0.11	0.48	–
Mean	3.29	3.00	2.57	2.71
Standard deviation	1.50	1.53	1.51	0.95

Similarly, the standardised partial regression coefficient between self-esteem and educational attainment is about 0.28 while the unstandardised partial regression coefficient is about 0.18:

$$B_2 = \frac{0.48 - (0.65 \times 0.36)}{1 - 0.36^2} = \frac{0.2460}{0.8704} = 0.2826$$

$$b_2 = \frac{0.95}{1.51} \times 0.2826 = 0.1778$$

Note that both the standardised and the unstandardised partial regression coefficients for parental acceptance are bigger than those for educational attainment which means that more of the variation in self-esteem is accounted for by parental acceptance than educational attainment.

We can calculate the intercept constant from the following formula:

$$a = \text{criterion mean} - (b_1 \times \text{predictor}_1 \text{ mean}) + (b_2 \times \text{predictor}_2 \text{ mean})$$

Substituting the appropriate values in the formula gives an intercept constant of about 1.10:

$$2.71 - (0.35 \times 3.29) + (0.18 \times 2.57)$$
$$= 2.71 - 1.15 + 0.46$$
$$= 1.10$$

The formula for computing the squared multiple correlation is as follows:

$$R^2 = \frac{r_{c1}^2 + r_{c2}^2 - (2 \times r_{c1} \times r_{c2} \times r_{12})}{1 - r_{12}^2}$$

Placing the appropriate correlations into this formula produces a squared multiple correlation of about 0.49:

$$\frac{0.65^2 + 0.48^2 - (2 \times 0.65 \times 0.48 \times 0.36)}{1 - 0.36^2}$$

$$= \frac{0.4225 + 0.2304 - 0.2246}{0.8704} = \frac{0.4283}{0.8704} = 0.492$$

The formula for the adjusted squared multiple correlation is

$$\text{adjusted } R^2 = R^2 - \frac{(1 - R^2) \times \text{no. of predictors}}{\text{no. of cases} - \text{no. of predictors} - 1}$$

Inserting the pertinent values into this formula we see that the adjusted squared multiple correlation for our example is about 0.24:

$$0.492 - \frac{(1 - 0.492) \times 2}{7 - 2 - 1} = 0.492 - \frac{1.016}{4}$$

$$= 0.492 - 0.254 = 0.238$$

The multiple correlation is the square root of the squared multiple correlation:

$$R = \sqrt{(R^2)}$$

Consequently, the multiple correlation for our example is about 0.70 ($\sqrt{(0.492)} = 0.70$).

The formula for computing the F ratio for testing the significance of the multiple correlation is

$$F = \frac{R^2 \times (\text{no. of cases} - \text{no. of predictors} - 1)}{(1 - R^2) \times \text{no. of predictors}}$$

The degrees of freedom is the number of predictors for the numerator and the number of cases minus the number of predictors minus 1 for the denominator.

The F ratio for our example is about 1.94:

$$\frac{0.492 \times (7 - 2 - 1)}{(1 - 0.492) \times 2} = \frac{0.492 \times 4}{0.508 \times 2} = 1.9370$$

Looking up this value in the table in Appendix 5, we see that with 2 and 4 degrees of freedom in the numerator and denominator respectively F has to be 6.9443 or bigger to be significant at the 0.05 level, which it is not. Consequently, we would conclude that the multiple correlation between self-esteem and the two predictors of parental acceptance and educational attainment is not significant.

Note that the size of the F test depends partly on the number of cases in the numerator. If the number of cases is increased, then the size of the F ratio increases. For example, with 12 cases F is about 4.36:

$$\frac{0.492 \times (12 - 2 - 1)}{(1 - 0.492) \times 2} = \frac{0.492 \times 9}{0.508 \times 2} = 4.3582$$

With 2 and 9 degrees of freedom respectively F has to be 4.2565 or larger to be significant at the 0.05 level which it is.

Multiple regressions are computed by the following general SPSS command:

regression variables criterion predictors
 /**dep** criterion
 /**method enter** predictors.

Since we calculated the multiple correlation from the means, standard deviations, intercorrelations and number of cases, we will use only this information with the **regression** command. Consequently, we will access these data in the form of a matrix with the following commands:

data list matrix/pa 1-4 pe ea se 5-22.
begin data.
3.29 3.00 2.57 2.71
1.50 1.53 1.51 0.95
1.00 0.15 0.36 0.65
0.15 1.00 0.87 0.11
0.36 0.87 1.00 0.48
0.65 0.11 0.48 1.00
7
end data.

The first line of the matrix contains the means of the four variables in the order in which they are listed on the **data list** command while the second line similarly presents the standard deviations of those variables. The following four lines hold the matrix of intercorrelations while the seventh line specifies the number of cases.

  The following **regression** command was used to run the multiple regression analysis:

regression variables pa pe ea se
 /**read mean stddev corr n**
 /**statistics r coeff zpp**
 /**dep se**
 /**enter pa ea.**

The data matrix was read by the **read** subcommand which states the order in which the data were presented. The criterion is named on the **dep** subcommand while the two predictors are listed on the **enter** subcommand. The only statistics requested are the multiple correlations, the standard error of estimate, the F ratio and its probability (**r**); the regression coefficients (**coeff**); and the zero-order, part and partial correlations (**zpp**).

  The relevant output for this command is presented in Table 11.11.

  Although the standardised and unstandardised partial regression coefficients provide an index of the contributions made by the predictors, they do not offer an estimate of the amount of variation in the criterion which is accounted for by each of the predictors. One coefficient which does this is the *part* (or *semipartial*) *correlation*. A first-order part correlation can be

Table 11.11 **Regression** output with two predictors

* * * * MULTIPLE REGRESSION * * * *

Listwise Deletion of Missing Data

Equation Number 1   **Dependent Variable ..**   **SE**

Block Number   1. **Method: Enter   PA   EA**

Variable(s) Entered on Step Number
   1..   EA
   2..   PA

Multiple R	.70145
R Square	.49203
Adjusted R Square	.23804
Standard Error	.82926

F =   1.93721   **Signif F =   .2580**

–––––––––––––– **Variables in the Equation** ––––––––––––––

Variable	B	SE B	Beta	T	Sig T
EA	.177813	.240313	.282629	.740	.5004
PA	.347227	.241915	.548254	1.435	.2245
(Constant)	1.110643	.871330		1.275	.2714

End Block Number   1   All requested variables entered.

thought of as a simple correlation between the residual of the criterion and the residual of the first predictor, from the latter of which the effect of the second predictor has been taken out. The squared first-order part correlation is the absolute increase in the amount of variation in the criterion which is explained by the first predictor taking the second predictor into account. Consequently, the squared part correlation is often used to determine whether adding a further variable to the regression equation provides a significant increase in the overall proportion of explained variation in the criterion.

The formula for the first-order part correlation between the criterion (c) and the first predictor (1) controlling for the second predictor (2) is

$$r_{c1.2} = \frac{r_{c1} - (r_{c2} \times r_{12})}{\sqrt{1 - r_{12}^2}}$$

We will calculate the first-order part correlation between the criterion of self-esteem and the two predictors of parental acceptance and educational attainment. Using this formula, we find that the first-order part correlation between self-esteem (c) and parental acceptance (1) controlling for educational attainment (2) is about 0.52:

$$\frac{0.65 - (0.48 \times 0.36)}{\sqrt{1 - 0.36^2}} = \frac{0.65 - 0.17}{\sqrt{1 - 0.13}} = \frac{0.48}{0.93} = 0.516$$

This first-order part correlation squared is about 0.27 (0.266) which means that adding the predictor of parental acceptance to that of educational attainment increases the percentage of variation explained in self-esteem by about 27.

To determine whether the increase in variation explained by the additional variable of parental acceptance is significant we carry out the following F test:

$$F = \frac{\text{squared partial correlation}/1}{(1 - R^2)/(\text{no. of cases} - \text{no. of predictors} - 1)}$$

The squared partial correlation involves the additional variable in question while the squared multiple correlation (R^2) includes both the additional variable and the others in the regression equation. The degrees of freedom for the numerator is 1 and for the denominator is the number of cases minus the number of predictors minus 1.

The F ratio for adding parental acceptance to the regression equation is about 2.09.

$$\frac{0.266/1}{(1 - 0.492)/(7 - 2 - 1)} = \frac{0.266}{0.508/4} = \frac{0.266}{0.127} = 2.094$$

Turning to the table in Appendix 5, we see that with 1 and 4 degrees of freedom respectively, F has to be 7.7086 or bigger to be significant at the 0.05 level. Consequently, adding parental acceptance to the regression equation does not provide a significant increase to the proportion of variation already explained. Note, however, that if the number of cases had been increased to 13, including parental acceptance would have made a significant contribution to the percentage of variation explained. With 13 cases, F is about 5.24 (0.266/(0.508/10) = 5.236). With 1 and 10 degrees of freedom respectively F has to be 4.9646 or larger to be significant at the 0.05 level which it is.

The first-order part correlation between self-esteem (c) and educational attainment (1) controlling for parental acceptance (2) is about 0.27:

$$\frac{0.48 - (0.65 \times 0.36)}{(1 - 0.36^2)^{1/2}} = \frac{0.48 - 0.23}{(1 - 0.13)^{1/2}} = \frac{0.25}{0.93} = 0.2688$$

This first-order part correlation squared is about 0.07. In other words, adding educational attainment to parental acceptance increases the percentage of variation explained in self-esteem by about 7.

The F ratio for adding educational attainment to the regression equation is about 0.55:

$$\frac{0.07/1}{(1 - 0.492)/(7 - 2 - 1)} = \frac{0.07}{0.508/4} = \frac{0.07}{0.127} = 0.551$$

With 1 and 4 degrees of freedom respectively, F has to be 7.7086 or bigger to be significant at the 0.05 level which it is not. Therefore, we could conclude that adding educational attainment to the regression equation does not result in a significant increase in the percentage of variation explained in self-esteem. Once again, however, note that, if the number of cases were increased to 35, adding educational attainment would have produced a significant increase in the proportion of variation explained. With 35 cases F is about 4.41 ($0.07/(0.508/32) = 4.409$). With 1 and 32 degrees of freedom, F has to be 4.1709 or bigger to be significant at the 0.05 level which it is.

The proportion of variation explained by an additional predictor can be determined by the following **regression** command:

regression variables criterion predictors
 /statistics r cha zpp
 /dep criterion
 /enter other predictor(s)/**enter** additional predictor.

The keyword **cha** on the **statistics** subcommand displays the change in the variation explained by the additional predictor, its F value and probability, and the F value for the regression equation and its probability.

The following SPSS command was run to calculate any change in variation by adding parental acceptance:

regression variables=pa pe ea se
 /read mean stddev corr n
 /statistics r cha zpp
 /dep se
 /enter ea/enter pa.

The relevant output for including parental acceptance in the second step of the regression equation is shown in Table 11.12. The part correlation (**Part Cor**) controlling for educational attainment (**EA**) is displayed as **.511495**. This part correlation squared (**R Square Change**) is **.26163**. The F test for this change (**F Change**) is

Table 11.12 **Regression** output with parental acceptance entered on the second step

* * * * MULTIPLE REGRESSION * * * *

Equation Number 1   Dependent Variable ..   **SE**

Block Number   2.   Method: Enter   PA

Variable(s) Entered on Step Number
  2 . .   PA

Multiple R	.70145		
R Square	.49203	**R Square Change**	.26163
Adjusted R Square	.23804	**F Change**	2.06016
Standard Error	.82926	**Signif F Change**	.2245
F = 1.93721		**Signif F =**	.2580

Equation Number 1   Dependent Variable ..   **SE**

– – – – Variables in the Equation – – – –

Variable	Correl	Part Cor	Partial
EA	.480000	.263679	.346976
PA	.650000	.511495	.583054

End Block Number   2   All requested variables entered.

$$\frac{\textbf{R Square Change}/1}{(1 - \textbf{R Square})/(\text{no. of cases} - \text{no. of predictors} - 1)}$$

which works out to be **2.06016**:

$$\frac{.26163}{(1 - .49203)/7 - 2 - 1} = \frac{.26163}{0.50797/4} = 2.06020$$

The statistical significance of this F ratio (**Signif F Change**) is **.2245**. The F ratio for the regression equation containing the two predictors of educational attainment (**EA**) and parental acceptance (**PA**) is **1.93721** which of course is the same as that shown in Table 11.11.

The following SPSS command was used to estimate any change in variation by adding educational attainment:

regression variables=pa pe ea se
 /read mean stddev corr n
 /statistics r cha zpp

/dep se
/enter pa/enter ea.

The relevant output for including educational attainment in the second step of the regression equation is presented in Table 11.13.

PROCEDURES FOR SELECTING PREDICTORS

The number of potential regression equations increases with the number of predictors and is a function of 2 to the power of the number of predictors minus 1. With only two predictors the maximum number of regression equations or models that can be tested is three ($2^2 - 1 = 3$): the two predictors on their own and combined. With three predictors seven different equations can be examined ($2^3 - 1 = 7$): three with only one predictor, three with two predictors and one with all three. With four predictors there are fifteen different equations ($2^4 - 1 = 15$). As the number of predictors increases it takes more and more time to investigate and compare the different equations. In order not to have to examine every possible equation, a number of different approaches for selecting and

Table 11.13 **Regression** output with educational attainment entered on the second step

---

* * * * MULTIPLE REGRESSION * * * *

Equation Number 1　　　　**Dependent Variable ..**　　**SE**
Block Number   2.   Method: Enter　　**EA**

Variable(s) Entered on Step Number
　2 ..　　**EA**

Multiple R	.70145		
R Square	.49203	**R Square Change**	.06953
Adjusted R Square	.23804	**F Change**	.54748
Standard Error	.82926	**Signif F Change**	.5004
F =　1.93721		**Signif F =**　.2580	

Equation Number 1　　　　**Dependent Variable ..**　　**SE**

　　– – – – Variables in the Equation – – – –

Variable	Correl	Part Cor	Partial
PA	.650000	.511495	.583054
EA	.480000	.263679	.346976

End Block Number   2   All requested variables entered.

testing predictors have been suggested, including *hierarchical* (or *block-wise*) *selection, forward selection, backward elimination* and *stepwise selection*. The first of these selects predictors on practical or theoretical grounds while the last three involve statistical criteria and are used to choose the smallest set of predictors that might explain most of the variation in the criterion. In contrast to these methods, entering all predictors into the equation is known as *standard* multiple regression while comparing all possible sets of predictors is called *setwise* regression. The method(s) used should mirror the purpose of the analysis.

In hierarchical selection predictors are entered singly or in blocks according to some rationale. For example, potentially confounding variables such as socio-demographic factors may be entered first in order to control for their effects. Or similar variables (such as attitudes) may be grouped together and entered as a block. The **regression** subcommand for entering variables in a particular order is **enter** which was demonstrated when estimating the increase in variation explained by the two variables of parental acceptance and educational attainment. Each new variable or set of variables is listed on a separate **enter** subcommand together with any previous variables. The **enter** subcommands listed first will be processed first. So, for example, in the following sequence

/enter gender/enter gender age/enter gender age income

gender will be entered first, followed by gender and age second, and gender, age and income third. The proportional increase in variation explained by age over gender is shown in the second step of the regression by **R Square Change**.

In forward selection the predictor that has the highest zero-order correlation with the criterion is considered first for entry into the regression equation. This predictor is entered into the equation if the previously specified F ratio (or, alternatively, its probability for entering predictors) is exceeded. If it is not, this variable is not entered and the analysis ends. If this value is exceeded, then this predictor is entered and the analysis continues. The next predictor considered for entry is that with the largest partial correlation (which will also have the largest F ratio). If it meets the statistical criterion, it will be entered into the regression equation and the next predictor with the largest partial correlation will be evaluated. The selection stops when no other predictor satisfies the entry criterion. Once a predictor has been entered into the equation it remains there even though it may no longer make a significant contribution to the amount of variance explained. The **regression** subcommand for forward selection is **forward**.

In backward elimination all the predictors are initially entered into the regression equation. The predictor with the smallest partial correlation is examined first. If it exceeds the previously specified F ratio (or, alternatively, its probability for removing predictors), it is excluded from the regression equation and the predictor with the next smallest partial correlation is considered. The analysis stops when no further predictors satisfy this criterion. The **regression** subcommand for backward elimination is **backward**.

Stepwise selection is a combination of forward selection and backward elimination. The predictor which has the highest zero-order correlation with the criterion is entered first if the previously specified F ratio (or, alternatively, its probability for entering predictors) is exceeded. The second predictor to be considered is that which has the highest partial correlation. If this meets the statistical criterion it enters the regression equation. At this stage the predictor which was entered first is examined to see if it still satisfies the statistical criterion to remain in the equation. If it does not, it is removed. The third predictor to be examined is that which has the next highest partial correlation. The procedure stops when no more predictors are to be entered into or removed from the equation. The **regression** subcommand for stepwise selection is **stepwise**. Note that these three different selection methods may give different results with the same data and so it may be worthwhile comparing the results of the three methods.

SUMMARY

The computation of bivariate regression and multiple regression with two predictors is described. One use of regression analysis is to estimate the likely score of a criterion from one or more predictors. Another use is to determine the minimum number of predictors needed to explain the maximum variation in the criterion. The regression coefficient (b) is the straight line lying closest to the points on the scatterplot. It provides a good index of the association between two variables when the assumptions of normality, linearity and homoscedasticity are met, which can be visually checked through a scatterplot of the residuals with the predicted values. The accuracy of prediction is given by the standard error of estimate. The proportion of variation in the criterion accounted for by the linear combination of predictors is assessed by the squared multiple correlation (R^2), the statistical significance of which is tested by the F ratio. A more conservative estimate of explained variance which takes account of the size of the sample and the number of predictors is the adjusted squared multiple correlation. Multiple regression uses partial regression coefficients. The squared part correlation is the absolute increase in the amount of variation in the criterion explained by the predictors and is often used to determine whether adding a further variable to the regression equation significantly increases the overall proportion of variation explained. With a large number of potential predictors, various procedures may be used to select those predictors which maximise the explained variation.

EXERCISES

Use the data in Table 6.18 for the following exercises.

1 Conduct a bivariate regression with educational interest at 15 as the criterion and educational interest at 12 as the predictor.
   (a) What is the unstandardised regression coefficient?
   (b) What is the standardised regression coefficient?
   (c) What is the intercept constant?
   (d) What is the predicted value of educational interest at 15 if the value of educational interest at 9 is 2?
   (e) What is the standard error of estimate?
   (f) What is the standard error of the regression coefficient?
   (g) What is the standard error of the intercept?
   (h) What is the squared multiple correlation?
   (i) What is the adjusted squared multiple correlation?
   (j) What is the F ratio of the squared multiple correlation?
   (k) What are its degrees of freedom?
   (l) What is its probability value?

2 Carry out a multivariate regression with educational interest at 15 as the criterion and educational interest at 12 and at 9 as the predictors.
   (a) What is the standardised partial regression coefficient between educational interest at 15 and at 12?
   (b) What is the unstandardised partial regression coefficient between educational interest at 15 and at 12?
   (c) What is the standardised partial regression coefficient between educational interest at 15 and at 9?
   (d) What is the unstandardised partial regression coefficient between educational interest at 15 and at 9?
   (e) What is the squared multiple correlation?
   (f) What is the adjusted squared multiple correlation?
   (g) What is the F ratio of the squared multiple correlation?
   (h) What are its degrees of freedom?
   (i) What is its probability value?
   (j) What is the part correlation between educational interest at 15 and educational interest at 12 controlling for educational interest at 9?
   (k) What is the F ratio for adding educational interest at 12 to the regression equation?
   (l) What are its degrees of freedom?
   (m) What is its probability value?
   (n) What is the part correlation between educational interest at 15 and educational interest at 9 controlling for educational interest at 12?
   (o) What is the F ratio for adding educational interest at 9 to the regression equation?
   (p) What are its degrees of freedom?
   (q) What is its probability value?

Chapter 12

Measurement reliability and agreement

This chapter describes statistical tests which provide an index of how reliable a particular measure is or how much agreement exists between two or more judges. For instance, we may wish to find out to what extent two or more judges categorise or rate cases in the same way, or to what extent the answers to questions devised to measure the same quality are consistent. The type of test to use depends on whether the data are categorical or not. The most widely recommended index of agreement between two or more judges is Cohen's *kappa coefficient* for categorical data. The most common measure of the reliability of non-categorical data from three or more judges is Ebel's *intraclass correlation* while the most frequently used index of the internal reliability of a set of questions is Cronbach's *alpha*.

KAPPA COEFFICIENT

Kappa indicates the extent of agreement for categorical data between two judges or raters and can be extended to apply to more than two judges (Fleiss 1971). It measures the proportion of agreements between two judges taking into account the proportion of agreements that may occur simply by chance. It has the following formula:

$$k = \frac{\text{observed proportion of agreement} - \text{chance-expected proportion of agreement}}{1 - \text{chance-expected proportion of agreement}}$$

which can be expressed in frequencies:

$$k = \frac{\text{observed frequency of agreement} - \text{chance-expected frequency of agreement}}{\text{no. of cases} - \text{chance-expected frequency of agreement}}$$

Kappas can range from -1 to $+1$. A kappa of 0 means that the observed agreement is exactly equal to the agreement that would be expected by chance, a negative kappa a less than chance agreement, a positive kappa a greater than chance agreement and a kappa of 1 perfect agreement. A kappa of 0.7 or more is usually considered to be an acceptable level of agreement. As will be demonstrated below, kappa is an index of agreement whereas tests such as the contingency coefficient and phi are measures of association. Both the contingency coefficient and phi vary between 0 and 1. If there is substantial disagreement between two judges on a dichotomous judgement task, then both the contingency coefficient and phi will be positive whereas kappa will be negative.

To illustrate the computation of kappa we will take the case where two judges are asked to indicate whether they consider each of 100 photographs of sexual scenes to be erotic or pornographic. The results of these two judges are shown in Table 12.1. Judge A thinks that 90 out of 100 or 90 per cent of the photographs are pornographic while Judge B believes that only 40 per cent of them are. The decisions of the two judges agree on only 30 per cent of the photographs.

To calculate kappa we first find the chance-expected frequency of agreement for the two cells. This is done for each cell by multiplying its row total by its column total and dividing by the overall total. So the chance-expected frequency for the erotic category is 6 ($10 \times 60/100 = 6$) and for the pornographic category 36 ($90 \times 40/100 = 36$) giving a total of 42.

Applying the above formula we find that kappa is about -0.21:

$$\frac{30 - 42}{100 - 42} = \frac{-12}{58} = -0.2069$$

This indicates that the agreement between the two judges is less than would be expected by chance which implies that they are using different criteria to make their judgements.

Let us now compare this kappa with the contingency coefficient and phi. To calculate these two coefficients we first have to find chi-square which is about 16.67:

$$\frac{(0 - 6)^2}{6} + \frac{(10 - 4)^2}{4} + \frac{(60 - 54)^2}{54} + \frac{(30 - 36)^2}{36}$$

$$= 6 + 9 + 0.67 + 1 = 16.67$$

Table 12.1 Categorisation of photos by two judges

		Judge B		
		Erotic	Porn	Total
Judge A	Erotic	0	10	10
	Porn	60	30	90
Total		60	40	100

Consequently, the contingency coefficient is about 0.38 ($\sqrt{16.67/(16.67 + 100)} = 0.378$) and phi is 0.41 ($\sqrt{16.67/100} = 0.408$). Note that both the contingency coefficient and phi are positive and larger than kappa even though the amount of disagreement is greater than the amount of agreement. What these two coefficients indicate is that there is a tendency for certain decisions of Judge A to be associated with certain decisions of Judge B but they provide no information as to whether the actual decisions are the same.

The SPSS command for computing kappa is **crosstabs** where the keyword **kappa** is added to the **statistics** subcommand:

crosstabs table=variable **by** variable
 /**statistics kappa**.

To calculate kappa as well as the contingency coefficient and phi for this example, we first have to enter the data table with the use of the **weight** command followed by the appropriate **crosstabs** command. The following commands could be used for computing these statistics:

data list/a 1 b 3 wt 5-7.
weight by wt.
begin data.
1 1 0
1 2 10
2 1 60
2 2 30
end data.
crosstabs table=a by b
 /**cells=count**
 /**statistics=cc phi kappa.**

The output for these three statistics is shown in Table 12.2.

Table 12.2 Kappa output

Statistic	Value	ASE1	T-value	Approximate Significance
Phi	.40825			.00004 *1
Cramer's V	.40825			.00004 *1
Contingency Coefficient	.37796			.00004 *1
Kappa	–.20690	.06308	–4.08248	

*1 Pearson chi-square probability

INTRACLASS CORRELATION

For non-categorical data the reliability of the ratings made by two judges can be estimated with Pearson's correlation. For more than two judges the intraclass correlation is used. The intraclass correlation can be thought of as the proportion of the true variance in the ratings of the cases (i.e. minus the error variance) to the total variance in the cases being rated:

$$\text{intraclass correlation} = \frac{\text{cases variance} - \text{error variance}}{\text{cases variance}}$$

The above formula gives the reliability of the average rating for all the judges, while the following formula estimates the reliability of the average rating for an individual judge:

$$\text{intraclass correlation} = \frac{\text{cases variance} - \text{error variance}}{\text{cases variance} + [\text{error variance} \times (\text{no. of judges} - 1)]}$$

The between-judges variance can either be excluded or be included in the error variance. It should be excluded from the error variance if differences in the mean levels of the judges are to be ignored. When it is to be included we can calculate the intraclass correlation as a one-way analysis of variance in which the cases are the only factor. When we wish to exclude it we should carry out a two-way analysis of variance in which the two factors are the cases and the judges. With a two-way analysis of variance we can add the between-judges sum of squares to the residual sum of squares when we wish to include the between-judges variance as part of the error variance.

We will demonstrate the calculation of the intraclass correlation for the ratings in Table 12.3 made by three judges of four cases. Note that while there is perfect agreement in the rank order of the four cases there is total disagreement over the particular ratings given. We will compute a two-way analysis of variance for these data. The means for the three judges and four cases are shown in Table 12.4 together with the grand mean.

The between-cases sum of squares is calculated by subtracting the grand

Table 12.3 Ratings by three judges

Cases	Judges		
	A	B	C
1	1	2	3
2	2	3	4
3	3	4	5
4	4	5	6

Table 12.4 Sums and means of ratings of cases and judges

Cases	Judges			Sum	Mean
	A	B	C		
1	1	2	3	6	2
2	2	3	4	9	3
3	3	4	5	12	4
4	4	5	6	15	5
Sum	10	14	18	42	
Mean	2.5	3.5	4.5		3.5

mean from each of the case means, squaring this difference, multiplying this squared difference by the number of judges and summing the products for all the cases. This makes it 15:

$$[(2-3.5)^2 \times 3] + [(3-3.5)^2 \times 3] + [(4-3.5)^2 \times 3] + [(5-3.5)^2 \times 3]$$
$$= [2.25 \times 3] + [0.25 \times 3] + [0.25 \times 3] + [2.25 \times 3]$$
$$= 6.75 + 0.75 + 0.75 + 6.75 = 15$$

The between-cases mean square is its sum of squares divided by its degrees of freedom (the number of cases minus 1) which gives 5.0 ($15/3 = 5$).

The between-judges sum of squares is calculated by subtracting the grand mean from the mean of each judge, squaring this difference, multiplying this squared difference by the number of cases and summing the products for all the judges. This makes it 8:

$$[(2.5-3.5)^2 \times 4] + [(3.5-3.5)^2 \times 4] + [(4.5-3.5)^2 \times 4]$$
$$= 4 + 0 + 4 = 8$$

The between-judges mean square is its sum of squares divided by its degrees of freedom (the number of judges minus 1) which gives 4.0 ($8/2 = 4$).

The residual or error sum of squares can be calculated by subtracting the between-cases and between-judges sum of squares from the total sum of squares. The total sum of squares is the grand mean subtracted from each rating, squared and added together, which makes it 23.0:

$$(1-3.5)^2 + (2-3.5)^2 + (3-3.5)^2 + (4-3.5)^2 + (2-3.5)^2$$
$$+ (3-3.5)^2 + (4-3.5)^2 + (5-3.5)^2 + (3-3.5)^2 + (4-3.5)^2$$
$$+ (5-3.5)^2 + (6-3.5)^2$$
$$= 6.25 + 2.25 + 0.25 + 0.25 + 2.25 + 0.25 + 0.25 + 2.25 + 0.25$$
$$+ 0.25 + 2.25 + 6.25$$
$$= 23.0$$

The error sum of squares is 0 ($23.0 - 15.0 - 8.0 = 0.0$). The degrees of freedom for the error sum of squares are the number of cases minus 1 multiplied by the number of judges minus 1. Since the error sum of squares is 0 its mean square is also 0 ($0/(4 - 1) \times (3 - 1) = 0$). The sums of squares, degrees of freedom and mean squares for these data are presented in Table 12.5.

Using the case and error mean square we find that the reliability of the average rating for an individual judge is 1.0:

$$\frac{5 - 0}{5 + [0 \times (3 - 1)]} = \frac{5}{5} = 1.0$$

If no account is taken of the differences in the average ratings of the judges, then the intraclass correlation indicates that there is perfect agreement between the judges even though no judge gave the same case the same rating. In other words, when the average ratings of the judges are ignored the intraclass correlation is similar to an average intercorrelation.

However, if the between-judges variance is included in the error term, the intraclass correlation is substantially smaller. To calculate the error sum of squares which includes the between-judges variance either subtract the cases between-groups sum of squares from the total sum of squares which gives 8.0 ($23.0 - 15.0 = 8.0$) or add the between-judges sum of squares to the residual sum of squares ($8.0 + 0.0 = 8.0$). The degrees of freedom for this residual sum of squares are 1 subtracted from the number of judges for each case summed together. Therefore the residual mean square is 1.0 ($8/(3 - 1 + 3 - 1 + 3 - 1 + 3 - 1) = 1$). Using this value, we find that the intraclass correlation is 0.57:

$$\frac{5 - 1}{5 + [1 \times (3 - 1)]} = \frac{4}{7} = 0.57$$

Note that the intraclass correlation is still positive even though none of the ratings is the same.

The SPSS command for producing the necessary statistics to calculate the intraclass correlation is **anova**:

Table 12.5 Analysis of variance table for the intraclass correlation

Sources of variation	SS	df	MS
Between cases	15.0	3	5.0
Between judges	8.0	2	4.0
Error	0.0	6	0.0
Total	23.0		

anova ratings **by** cases (lowest value, highest value) judges (lowest value, highest value)

To suppress the cases by judges interaction effect add the following **options** subcommand:

/**options 3.**

The following SPSS commands were used to produce a two-way analysis of variance for this example:

data list/cases 1 judges 3 rating 5.
begin data.
1 1 1
2 1 2
3 1 3
4 1 4
1 2 2
2 2 3
3 2 4
4 2 5
1 3 3
2 3 4
3 3 5
4 3 6
end data.
anova rating by cases(1,4) judges(1,3)
  /**options 3.**

Note that each rating is treated as if it were a separate record (i.e. case).
  The output for these commands is displayed in Table 12.6.

Table 12.6 **Anova** output of analysis of variance table

* * * ANALYSIS OF VARIANCE * * *

RATING
BY CASES
JUDGES

Source of Variation	Sum of Squares	DF	Mean Square	F	Signif of F
Main Effects	23.000	5	4.600		
CASES	15.000	3	5.000		
JUDGES	8.000	2	4.000		
Explained	23.000	5	4.600		
Residual	.000	6	.000		
Total	23.000	11	2.091		

ALPHA

The alpha coefficient determines the internal reliability or consistency of a set of items (or judges) designed to measure a particular characteristic. It can be thought of as the proportion of variation in the cases which is explained by the items:

$$\text{alpha} = \frac{\text{cases variance} - \text{error variance}}{\text{cases variance}}$$

or

$$1 - \frac{\text{error variance}}{\text{cases variance}}$$

The difference between this formula and that for the intraclass correlation lies in the different way in which the error variance is derived. We can calculate alpha as a single factor repeated measures analysis of variance in which the error variance is divided by the between-subjects (or cases) factor and the result is subtracted from 1:

$$\text{alpha} = 1 - \frac{\text{error variance}}{\text{between-cases variance}}$$

We will illustrate the computation of alpha with the data shown in Table 12.7 which represent the dichotomous answers of four cases to three items measuring, say, self-esteem. A '1' might indicate a 'No' or 'Disagree' response and a '2' a 'Yes' or 'Agree' answer. Each of the three items is worded so that a 'Yes' reply indicates greater self-esteem than a 'No' response. Apart from the fourth case the scores for each person are the same for all three items so that if a person answers 'Yes' to one question they answer 'Yes' to the other two. This pattern of responding implies that the items are measuring the same characteristic. If some of the items had been worded so that a 'Yes' signified lower self-esteem than a 'No', then the scoring of these items would have to be reversed (i.e. a 'Yes' coded as a '1' and a 'No' as '2') so that the direction of the scoring was consistent.

Table 12.7 Dichotomous answers to three items

Cases	Items		
	1	*2*	*3*
1	1	1	1
2	2	2	2
3	1	1	1
4	1	2	2

The total and mean scores for the cases and items are presented in Table 12.8 together with the grand mean. To calculate the between-cases and error mean squares carry out the following steps.

Step 1   Calculate the total sum of squares by subtracting the grand mean from each score, squaring them and adding them together.
The total sum of squares for our example is 2.92:

$$(1 - 1.42)^2 + (2 - 1.42)^2 + (1 - 1.42)^2 + (1 - 1.42)^2 + (1 - 1.42)^2$$
$$+ (2 - 1.42)^2 + (1 - 1.42)^2 + (2 - 1.42)^2 + (1 - 1.42)^2 + (2 - 1.42)^2$$
$$+ (1 - 1.42)^2 + (2 - 1.42)^2$$
$$= 2.917$$

Step 2   Compute the between-cases sum of squares by subtracting the grand mean from the mean score for each case, squaring them, multiplying them by the number of items and adding them together.
The between-cases sum of squares for our example is 2.25:

$$[(1.00 - 1.42)^2 \times 3] + [(2.00 - 1.42)^2 \times 3] + [(1.00 - 1.42)^2 \times 3]$$
$$+ [(1.67 - 1.42)^2 \times 3]$$
$$= 0.529 + 1.009 + 0.529 + 0.188$$
$$= 2.25$$

Step 3   Work out the within-factor (i.e. items) sum of squares by subtracting the grand mean from the mean score for each of the items, squaring them, multiplying them by the number of cases and summing them.
The within-factor sum of squares for our example is 0.17:

$$[(1.25 - 1.42)^2 \times 4] + [(1.5 - 1.42)^2 \times 4] + [(1.5 - 1.42)^2 \times 4]$$
$$= 0.116 + 0.026 + 0.026$$
$$= 0.168$$

Table 12.8 Sum and means of items and cases

Cases	Items			Sum	Mean
	1	*2*	*3*		
1	1	1	1	3	1
2	2	2	2	6	2
3	1	1	1	3	1
4	1	2	2	5	1.67
Sum	5	6	6	17	
Mean	1.25	1.5	1.5		1.42

Step 4   Calculate the residual sum of squares by adding together the between-cases and within-cases sum of squares and subtracting them from the total sum of squares.

For our example the residual sum of squares is 0.50 (2.92 − (2.25 + 0.17) = 0.50).

Step 5   Calculate the error mean square by dividing its sum of squares by its degrees of freedom which is the number of cases minus 1 multiplied by the number of items minus 1.

For our example the degrees of freedom are 6 ((4 − 1) × (3 − 1) = 6) and so the error mean square is 0.08 (0.50/6 = 0.08).

Step 6   Calculate the between-cases mean square by dividing its sum of squares by its degrees of freedom which are the number of cases minus 1.

The between-cases mean square for our example is 0.75 (2.25/3 = 0.75).

The results of these steps are presented in Table 12.9.

To calculate alpha divide the error mean square by the between-cases mean square and subtract the result from 1.

For our example alpha for the three items is 0.89:

$$1 - \frac{0.08}{0.75} = 1 - 0.1067 = 0.8933$$

Since an alpha of 0.80 or higher is generally thought to indicate an acceptable level of internal reliability, this set of three items would be considered as constituting a reliable scale.

The basic SPSS command for calculating alpha is the following **reliability** command:

reliability item names
 /**scale**(scale name)=item names.

The **summary** subcommand with the keyword **total** is worth including since

Table 12.9 Analysis of variance table for alpha

Sources of variation	SS	df	MS
Between-cases	2.25	3	0.75
Within-cases			
Within-factor	0.17		
Residual	0.50	6	0.08
Total	2.92		

it provides alpha when each item is removed from the scale. This information can be used to construct a scale which has a higher alpha and which therefore is more reliable.

The following SPSS commands could be used to compute alpha for our example:

data list/cno 1 q1 q2 q3 2-13.
begin data.
1 1 1 1
2 2 2 2
3 1 1 1
4 1 2 2
end data.
reliability variables q1 to q3
 /scale(se) q1 to q3
 /summary total.

The output for these commands is displayed in Table 12.10. Note that if the first item is omitted alpha for the remaining two items increases to **1.0000** while if either of the other two items is dropped alpha decreases to **.7273**.

If the wording of one or more of a series of items was reversed, then the **recode** command could be used to reverse the scores of these items.

Table 12.10 Alpha output

RELIABILITY ANALYSIS – SCALE (SE)

1. Q1
2. Q2
3. Q3

ITEM-TOTAL STATISTICS

	SCALE MEAN IF ITEM DELETED	SCALE VARIANCE IF ITEM DELETED	CORRECTED ITEM– TOTAL CORRELATION	ALPHA IF ITEM DELETED
Q1	3.0000	1.3333	.5774	1.0000
Q2	2.7500	.9167	.9045	.7273
Q3	2.7500	.9167	.9045	.7273

RELIABILITY COEFFICIENTS

N OF CASES =   4.0   N OF ITEMS =   3

ALPHA =   .8889

Imagine, for example, that of a scale of 10 dichotomously scored items the wording of the odd-numbered ones was reversed. We could reconvert the scores for these items so that a 1 becomes a 2 and a 2 a 1 using the following **recode** command:

recode q1 q3 q5 q7 q9 (1=2)(2=1).

This command always comes after commands which have already defined the variables such as the **data list** command. The variable names precede the values to be changed. The values for each case are recoded from left to right and are only changed once so that when 1 is initially recoded as 2 [**(1=2)**] it is not then reconverted as 1 in the next step [(2=1)]. The values to be changed must always be placed in parentheses.

SPEARMAN–BROWN PROPHECY FORMULA

One way of estimating the number of judges or items necessary for providing a measure of acceptable reliability is to use the following Spearman–Brown prophecy formula:

$$\text{estimated reliability} = \frac{n \times \text{known reliability}}{1 + [(n-1) \times \text{known reliability}]}$$

where n is the ratio by which the number of judges or items is to be increased or decreased. For example, we could use this formula to estimate the reliability of having six rather than three items to assess self-esteem where the alpha reliability of the three items was 0.89. The estimated reliability of the six-item scale is 0.94:

$$\frac{2 \times 0.89}{1 + [(2-1) \times 0.89]} = \frac{1.78}{1.89} = 0.94$$

We can check the accuracy of this estimate by adding to our data an identical set of three scores as shown in Table 12.11. Alpha for these six items as calculated by SPSS is 0.9556 which is close to the estimate

Table 12.11 Dichotomous answers to six items

Cases	Items					
	1	2	3	4	5	6
1	1	1	1	1	1	1
2	2	2	2	2	2	2
3	1	1	1	1	1	1
4	1	2	2	1	2	2

provided by the Spearman–Brown prophecy formula.

The following formula is used for estimating the ratio by which the number of judges or items has to be changed in order to achieve a measure of a specified reliability:

$$\text{ratio} = \frac{\text{specified reliability} \times (1 - \text{known reliability})}{\text{known reliability} \times (1 - \text{specified reliability})}$$

Suppose, for instance, we had a scale of three items with an alpha of 0.5 and we wished to increase it to about 0.9. According to this formula, the number of items we would need to do this is 9 times 3 (i.e. 27):

$$\frac{0.9 \times (1 - 0.5)}{0.5 \times (1 - 0.9)} = \frac{0.45}{0.05} = 9$$

CORRECTION FOR ATTENUATION

Many variables are measured with a certain degree of unreliability. Consequently, the correlation between unreliably measured variables will always be less strong than that between reliably measured variables. This reduced correlation is known as *attenuation*. If we wanted to find out the 'true' or theoretical correlation between two measures which had been assessed without error then we would need to make a correction for their unreliability.

The following formula has been proposed for calculating the correlation between two variables where the unreliability of both measures has been taken into account:

$$r_c = \frac{\text{correlation between measure}_1 \text{ and measure}_2}{\sqrt{(\text{measure}_1 \text{ reliability} \times \text{measure}_2 \text{ reliability})}}$$

When the reliability of only one of the measures is being adjusted, then the formula is

$$r_c = \frac{\text{correlation between measure}_1 \text{ and measure}_2}{\sqrt{(\text{measure}_1 \text{ or measure}_2 \text{ reliability})}}$$

For instance, if the observed correlation between self-esteem and parental acceptance was 0.30 and the reliabilities of the self-esteem and parental acceptance measure were 0.80 and 0.70 respectively, then the theoretical correlation between self-esteem and parental acceptance would be 0.40:

$$\frac{0.30}{\sqrt{0.80 \times 0.70}} = \frac{0.30}{0.75} = 0.40$$

If the attenuated correlation between two measures is close to 1.0, then the two measures would be interpreted as two forms of the same measure.

SUMMARY

The computation of various tests for assessing the agreement and reliability between judges and the internal reliability of a scale of items is described. Kappa indicates the amount of agreement for categorical data between two judges taking into account the agreement expected by chance. While it can range from −1 to +1, a kappa of 0.7 or higher indicates an acceptable level of agreement. For non-categorical data Pearson's correlation assesses the reliability of the ratings made by two judges and the intraclass correlation the reliability of three or more judges. Alpha assesses the internal reliability of a set of items (or judges) for measuring a particular characteristic. Spearman–Brown's prophecy formula estimates the number of judges or items needed to provide a specified level of reliability. The correlation between two variables can be corrected for the known unreliability of both or either measure.

EXERCISES

1   Two clinicians categorise the problems of 100 patients into the three classes of anxiety, depression and other as shown in Table 12.12. What is the kappa coefficient of agreement for the diagnoses of the two clinicians?

2   Three judges rate the physical attractiveness of four people on a four-point scale as presented in Table 12.13.
   (a) What is the reliability of the average rating for an individual judge not taking into account the mean levels of the judges' ratings?
   (b) What is the reliability of the average rating for an individual judge taking into account the mean levels of the judges' ratings?
   (c) What is the reliability of the average rating for all three judges not taking into account the mean levels of the judges' ratings?

Table 12.12 Categorisation of patients' problems by two clinicians

Clinician A	Clinician B		
	Anxiety	Depression	Other
Anxiety	7	2	1
Depression	6	35	4
Other	2	13	30

Table 12.13 Physical attractiveness ratings by three judges

Cases	Judges		
	A	B	C
1	1	2	2
2	2	2	1
3	3	1	2
4	4	3	2

(d) What is the reliability of the average rating for all three judges taking into account the mean levels of the judges' ratings?

(e) What is the alpha reliability of the judges' ratings?

(f) By what factor would we have to increase the number of judges to achieve an alpha of 0.80?

(g) How many judges would be needed to attain this alpha?

Appendices

APPENDIX 1: SPSS/PC+ 4.0 COMMANDS

This appendix provides a convenient summary of SPSS/PC + 4.0 commands described in this book, listed in alphabetical order. Only SPSS terms are printed in bold. Optional SPSS terms are enclosed in square brackets. 'Variable(s)' refer to the SPSS names given to those variable(s). Note that each command should end with a full stop.

anova variables **by** first-grouping-variable (value of first group,value of last group) second-grouping-variable (value of first group,value of last group) **with** covariate
/**statistics**=1 3

begin data
lines of data
end data

compute new-variable=transformed old-variables
+   addition
-            subtraction
*   multiplication
/   division
sqrt(variable)   square root
lg10(variable)   base 10 logarithm
ln(variable)   natural logarithm

correlation variables
/**options** 5
/**statistics** 1 2

crosstabs table=first-variable **by** second-variable
/**cells**=**count expected**
/**statistics**=**chisq phi cc lambda btau ctau gamma d corr**
eta kappa

crosstabs variables=first-variable (minimum value,maximum value)
second-variable (minimum value,maximum value) third-variable
(minimum value,maximum value)
/**tables**=first-variable **by** second-variable **by** third-variable
/**statistics gamma**

data list [**file**='filename' if data in separate file] [**free** if format is not fixed]
[**matrix** if data are in a matrix]
/variable columns variable columns (first line of data
for same case)
/...... (second line of data for same case)

descriptives variables
/**statistics**
              1 mean
              5 standard deviation
              6 variance
              7 kurtosis
              8 skewness
              9 range

frequencies variables
/**ntiles** number of groups
/**statistics mode median mean range variance stddev
skewness seskew kurtosis sekurt**
/**histogram normal [percent]**

if (logical expression) new-variable=transformed old-
variables
and or **&**	and
or	or
not or ~	not
eq or =	equal to
ne or ~ = or < >	not equal to
le or < =	less than or equal to
lt or <	less than
ge or > =	greater than or equal to
gt or >	greater than

list [variables]

manova dependent-variables **by** grouping-variables (value of first
group,value of last group) **with** covariates
/**wsfactor**=name(number of conditions)
/**print**=**cellinfo(means) signif(brief)**
/**pmeans**

/**design**
/**analysis**=dependent-variables
/**design**=covariates grouping-variable, grouping-variable **by** covariates

missing value variables (same missing value)
/variables (different missing value)

npar tests binomial(proportion of value 1)=variable (lowest value, highest
value)
npar tests cochran=variables
npar tests friedman=variables
npar tests k-s=ordinal variable **by** grouping-variable (value of one
group,value of other group)
npar tests k-w=ordinal variable **by** grouping-variable (value of first
group,value of last group)
npar tests m-w=ordinal variable **by** grouping-variable (value of one
group,value of other group)
npar tests mcnemar=first-variable second-variable
npar tests sign=first-variable second-variable
npar tests wilcoxon=first-variable second-variable

oneway variable **by** grouping-variable (value of first group,value of last
group)
/**statistics**=1 3
/**ranges**=scheffe

plot
/**symbols** 'symbol'
/**vertical** 'name'
/**horizontal** 'title' **min**(value) **max**(value)
/**title** 'title'
/**format regression**
/**plot** vertical-axis-variable **with** horizontal-axis-variable

recode variables (old-value/s=new-value)

regression variables criterion predictors
/**statistics r anova coeff ci cha**
/**dep** criterion
/**method** [**enter**] [**forward**] [**backward**] [**stepwise**] predictors
/**scatterplot** (*resid,*pred)

reliability items
/**scale**(scale)=items
/**summary total**

select if (logical expression)
and or **&**   and

or	or
not or ~	not
eq or =	equal to
ne or ~ = or < >	not equal to
le or < =	less than or equal to
lt or <	less than
ge or > =	greater than or equal to
gt or >	greater than

set automenu off

t-test groups=variable(value of one group,value of other group)/**variables**=variables

t-test pair=first-variable second-variable

weight by variable

APPENDIX 2: SPSS/PC+ 3.0 DIFFERENCES

crosstabs table=first-variable **by** second-variable
   /**options**=14 for expected frequencies
   /**statistics**=1 for chi-square
              2 for phi and Cramer's *V*
              3 for contingency coefficient
              4 for lambda
              6 for Kendall's tau *b*
              7 for Kendall's tau *c*
              8 for gamma
              9 for Somer's *d*
             10 for eta
             11 for Pearson's *r*
No partial gamma or kappa

APPENDIX 3: SPSS 4.0 DIFFERENCES

The continuation of a command beyond the first line needs to begin in the second column of any subsequent lines.

anova variables **by** first-grouping-variable (value of first group,value of last group) second-grouping-variable (value of first group,value of last group) **with** covariate
   /**statistics**=**mca mean**

correlation variables
  /print [**twotail**] [**onetail**] [**sig**]
  /statistics [**descriptives** for means, etc.] [**xprod** for cross-product deviations, etc.]

data list [**file**='filename' if data in separate file] [**free** if format is not fixed] [**matrix** if data are in a matrix]
  /1 (record) variable columns variable columns (first line of data for same case)
  /2 (record) ...... (second line of data for same case)

descriptives variables
  /statistics mean stddev variance kurtosis skewness range

matrix data variables=rowtype_ variables

oneway variable **by** grouping-variable (value of first group,value of last group)
  /statistics=descriptives homogeneity
  /ranges=scheffe

partial corr variables=variables **by** control-variables (order of partial correlation)
  [**/matrix=in(*)** if data are read from a matrix]
  /statistics corr descriptives

APPENDIX 4: SPSS^X 3.0 DIFFERENCES

crosstabs no kappa

APPENDIX 5: TWO-TAILED 0.05 VALUES OF F

| df_2 | \multicolumn{9}{c}{df_1} |
	1	2	3	4	5	6	7	8	9
1	161.45	199.50	215.71	224.58	230.16	233.99	236.77	238.88	240.54
2	18.513	19.000	19.164	19.247	19.296	19.330	19.353	19.371	19.385
3	10.128	9.5521	9.2766	9.1172	9.0135	8.9406	8.8867	8.8452	8.8323
4	7.7086	6.9443	6.5914	6.3882	6.2561	6.1631	6.0942	6.0410	5.9938
5	6.6079	5.7861	5.4095	5.1922	5.0503	4.9503	4.8759	4.8183	4.7725
6	5.9874	5.1433	4.7571	4.5337	4.3874	4.2839	4.2067	4.1468	4.0990
7	5.5914	4.7374	4.3468	4.1203	3.9715	3.8660	3.7870	3.7257	3.6767
8	5.3177	4.4590	4.0662	3.8379	3.6875	3.5806	3.5005	3.4381	3.3881
9	5.1174	4.2565	3.8625	3.6331	3.4817	3.3738	3.2927	3.2296	3.1789
10	4.9646	4.1028	3.7083	3.4780	3.3258	3.2172	3.1355	3.0717	3.0204
11	4.8443	3.9823	3.5874	3.3567	3.2039	3.0946	3.0123	2.9480	2.8962
12	4.7472	3.8853	3.4903	3.2592	3.1059	2.9961	2.9134	2.8486	2.7964
13	4.6672	3.8056	3.4105	3.1791	3.0254	2.9153	2.8321	2.7669	2.7444
14	4.6001	3.7389	3.3439	3.1122	2.9582	2.8477	2.7642	2.6987	2.6458
15	4.5431	3.6823	3.2874	3.0556	2.9013	2.7905	2.7066	2.6408	2.5876
16	4.4940	3.6337	3.2389	3.0069	2.8524	2.7413	2.6572	2.5911	2.5377
17	4.4513	3.5915	3.1968	2.9647	2.8100	2.6987	2.6143	2.5480	2.4443
18	4.4139	3.5546	3.1599	2.9277	2.7729	2.6613	2.5767	2.5102	2.4563
19	4.3807	3.5219	3.1274	2.8951	2.7401	2.6283	2.5435	2.4768	2.4227
20	4.3512	3.4928	3.0984	2.8661	2.7109	2.5990	2.5140	2.4471	2.3928
21	4.3248	3.4668	3.0725	2.8401	2.6848	2.5727	2.4876	2.4205	2.3660
22	4.3009	3.4434	3.0491	2.8167	2.6613	2.5491	2.4638	2.3965	2.3219
23	4.2793	3.4221	3.0280	2.7955	2.6400	2.5277	2.4422	2.3748	2.3201
24	4.2597	3.4028	3.0088	2.7763	2.6207	2.5082	2.4226	2.3551	2.3002
25	4.2417	3.3852	2.9912	2.7587	2.6030	2.4904	2.4047	2.3371	2.2821
26	4.2252	3.3690	2.9752	2.7426	2.5868	2.4741	2.3883	2.3205	2.2655
27	4.2100	3.3541	2.9604	2.7278	2.5719	2.4591	2.3732	2.3053	2.2501
28	4.1960	3.3404	2.9467	2.7141	2.5581	2.4453	2.3593	2.2913	2.2360
29	4.1830	3.3277	2.9340	2.7014	2.5454	2.4324	2.3463	2.2783	2.2329
30	4.1709	3.3158	2.9223	2.6896	2.5336	2.4205	2.3343	2.2662	2.2507
40	4.0847	3.2317	2.8387	2.6060	2.4495	2.3359	2.2490	2.1802	2.1240
60	4.0012	3.1504	2.7581	2.5252	2.3683	2.2541	2.1665	2.0970	2.0401
120	3.9201	3.0718	2.6802	2.4472	2.2899	2.1750	2.0868	2.0164	1.9688
∞	3.8415	2.9957	2.6049	2.3719	2.2141	2.0986	2.0096	1.9384	1.8799

Source: Adapted from M. Merrington and C.M. Thompson (1943) 'Table of percentage points of the inverted beta (F) distribution', *Biometrika* 33: 73–88

Notes: df_1 are the degrees of freedom for the numerator; df_2 are the degrees of freedom for the denominator

APPENDIX 5: *continued*

					df_1				
10	12	15	20	24	30	40	60	120	∞
241.88	243.91	245.95	248.01	249.05	250.10	251.14	252.20	253.25	254.31
19.396	19.413	19.429	19.446	19.454	19.462	19.471	19.479	19.487	19.496
8.7855	8.7446	8.7029	8.6602	8.6385	8.6166	8.5944	8.5720	8.5594	8.5264
5.9644	5.9117	5.8578	5.8025	5.7744	5.7459	5.7170	5.6877	5.6381	5.6281
4.7351	4.6777	4.6188	4.5581	4.5272	4.4957	4.4638	4.4314	4.3085	4.3650
4.0600	3.9999	3.9381	3.8742	3.8415	3.8082	3.7743	3.7398	3.7047	3.6689
3.6365	3.5747	3.5107	3.4445	3.4105	3.3758	3.3404	3.3043	3.2674	3.2298
3.3472	3.2839	3.2184	3.1503	3.1152	3.0794	3.0428	3.0053	2.9669	2.9276
3.1373	3.0729	3.0061	2.9365	2.9005	2.8637	2.8259	2.7872	2.7475	2.7067
2.9782	2.9130	2.8450	2.7740	2.7372	2.6996	2.6609	2.6211	2.5801	2.5379
2.8536	2.7876	2.7186	2.6464	2.6090	2.5705	2.5309	2.4901	2.4480	2.4045
2.7534	2.6866	2.6169	2.5436	2.5055	2.4663	2.4259	2.3842	2.3410	2.2962
2.6710	2.6037	2.5331	2.4589	2.4202	2.3803	2.3392	2.2966	2.2524	2.2064
2.6022	2.5342	2.4630	2.3879	2.3487	2.3082	2.2664	2.2229	2.1778	2.1307
2.5437	2.4753	2.4034	2.3275	2.2878	2.2468	2.2043	2.1601	2.1141	2.0658
2.4935	2.4247	2.3522	2.2756	2.2354	2.1938	2.1507	2.1058	2.0589	2.0096
2.4499	2.3807	2.3077	2.2304	2.1898	2.1477	2.1040	2.0584	2.0107	1.9604
2.4117	2.3421	2.2686	2.1906	2.1497	2.1071	2.0629	2.0166	1.9681	1.9168
2.3779	2.3080	2.2341	2.1555	2.1141	2.0712	2.0264	1.9795	1.9302	1.8780
2.3479	2.2776	2.2033	2.1242	2.0825	2.0391	1.9938	1.9464	1.8963	1.8432
2.3210	2.2504	2.1757	2.0960	2.0540	2.0102	1.9645	1.9165	1.8657	1.8117
2.2967	2.2258	2.1508	2.0707	2.0283	1.9842	1.9380	1.8894	1.8380	1.7831
2.2747	2.2036	2.1282	2.0476	2.0050	1.9605	1.9139	1.8648	1.8128	1.7570
2.2547	2.1834	2.1077	2.0267	1.9838	1.9390	1.8920	1.8424	1.7896	1.7330
2.2365	2.1649	2.0889	2.0075	1.9643	1.9192	1.8718	1.8217	1.7684	1.7110
2.2197	2.1479	2.0716	1.9898	1.9464	1.9010	1.8533	1.8027	1.7488	1.6906
2.2043	2.1323	2.0558	1.9736	1.9299	1.8842	1.8361	1.7851	1.7306	1.6717
2.1900	2.1179	2.0411	1.9586	1.9147	1.8687	1.8203	1.7689	1.7138	1.6541
2.1768	2.1045	2.0275	1.9446	1.9005	1.8543	1.8055	1.7537	1.6981	1.6376
2.1646	2.0921	2.0148	1.9317	1.8874	1.8409	1.7918	1.7396	1.6835	1.6223
2.0772	2.0035	1.9245	1.8389	1.7929	1.7444	1.6928	1.6373	1.5766	1.5089
1.9926	1.9174	1.8364	1.7480	1.7001	1.6491	1.5943	1.5343	1.4673	1.3893
1.9105	1.8337	1.7505	1.6587	1.6084	1.5543	1.4952	1.4290	1.3519	1.2539
1.8307	1.7522	1.6664	1.5705	1.5173	1.4591	1.3940	1.3180	1.0214	1.0000

APPENDIX 6: STANDARD NORMAL DISTRIBUTION

z	0.00	0.01	0.02	0.03	0. 04	0.05	0.06	0.07	0.08	0.09
0.0	0.0000	0.0040	0.0080	0.0120	0.0160	0.0199	0.0239	0.0279	0.0319	0.0359
0.1	0.0398	0.0438	0.0478	0.0517	0.0557	0.0596	0.0636	0.0675	0.0714	0.0754
0.2	0.0793	0.0832	0.0871	0.0910	0.0948	0.0987	0.1026	0.1064	0.1103	0.1141
0.3	0.1179	0.1217	0.1255	0.1293	0.1331	0.1368	0.1406	0.1443	0.1480	0.1517
0.4	0.1554	0.1591	0.1628	0.1664	0.1736	0.1700	0.1772	0.1808	0.1844	0.1879
0.5	0.1915	0.1950	0.1985	0.2019	0.2054	0.2088	0.2123	0.2157	0.2190	0.2224
0.6	0.2258	0.2291	0.2324	0.2357	0.2389	0.2422	0.2454	0.2486	0.2518	0.2549
0.7	0.2580	0.2612	0.2642	0.2673	0.2704	0.2734	0.2764	0.2794	0.2823	0.2852
0.8	0.2881	0.2910	0.2939	0.2967	0.2996	0.3023	0.3051	0.3078	0.3106	0.3133
0.9	0.3159	0.3186	0.3212	0.3238	0.3264	0.3289	0.3315	0.3340	0.3365	0.3389
1.0	0.3413	0.3438	0.3461	0.3485	0.3508	0.3531	0.3554	0.3577	0.3599	0.3621
1.1	0.3643	0.3665	0.3686	0.3708	0.3729	0.3749	0.3770	0.3790	0.3810	0.3830
1.2	0.3849	0.3869	0.3888	0.3907	0.3925	0.3944	0.3962	0.3980	0.3997	0.4015
1.3	0.4032	0.4049	0.4066	0.4082	0.4099	0.4115	0.4131	0.4147	0.4162	0.4177
1.4	0.4192	0.4207	0.4222	0.4236	0.4251	0.4265	0.4279	0.4292	0.4306	0.4319
1.5	0.4332	0.4345	0.4357	0.4370	0.4382	0.4394	0.4406	0.4418	0.4429	0.4441
1.6	0.4452	0.4463	0.4474	0.4484	0.4495	0.4505	0.4515	0.4525	0.4535	0.4545
1.7	0.4554	0.4564	0.4573	0.4582	0.4591	0.4599	0.4608	0.4616	0.4625	0.4633
1.8	0.4641	0.4649	0.4656	0.4664	0.4671	0.4678	0.4686	0.4693	0.4699	0.4706
1.9	0.4713	0.4719	0.4726	0.4732	0.4738	0.4744	0.4750	0.4756	0.4761	0.4767
2.0	0.4772	0.4778	0.4783	0.4788	0.4793	0.4798	0.4803	0.4808	0.4812	0.4817
2.1	0.4821	0.4826	0.4830	0.4834	0.4838	0.4842	0.4846	0.4850	0.4854	0.4857
2.2	0.4861	0.4864	0.4868	0.4871	0.4875	0.4878	0.4881	0.4884	0.4887	0.4890
2.3	0.4893	0.4896	0.4898	0.4901	0.4904	0.4906	0.4909	0.4911	0.4913	0.4916
2.4	0.4918	0.4920	0.4922	0.4925	0.4927	0.4929	0.4931	0.4932	0.4934	0.4936
2.5	0.4938	0.4940	0.4941	0.4943	0.4945	0.4946	0.4948	0.4949	0.4951	0.4952
2.6	0.4953	0.4955	0.4956	0.4957	0.4959	0.4960	0.4961	0.4962	0.4963	0.4964
2.7	0.4965	0.4966	0.4967	0.4968	0.4969	0.4970	0.4971	0.4972	0.4973	0.4974
2.8	0.4974	0.4975	0.4976	0.4977	0.4977	0.4978	0.4979	0.4979	0.4980	0.4981
2.9	0.4981	0.4982	0.4982	0.4983	0.4984	0.4984	0.4985	0.4985	0.4986	0.4986
3.0	0.4987	0.4987	0.4987	0.4988	0.4988	0.4989	0.4989	0.4989	0.4990	0.4990
3.1	0.4990	0.4991	0.4991	0.4991	0.4992	0.4992	0.4992	0.4992	0.4992	0.4993
3.2	0.4993	0.4993	0.4994	0.4994	0.4994	0.4994	0.4994	0.4995	0.4995	0.4995
3.3	0.4995	0.4995	0.4995	0.4996	0.4996	0.4996	0.4996	0.4996	0.4996	0.4997
3.4	0.4997	0.4997	0.4997	0.4997	0.4997	0.4997	0.4997	0.4997	0.4997	0.4998
3.5	0.4998	0.4998	0.4998	0.4998	0.4998	0.4998	0.4998	0.4998	0.4998	0.4998
3.6	0.4998	0.4998	0.4999	0.4999	0.4999	0.4999	0.4999	0.4999	0.4999	0.4999
3.7	0.4999	0.4999	0.4999	0.4999	0.4999	0.4999	0.4999	0.4999	0.4999	0.4999
3.8	0.4999	0.4999	0.4999	0.4999	0.4999	0.4999	0.4999	0.4999	0.4999	0.4999
3.9	0.5000	0.5000	0.5000	0.5000	0.5000	0.5000	0.5000	0.5000	0.5000	0.5000

Note: Proportion of area from the mean (0) to z

APPENDIX 7: ONE-TAILED PROBABILITIES OF SMALL OBSERVED VALUES IN THE BINOMIAL TEST

n

N	0	1	2	3	4	5	6	7	8	9	10	11	12	13	14	15
1	0.500															
2	0.250	0.750														
3	0.125	0.500	0.875													
4	0.062	0.312	0.687	0.937												
5	0.031	0.188	0.500	0.812	0.969	*										
6	0.016	0.109	0.344	0.656	0.891	0.984	*									
7	0.008	0.062	0.227	0.500	0.773	0.938	0.992	*								
8	0.004	0.035	0.145	0.363	0.637	0.855	0.965	0.996	*							
9	0.002	0.020	0.090	0.254	0.500	0.746	0.910	0.980	0.998	*						
10	0.001	0.011	0.055	0.172	0.377	0.623	0.828	0.945	0.989	0.999	*					
11		0.006	0.033	0.113	0.274	0.500	0.726	0.887	0.967	0.994	*	*				
12		0.003	0.019	0.073	0.194	0.387	0.613	0.806	0.927	0.981	0.997	*	*			
13		0.002	0.011	0.046	0.133	0.291	0.500	0.709	0.867	0.954	0.989	0.998	*	*		
14		0.001	0.006	0.029	0.090	0.212	0.395	0.605	0.788	0.910	0.971	0.994	0.999	*	*	
15			0.004	0.018	0.059	0.151	0.304	0.500	0.696	0.849	0.941	0.982	0.996	*	*	*
16			0.002	0.011	0.038	0.105	0.227	0.402	0.598	0.773	0.895	0.962	0.989	0.998	*	*
17			0.001	0.006	0.025	0.072	0.166	0.315	0.500	0.685	0.834	0.928	0.975	0.994	0.999	*
18			0.001	0.004	0.015	0.048	0.119	0.240	0.407	0.593	0.760	0.881	0.952	0.985	0.996	0.999
19				0.002	0.010	0.032	0.084	0.180	0.324	0.500	0.676	0.820	0.916	0.968	0.990	0.998
20				0.001	0.006	0.021	0.058	0.132	0.252	0.412	0.588	0.748	0.868	0.942	0.979	0.994
21				0.001	0.004	0.013	0.039	0.095	0.192	0.332	0.500	0.668	0.808	0.905	0.961	0.987
22					0.002	0.008	0.026	0.067	0.143	0.262	0.416	0.584	0.738	0.857	0.933	0.974
23					0.001	0.005	0.017	0.047	0.105	0.202	0.339	0.500	0.661	0.798	0.895	0.953
24					0.001	0.003	0.011	0.032	0.076	0.154	0.271	0.419	0.581	0.729	0.846	0.924
25						0.002	0.007	0.022	0.054	0.115	0.212	0.345	0.500	0.655	0.788	0.885

Source: Adapted from Table IV, B of H. Walker and J. Lev (1953) *Statistical Inference*, New York: Holt, Rinehart & Winston, by permission of the publishers

APPENDIX 8: TWO-TAILED CRITICAL VALUES OF CHI-SQUARE

df	Level of significance		
	0.10	0.05	0.01
1	2.71	3.84	6.64
2	4.60	5.99	9.21
3	6.25	7.82	11.34
4	7.78	9.49	13.28
5	9.24	11.07	15.09
6	10.64	12.59	16.81
7	12.02	14.07	18.48
8	13.36	15.51	20.09
9	14.68	16.92	21.67
10	15.99	18.31	23.21
11	17.28	19.68	24.72
12	18.55	21.03	26.22
13	19.81	22.36	27.69
14	21.06	23.68	29.14
15	22.31	25.00	30.58
16	23.54	26.30	32.00
17	24.77	27.59	33.41
18	25.99	28.87	34.80
19	27.20	30.14	36.19
20	28.41	31.41	37.57
21	29.62	32.67	38.93
22	30.81	33.92	40.29
23	32.01	35.17	41.64
24	33.20	36.42	42.98
25	34.38	37.65	44.31
26	35.56	38.88	45.64
27	36.74	40.11	46.96
28	37.92	41.34	48.28
29	39.09	42.69	49.59
30	40.26	43.77	50.89

Source: Adapted from Table IV of R.A. Fisher and F. Yates (1974) *Statistical Tables for Biological, Agricultural and Medical Research*, 6th edn, London: Longman, by permission of the publishers

APPENDIX 9: ONE- AND TWO-TAILED CRITICAL VALUES OF THE KOLMOGOROV–SMIRNOV TEST FOR SMALL SAMPLES

n	One-tailed		Two-tailed	
	0.05	0.01	0.05	0.01
3	3	–	–	–
4	4	–	4	–
5	4	5	5	5
6	5	6	5	6
7	5	6	6	6
8	5	6	6	7
9	6	7	6	7
10	6	7	7	8
11	6	8	7	8
12	6	8	7	8
13	7	8	7	9
14	7	8	8	9
15	7	9	8	9
16	7	9	8	10
17	8	9	8	10
18	8	10	9	10
19	8	10	9	10
20	8	10	9	11
21	8	10	9	11
22	9	11	9	11
23	9	11	10	11
24	9	11	10	12
25	9	11	10	12
26	9	11	10	12
27	9	12	10	12
28	10	12	11	13
29	10	12	11	13
30	10	12	11	13
35	11	13	12	
40	11	14	13	

Source: Adapted from Table L of S. Siegel (1956) *Nonparametric Statistics for the Behavioral Sciences*, New York: McGraw-Hill, by permission of the publishers

APPENDIX 10: TWO-TAILED CRITICAL VALUES OF THE KOLMOGOROV–SMIRNOV TEST FOR LARGE SAMPLES

Significance level	D
0.10	$1.22 \sqrt{\dfrac{n_i + n_2}{n_1 \times n_2}}$
0.05	$1.36 \sqrt{\dfrac{n_i + n_2}{n_1 \times n_2}}$
0.025	$1.48 \sqrt{\dfrac{n_i + n_2}{n_1 \times n_2}}$
0.01	$1.63 \sqrt{\dfrac{n_i + n_2}{n_1 \times n_2}}$
0.005	$1.73 \sqrt{\dfrac{n_i + n_2}{n_1 \times n_2}}$
0.001	$1.95 \sqrt{\dfrac{n_i + n_2}{n_1 \times n_2}}$

Source: Adapted from Table M of S. Siegel (1956) *Nonparametric Statistics for the Behavioral Sciences*, New York: McGraw-Hill, by permission of the publishers

APPENDIX 11: CRITICAL VALUES OF U AT 0.05 ONE-TAILED LEVEL AND 0.10 TWO-TAILED LEVEL

n_2 \\ n_1	1	2	3	4	5	6	7	8	9	10	11	12	13	14	15	16	17	18	19	20
1	—	—	—	—	—	—	—	—	—	—	—	—	—	—	—	—	—	—	0	0
2	—	—	—	—	0	0	0	1	1	1	1	2	2	2	3	3	3	4	4	4
3	—	—	0	0	1	2	2	3	3	4	5	5	6	7	7	8	9	9	10	11
4	—	—	0	1	2	3	4	5	6	7	8	9	10	11	12	14	15	16	17	18
5	—	0	1	2	4	5	6	8	9	11	12	13	15	16	18	19	20	22	23	25
6	—	0	2	3	5	7	8	10	12	14	16	17	19	21	23	25	26	28	30	32
7	—	0	2	4	6	8	11	13	15	17	19	21	24	26	28	30	33	35	37	39
8	—	1	3	5	8	10	13	15	18	20	23	26	28	31	33	36	39	41	44	47
9	—	1	3	6	9	12	15	18	21	24	27	30	33	36	39	42	45	48	51	54
10	—	1	4	7	11	14	17	20	24	27	31	34	37	41	44	48	51	55	58	62
11	—	1	5	8	12	16	19	23	27	31	34	38	42	46	50	54	57	61	65	69
12	—	2	5	9	13	17	21	26	30	34	38	42	47	51	55	60	64	68	72	77
13	—	2	6	10	15	19	24	28	33	37	42	47	51	56	61	65	70	75	80	84
14	—	2	7	11	16	21	26	31	36	41	46	51	56	61	66	71	77	82	87	92
15	—	3	7	12	18	23	28	33	39	44	50	55	61	66	72	77	83	88	94	100
16	—	3	8	14	19	25	30	36	42	48	54	60	65	71	77	83	89	95	101	107
17	—	3	9	15	20	26	33	39	45	51	57	64	70	77	83	89	96	102	109	115
18	—	4	9	16	22	28	35	41	48	55	61	68	75	82	88	95	102	109	116	123
19	0	4	10	17	23	30	37	44	51	58	65	72	80	87	94	101	109	116	123	130
20	0	4	11	18	25	32	39	47	54	62	69	77	84	92	100	107	115	123	130	138

Source: Adapted from Table I of R.P. Runyon and A. Haber (1989) *Fundamentals of Behavioral Statistics*, 6th edn, New York: McGraw-Hill, by permission of the publishers

Note: —, no decision possible at the stated level of significance

APPENDIX 12: CRITICAL VALUES OF U AT 0.025 ONE-TAILED LEVEL AND 0.05 TWO-TAILED LEVEL

n_2 \ n_1	1	2	3	4	5	6	7	8	9	10	11	12	13	14	15	16	17	18	19	20
1	—	—	—	—	—	—	—	—	—	—	—	—	—	—	—	—	—	—	—	—
2	—	—	—	—	—	—	—	0	0	0	0	1	1	1	1	1	2	2	2	2
3	—	—	—	—	0	1	1	2	2	3	3	4	4	5	5	6	6	7	7	8
4	—	—	—	0	1	2	3	4	4	5	6	7	8	9	10	11	11	12	13	13
5	—	—	0	1	2	3	5	6	7	8	9	11	12	13	14	15	17	18	19	20
6	—	—	1	2	3	5	6	8	10	11	13	14	16	17	19	21	22	24	25	27
7	—	—	1	3	5	6	8	10	12	14	16	18	20	22	24	26	28	30	32	34
8	—	0	2	4	6	8	10	13	15	17	19	22	24	26	29	31	34	36	38	41
9	—	0	2	4	7	10	12	15	17	20	23	26	28	31	34	37	39	42	45	48
10	—	0	3	5	8	11	14	17	20	23	26	29	33	36	39	42	45	48	52	55
11	—	0	3	6	9	13	16	19	23	26	30	33	37	40	44	47	51	55	58	62
12	—	1	4	7	11	14	18	22	26	29	33	37	41	45	49	53	57	61	65	69
13	—	1	4	8	12	16	20	24	28	33	37	41	45	50	54	59	63	67	72	76
14	—	1	5	9	13	17	22	26	31	36	40	45	50	55	59	64	67	74	78	83
15	—	1	5	10	14	19	24	29	34	39	44	49	54	59	64	70	75	80	85	90
16	—	1	6	11	15	21	26	31	37	42	47	53	59	64	70	75	81	86	92	98
17	—	2	6	11	17	22	28	34	39	45	51	57	63	67	75	81	87	93	99	105
18	—	2	7	12	18	24	30	36	42	48	55	61	67	74	80	86	93	99	106	112
19	—	2	7	13	19	25	32	38	45	52	58	65	72	78	85	92	99	106	113	119
20	—	2	8	13	20	27	34	41	48	55	62	69	76	83	90	98	105	112	119	127

Source: Adapted from Table I of R.P. Runyon and A. Haber (1989) *Fundamentals of Behavioral Statistics*, 6th edn, New York: McGraw-Hill, by permission of the publishers

Note: —, no decision possible at the stated level of significance

APPENDIX 13: TWO-TAILED CRITICAL VALUES OF T FOR THE WILCOXON TEST

N	Significance level			N	Significance level		
	0.10	0.05	0.02		0.10	0.05	0.02
5	0	–	–	28	130	116	101
6	2	0	–	29	140	126	110
7	3	2	0	30	151	137	120
8	5	3	1	31	163	147	130
9	8	5	3	32	175	159	140
10	10	8	5	33	187	170	151
11	13	10	7	34	200	182	162
12	17	13	9	35	213	195	173
13	21	17	12	36	227	208	185
14	25	21	15	37	241	221	198
15	30	25	19	38	256	235	211
16	35	29	23	39	271	249	224
17	41	34	27	40	286	264	238
18	47	40	32	41	302	279	252
19	53	46	37	42	319	294	266
20	60	52	43	43	336	310	281
21	67	58	49	44	353	327	296
22	75	65	55	45	371	343	312
23	83	73	62	46	389	361	328
24	91	81	69	47	407	378	345
25	100	89	76	48	426	396	362
26	110	98	84	49	446	415	379
27	119	107	92	50	466	434	397

Source: Adapted from Table I of F. Wilcoxon (1949) *Some Rapid Approximate Statistical Procedures*, New York: American Cyanamid Company

APPENDIX 14:   TWO-TAILED CRITICAL VALUES OF χ^2_r FOR THE FRIEDMAN TEST

N	C = 3		C = 4		C = 5	
	0.05	0.01	0.05	0.01	0.05	0.01
2	–	–	6.000	–	7.600	8.000
3	6.000	–	7.400	9.000	8.533	10.23
4	6.500	8.000	7.800	9.600	8.800	11.20
5	6.400	8.400	7.800	9.960	8.960	11.68
6	7.000	9.000	7.600	10.20	9.067	11.87
7	7.143	8.857	7.800	10.54	9.143	12.11
8	6.250	9.000	7.650	10.50	9.200	12.30
9	6.222	9.556	7.667	10.73	9.244	12.44
10	6.200	9.600	7.680	10.68		
11	6.545	9.455	7.691	10.75		
12	6.500	9.500	7.700	10.80		
13	6.615	9.385	7.800	10.85		
14	6.143	9.143	7.714	10.89		
15	6.400	8.933	7.720	10.92		
16	6.500	9.375	7.800	10.95		
17	6.118	9.294	7.800	11.05		
18	6.333	9.000	7.733	10.93		
19	6.421	9.579	7.863	11.02		
20	6.300	9.300	7.800	11.10		
21	6.095	9.238	7.800	11.06		
22	6.091	9.091	7.800	11.07		

Source: Adapted from Table 4.3 of H.R. Neave (1978) Statistical Tables, London: George Allen & Unwin, by permission of the publishers

APPENDIX 15: TWO-TAILED CRITICAL VALUES OF t

df	Significance level		
	0.10	0.05	0.02
1	6.314	12.706	31.821
2	2.920	4.303	6.965
3	2.353	3.182	4.541
4	2.132	2.776	3.747
5	2.015	2.571	3.365
6	1.943	2.447	3.143
7	1.895	2.365	2.998
8	1.860	2.306	2.896
9	1.833	2.262	2.821
10	1.812	2.228	2.764
11	1.796	2.201	2.718
12	1.782	2.179	2.681
13	1.771	2.160	2.650
14	1.761	2.145	2.624
15	1.753	2.131	2.602
16	1.746	2.120	2.583
17	1.740	2.110	2.567
18	1.734	2.101	2.552
19	1.729	2.093	2.539
20	1.725	2.086	2.528
21	1.721	2.080	2.518
22	1.717	2.074	2.508
23	1.714	2.069	2.500
24	1.711	2.064	2.492
25	1.708	2.060	2.485
26	1.706	2.056	2.479
27	1.703	2.052	2.473
28	1.701	2.048	2.467
29	1.699	2.045	2.462
30	1.697	2.042	2.457
40	1.684	2.021	2.423
60	1.671	2.000	2.390
120	1.658	1.980	2.358
∞	1.645	1.960	2.326

Source: Adapted from Table III of R.A. Fisher and F. Yates (1974) *Statistical Tables for Biological, Agricultural and Medical Research*, 6th edn, London: Longman, by permission of the publishers

APPENDIX 16: TWO-TAILED CRITICAL VALUES OF F_{max}

$n-1$	Number of groups								
	2	3	4	5	6	7	8	9	10
4	9.60	15.5	20.6	25.2	29.5	33.6	37.5	41.4	44.6
5	7.15	10.8	13.7	16.3	18.7	20.8	22.9	24.7	26.5
6	5.82	8.38	10.4	12.1	13.7	15.0	16.3	17.5	18.6
7	4.99	6.94	8.44	9.70	10.8	11.8	12.7	13.5	14.3
8	4.43	6.00	7.18	8.12	9.03	9.78	10.5	11.1	11.7
9	4.03	5.34	6.31	7.11	7.80	8.41	8.95	9.45	9.91
10	3.72	4.85	5.67	6.34	6.92	7.42	7.87	8.28	8.66
12	3.28	4.16	4.79	5.30	5.72	6.09	6.42	6.72	7.00
15	2.86	3.54	4.01	4.37	4.68	4.95	5.19	5.40	5.59
20	2.46	2.95	3.29	3.54	3.76	3.94	4.10	4.24	4.37
30	2.07	2.40	2.61	2.78	2.91	3.02	3.12	3.21	3.29
60	1.67	1.85	1.96	2.04	2.11	2.17	2.22	2.26	2.30
∞	1.00	1.00	1.00	1.00	1.00	1.00	1.00	1.00	1.00

Source: Adapted from Table 31 of E.S. Pearson and H.O. Hartley (1958) *Biometrika Tables for Statisticians*, vol. 1, 2nd edn, New York: Cambridge University Press, by permission of the Biometrika Trustees

APPENDIX 17: TWO-TAILED CRITICAL VALUES OF COCHRAN'S C

$n-1$	Number of groups										
	2	3	4	5	6	7	8	9	10	15	20
1	0.9985	0.9669	0.9065	0.8412	0.7808	0.7271	0.6798	0.6385	0.6020	0.4709	0.3894
2	0.9750	0.8709	0.7679	0.6838	0.6161	0.5612	0.5157	0.4775	0.4450	0.3346	0.2705
3	0.9392	0.7977	0.6841	0.5981	0.5321	0.4800	0.4377	0.4027	0.3733	0.2758	0.2205
4	0.9057	0.7457	0.6287	0.5441	0.4803	0.4307	0.3910	0.3584	0.3311	0.2419	0.1921
5	0.8772	0.7071	0.5895	0.5065	0.4447	0.3974	0.3595	0.3286	0.3029	0.2195	0.1735
6	0.8534	0.6771	0.5598	0.4783	0.4184	0.3726	0.3362	0.3067	0.2823	0.2034	0.1602
7	0.8332	0.6530	0.5365	0.4564	0.3980	0.3535	0.3185	0.2901	0.2666	0.1911	0.1501
8	0.8159	0.6333	0.5175	0.4387	0.3817	0.3384	0.3043	0.2768	0.2541	0.1815	0.1422
9	0.8010	0.6167	0.5017	0.4241	0.3682	0.3259	0.2926	0.2659	0.2439	0.1736	0.1357
16	0.7341	0.5466	0.4366	0.3645	0.3135	0.2756	0.2462	0.2226	0.2032	0.1429	0.1108
36	0.6602	0.4748	0.3720	0.3066	0.2612	0.2278	0.2022	0.1820	0.1655	0.1144	0.0879
144	0.5813	0.4031	0.3093	0.2513	0.2119	0.1833	0.1616	0.1446	0.1308	0.0889	0.0675

Source: Adapted from C. Eisenhart, M.W. Hastay and A. Wallis (1947) *Techniques of Statistical Analysis*, New York: McGraw-Hill, by permission of the publishers

APPENDIX 18: TWO-TAILED CRITICAL VALUES OF SPEARMAN'S rho

N	Significance level	
	0.10	*0.05*
5	0.900	1.000
6	0.829	0.886
7	0.715	0.786
8	0.620	0.715
9	0.600	0.700
10	0.564	0.649
11	0.537	0.619
12	0.504	0.588
13	0.484	0.561
14	0.464	0.539
15	0.447	0.522
16	0.430	0.503
17	0.415	0.488
18	0.402	0.474
19	0.392	0.460
20	0.381	0.447
21	0.371	0.437
22	0.361	0.426
23	0.353	0.417
24	0.345	0.407
25	0.337	0.399
26	0.331	0.391
27	0.325	0.383
28	0.319	0.376
29	0.312	0.369
30	0.307	0.363

Source: Adapted from G.J. Glasser and R.F. Winter (1961) 'Critical values of the coefficient of rank correlation for testing the hypothesis of independence', *Biometrika* 48: 444–8

APPENDIX 19: TWO-TAILED CRITICAL VALUES OF PEARSON'S r

$N-2$	Significance level	
	0.10	0.05
1	0.9877	0.9969
2	0.9000	0.9500
3	0.8054	0.8783
4	0.7293	0.8114
5	0.6694	0.7545
6	0.6215	0.7067
7	0.5822	0.6664
8	0.5494	0.6319
9	0.5214	0.6021
10	0.4973	0.5760
11	0.4762	0.5529
12	0.4575	0.5324
13	0.4409	0.5139
14	0.4259	0.4973
15	0.4124	0.4821
16	0.4000	0.4683
17	0.3887	0.4555
18	0.3783	0.4438
19	0.3687	0.4329
20	0.3598	0.4227
25	0.3233	0.3809
30	0.2960	0.3494
35	0.2746	0.3246
40	0.2573	0.3044
45	0.2428	0.2875
50	0.2306	0.2732
60	0.2108	0.2500
70	0.1954	0.2319
80	0.1829	0.2172
90	0.1726	0.2050
100	0.1638	0.1946

Source: Adapted from Table VII of R.A. Fisher and F. Yates (1974) *Statistical Tables for Biological, Agricultural and Medical Research*, 6th edn, London: Longman, by permission of the publishers

APPENDIX 20: TRANSFORMATION OF PEARSON'S r TO z_r

r	z_r	r	z_r	r	z_r	r	z_r	r	z_r
0.000	0.000	0.200	0.203	0.400	0.424	0.600	0.693	0.800	1.099
0.005	0.005	0.205	0.208	0.405	0.430	0.605	0.701	0.805	1.113
0.010	0.010	0.210	0.213	0.410	0.436	0.610	0.709	0.810	1.127
0.015	0.015	0.215	0.218	0.415	0.442	0.615	0.717	0.815	1.142
0.020	0.020	0.220	0.224	0.420	0.448	0.620	0.725	0.820	1.157
0.025	0.025	0.225	0.229	0.425	0.454	0.625	0.733	0.825	1.172
0.030	0.030	0.230	0.234	0.430	0.460	0.630	0.741	0.830	1.188
0.035	0.035	0.235	0.239	0.435	0.466	0.635	0.750	0.835	1.204
0.040	0.040	0.240	0.245	0.440	0.472	0.640	0.758	0.840	1.221
0.045	0.045	0.245	0.250	0.445	0.478	0.645	0.767	0.845	1.238
0.050	0.050	0.250	0.255	0.450	0.485	0.650	0.775	0.850	1.256
0.055	0.055	0.255	0.261	0.455	0.491	0.655	0.784	0.855	1.274
0.060	0.060	0.260	0.266	0.460	0.497	0.660	0.793	0.860	1.293
0.065	0.065	0.265	0.271	0.465	0.504	0.665	0.802	0.865	1.313
0.070	0.070	0.270	0.277	0.470	0.510	0.670	0.811	0.870	1.333
0.075	0.075	0.275	0.282	0.475	0.517	0.675	0.820	0.875	1.354
0.080	0.080	0.280	0.288	0.480	0.523	0.680	0.829	0.880	1.376
0.085	0.085	0.285	0.293	0.485	0.530	0.685	0.838	0.885	1.398
0.090	0.090	0.290	0.299	0.490	0.536	0.690	0.848	0.890	1.422
0.095	0.095	0.295	0.304	0.495	0.543	0.695	0.858	0.895	1.447
0.100	0.100	0.300	0.310	0.500	0.549	0.700	0.867	0.900	1.472
0.105	0.105	0.305	0.315	0.505	0.556	0.705	0.877	0.905	1.499
0.110	0.110	0.310	0.321	0.510	0.563	0.710	0.887	0.910	1.528
0.115	0.116	0.315	0.326	0.515	0.570	0.715	0.897	0.915	1.557
0.120	0.121	0.320	0.332	0.520	0.576	0.720	0.908	0.920	1.589
0.125	0.126	0.325	0.337	0.525	0.583	0.725	0.918	0.925	1.623
0.130	0.131	0.330	0.343	0.530	0.590	0.730	0.929	0.930	1.658
0.135	0.136	0.335	0.348	0.535	0.597	0.735	0.940	0.935	1.697
0.140	0.141	0.340	0.354	0.540	0.604	0.740	0.950	0.940	1.738
0.145	0.146	0.345	0.360	0.545	0.611	0.745	0.962	0.945	1.783
0.150	0.151	0.350	0.365	0.550	0.618	0.750	0.973	0.950	1.832
0.155	0.156	0.355	0.371	0.555	0.626	0.755	0.984	0.955	1.886
0.160	0.161	0.360	0.377	0.560	0.633	0.760	0.996	0.960	1.946
0.165	0.167	0.365	0.383	0.565	0.640	0.765	1.008	0.965	2.014
0.170	0.172	0.370	0.388	0.570	0.648	0.770	1.020	0.970	2.092
0.175	0.177	0.375	0.394	0.575	0.655	0.775	1.033	0.975	2.185
0.180	0.182	0.380	0.400	0.580	0.662	0.780	1.045	0.980	2.298
0.185	0.187	0.385	0.406	0.585	0.670	0.785	1.058	0.985	2.443
0.190	0.192	0.390	0.412	0.590	0.678	0.790	1.071	0.990	2.647
0.195	0.198	0.395	0.418	0.595	0.685	0.795	1.085	0.995	2.994

Source: Adapted from A.L. Edwards (1967) *Statistical Methods*, 2nd edn, New York: Holt, Rinehart & Winston

Answers to exercises

2 MEASUREMENT AND UNIVARIATE ANALYSIS

1   Ordinal
2   Ratio
3   (a) 3 and 4
    (b) 7
    (c) 4.0
    (d) 3.5
    (e) 4.3
    (f) 44.1
    (g) 4.9
    (h) 2.21

3 INTRODUCING THE STATISTICAL PACKAGE FOR THE SOCIAL SCIENCES

1   You could assign a single number to each category such as 1 for single
    and never married, 2 for married, 3 for separated, 4 for divorced and 5
    for widowed
2   With no other information, you could code marital status for this
    person as missing
3   age=2000-year-of-birth.
4   (a) A file such as the following:

>   **data list/cno 1-2 age 4-5 gen 7 q1 to q10 8-27.**
>   **begin data.**
>   **01 .. . .**
>   **02**
>   **.**
>   **. (data)**
>   **.**
>   **10 .. . .**
>   **end data.**

(b) **compute** new-name$_1$=q1+q2+q3+q4+q5+q6+q7+q8+q9+q10.

(c) **compute** new-name$_2$=new-name$_1$/**10.**

or

compute new-name$_2$=(q1+q2+q3+q4+q5+q6+q7+q8+q9 +q10)/**10.**

(d) The total score for individuals with missing individual question scores will always be less than their maximum potential total score. For ways of handling this situation, see Bryman and Cramer (1990)

(e) **descriptives** new-name$_2$
   /**statistics 1.**

4 STATISTICAL SIGNIFICANCE AND CHOICE OF TEST

1   1 out of 64 ($2 \times 2 \times 2 \times 2 \times 2 \times 2 = 64$) or 0.015625 (1/64 or $0.5 \times 0.5 \times 0.5 \times 0.5 \times 0.5 \times 0.5 = 0.015625$)

2   1 out of 8 ($2 \times 2 \times 2 = 8$) or 0.125 (1/8 or $0.5 \times 0.5 \times 0.5 = 0.125$)

3   0.421875 ($0.75 \times 0.75 \times 0.75 = 0.421875$)

4   25

5   No

6   Two-tailed

7   (a) 24.27
   (b) 5
   (c) 6
   (d) Less than 0.05
   (e) Yes

8   (a) 0.661
   (b) 0.717
   (c) 0.92
   (d) 0.4641
   (e) 0.9282
   (f) Symmetrical with a nonsignificant tendency of a positive skew
   (g) −0.153
   (h) 1.400
   (i) 0.11
   (j) 0.4562
   (k) 0.9124
   (l) Mesokurtic with a nonsignificant tendency towards platykurtosis

5 TESTS OF DIFFERENCE FOR CATEGORICAL DATA

1   (a) Chi-square
   (b) 6.95
   (c) 1

(d) Two-tailed
(e) Less than 0.05
(f) Yes
2 (a) McNemar test
   (b) 4.05
   (c) 1
   (d) One-tailed
   (e) Less than 0.05
   (f) Yes

6 TESTS OF DIFFERENCE FOR ORDINAL DATA

1 (a) −2.9569 (corrected for ties)
   (b) 0.003
   (c) Yes
2 (a) 12.3712
   (b) 2
   (c) Less than 0.01
   (d) Yes
3 (a) 0.1250
   (b) No
4 (a) −1.8593
   (b) 0.0628
5 (a) 3.5556
   (b) 2
   (c) Greater than 0.05
   (d) No

7 TESTS OF DIFFERENCE FOR INTERVAL/RATIO DATA IN UNRELATED SAMPLES

1 (a) 2.80
   (b) 4 in the numerator and 8 in the denominator
   (c) Greater than 0.05
   (d) No
   (e) No
   (f) 5.29
   (g) 12
   (h) Less than 0.02
   (i) Yes
2 (a) 28.0
   (b) 1 in the numerator and 12 in the denominator
   (c) Less than 0.05

(d) Yes
(e) 0.71
3 (a) 4.26
   (b) 2 in the numerator and 11 in the denominator
   (c) Less than 0.05
   (d) Yes
   (e) 2.14
   (f) 2.08
   (g) 1.50
   (h) Higher and lower socio-economic status
4 (a) 3.04
   (b) 2 in the numerator and 9 in the denominator
   (c) Greater than 0.05
   (d) No
   (e) 35.63
   (f) 1 in the numerator and 9 in the denominator
   (g) Less than 0.05
   (h) Yes
   (i) 28.13
   (j) 1 in the numerator and 9 in the denominator
   (k) Less than 0.05
   (l) Yes

8 TESTS OF DIFFERENCE FOR INTERVAL/RATIO DATA IN RELATED AND MIXED SAMPLES

1 (a) 2.40
   (b) 8
   (c) Less than 0.05
   (d) Yes
2 (a) 3.70
   (b) 2 in the numerator and 16 in the denominator
   (c) Less than 0.05
   (d) Yes
3 (a) 1.50
   (b) 1 in the numerator and 12 in the denominator
   (c) Greater than 0.05
   (d) No
4 (a) 13.55
   (b) 1 in the numerator and 11 in the denominator
   (c) Less than 0.05
   (d) 2.93
   (e) 1 in the numerator and 11 in the denominator
   (f) Greater than 0.05

(g) Yes
(h) 3.04
(i) 1.50
(j) Yes

9 TESTS OF ASSOCIATION FOR CATEGORICAL AND ORDINAL DATA

1   (a) 0.21
    (b) 0.20
    (c) 0.15
    (d) 0.00
    (e) 0.02
2   (a) 0.32
    (b) 0.30
    (c) 0.42
    (d) 0.32
    (e) 0.38
    (f) 0.40
    (g) 0.62

10 TESTS OF ASSOCIATION FOR INTERVAL/RATIO DATA

1   (a) 0.37
    (b) 12
    (c) Greater than 0.05
    (d) No
2   (a) z test
    (b) −0.43
    (c) −0.11
    (d) 0.49
    (e) 0.62
    (f) No
3   (a) T_2 test
    (b) 0.60
    (c) −0.68
    (d) 11
    (e) Greater than 0.05
    (f) No
4   (a) Z_2^* test
    (b) −0.52
    (c) −2.28
    (d) 0.0226

(e) Yes
5   0.51
6   0.28

11 BIVARIATE AND MULTIPLE REGRESSION

1   (a) 0.31
    (b) 0.37
    (c) 1.875
    (d) 2.495
    (e) 0.91
    (f) 0.23
    (g) 0.52
    (h) 0.14
    (i) 0.06
    (j) 1.89
    (k) 1 in the numerator and 12 in the denominator
    (l) Greater than 0.05
2   (a) 0.64
    (b) 0.54
    (c) −0.45
    (d) −0.74
    (e) 0.27
    (f) 0.135
    (g) 2.02
    (h) 2 in the numerator and 11 in the denominator
    (i) Greater than 0.05
    (j) 0.51
    (k) 0.06
    (l) 1 in the numerator and 11 in the denominator
    (m) Greater than 0.05
    (n) −0.36
    (o) 1.89
    (p) 1 in the numerator and 11 in the denominator
    (q) Greater than 0.05

12 MEASUREMENT RELIABILITY AND AGREEMENT

1   0.54
2   (a) −0.18
    (b) −0.17
    (c) −0.46
    (d) −0.78

(e) 0.42
(f) 5.5
(g) 17

Bibliography

Bliss, C. I. (1967) *Statistics in Biology, Statistical Methods for Research in the Natural Sciences*, vol. 1, New York: McGraw-Hill.

Boneau, C. A. (1960) 'The effects of violations of assumptions underlying the *t* test', *Psychological Bulletin* 57: 49–64.

Bryman, A. and Cramer, D. (1990) *Quantitative Data Analysis for Social Scientists*, London and New York: Routledge.

Campbell, D. T. and Stanley, J. C. (1966) *Experimental and Quasi-Experimental Designs for Research*, Chicago, IL: Rand McNally.

Dinneen, L. C. and Blakesley, B. C. (1973) 'Algorithm AS62: A generator for the sampling distribution of the Mann–Whitney *U* statistic', *Applied Statistics* 22: 269–73.

Fleiss, J. L. (1971) 'Measuring nominal scale agreement among many raters', *Psychological Bulletin* 76: 378–82.

Hays, W. L. (1988) *Statistics*, 4th edn, New York: Holt, Rinehart & Winston.

Lord, F. M. (1953) 'On the statistical treatment of football numbers', *American Psychologist* 8: 750–1.

Norušis, M. J./SPSS Inc. (1988a) *SPSS/PC+ V2.0 Base Manual*, Chicago.

Norušis, M. J./SPSS Inc. (1988b) *SPSS/PC+ V2.0 Advanced Statistics V2.0*, Chicago.

Norušis, M. J./SPSS Inc. (1988c) *SPSS/PC+ V3.0 Update Manual*, Chicago.

Norušis, M. J./SPSS Inc. (1990a) *SPSS/PC+ 4.0 Base Manual*, Chicago.

Norušis, M. J./SPSS Inc. (1990b) *SPSS/PC+ Statistics 4.0*, Chicago.

Norušis, M. J./SPSS Inc. (1990c) *SPSS Base System User's Guide*, Chicago.

Norušis, M. J./SPSS Inc. (1990d) *SPSS Advanced Statistics User's Guide*, Chicago.

Siegel, S. (1956) *Nonparametric Statistics for the Behavioral Sciences*, New York: McGraw-Hill.

Smirnov, N. V. (1948) 'Table for estimating the goodness of fit of empirical distributions', *Annals of Mathematical Statistics* 19: 279–81.

SPSS Inc. (1983) *SPSS^X Statistical Algorithms*, Chicago.

SPSS Inc. (1988) *SPSS-X User's Guide*, 3rd edn, Chicago.

SPSS Inc. (1990) *SPSS Reference Guide*, Chicago.

Steiger, J. H. (1980) 'Tests for comparing elements of a correlation matrix', *Psychological Bulletin* 87: 245–51.

Stevens, S. S. (1946) 'On the theory of scales of measurement', *Science* 103: 677–80.

Tabachnick, B. G. and Fidell, L. S. (1989) *Using Multivariate Statistics*, 2nd edn, New York: Harper & Row.

Walker, H. M. (1940) 'Degrees of freedom', *Journal of Educational Psychology* 31: 253–69.

Index